THE POLITICS OF THE FAMILY

This

swell Ltd., London, N.21   Cat. No. 1207   DG 02242/71

The Politics of the Family

Edited by
HELEN JONES
JANE MILLAR

Avebury

Aldershot • Brookfield USA • Hong Kong • Singapore • Sydney

Published by
Avebury
Ashgate Publishing Limited
Gower House
Croft Road
Aldershot
Hants GU11 3HR
England

Ashgate Publishing Company
Old Post Road
Brookfield
Vermont 05036
USA

A CIP catalogue record for this book is available from the British Library

Library of Congress Catalog Card Number: 95-81227

ISBN 1 85972 086 2

Typeset by
Karen McGowan
University of Liverpool

Printed and bound by Athenaeum Press, Ltd.,
Gateshead, Tyne & Wear.

The Social Policy Association

The Social Policy Association was founded in 1967 as the Social Administration Association. It brings together teachers, researchers, practitioners and students of social policy and administration. Its members include academics and students in universities, colleges and schools, as well as other practitioners of social policy. Its object is to encourage teaching, research and scholarship in social policy and administration.

Publications

The Journal of Social Policy

The SPA's major intellectual activity is the publication, with the Cambridge University Press, of the *Journal of Social Policy*. It is a leading international journal with a worldwide circulation and the most authoritative journal on the subject in the United Kingdom. The *Journal of Social Policy* is published quarterly and full members of the SPA receive copies free. An elected editorial board is responsible for the Journal's content.

Social Policy Review

Since 1992 the Association has assumed full responsibility for the commissioning, publication and distribution of the *Social Policy Review* (formerly published by Routledge and Longman under the title of the *Year Book of Social Policy*. The most recent issues are N. Manning and R. Page (eds) (1992) *Social Policy Review 4*; R. Page and J. Baldock (eds) (1993) *Social Policy Review 5 : the evolving welfare state*; R. Page and J.

Baldock (eds) (1994) *Social Policy Review 6*; J. Baldock and M. May (eds) (1995) *Social Policy Review 7*. Copies of the Review can be obtained from Steve Martin, SPA, 16 Creighton Avenue, London, N10 1NU.

Newsletter

The SPA also publishes a *Newsletter* three times a year to keep members in touch with current events such as lectures, seminars, conferences and workshops.

Membership

Membership of the Social Policy Association is open to both individuals and organisations.

Contents

Figures and tables

Contributors

John Baldock, Department of Social Policy and Administration, University of Kent.

Alan Deacon, School of Sociology and Social Policy, University of Leeds.

Hartley Dean, Faculty of Health Care and Social Studies, University of Luton.

Janet Finch, Vice Chancellor, University of Keele.

Carl Hylton, School of Sociology and Social Policy, University of Leeds.

Helen Jones, Department of Social Policy and Politics, Goldsmiths' College, University of London.

Alyas Karmani, School of Sociology and Social Policy, University of Leeds.

Ian Law, School of Sociology and Social Policy, University of Leeds.

Ruth Lister, Department of Social Sciences, Loughborough University.

Peter McCarthy, Relate Centre for Family Studies, University of Newcastle.

Jane Millar, School of Social Sciences, University of Bath.

Sue Morris, Department of Social Policy, University of Edinburgh.

Ilona Ostner, Zentrum für Sozialpolitick, Universität Bremen.

Gillian Reynolds, School of Social Sciences, Staffordshire University.

Peter Selman, Department of Social Policy, University of Newcastle.

Di Thompson, Faculty of Health Care and Social Studies, University of Luton.

Clare Ungerson, Department of Sociology, University of Southampton.

Fran Wasoff, Department of Social Policy, University of Edinburgh.

Introduction

Helen Jones and Jane Millar

In December 1994 Virginia Bottomley, then minister for the family, claimed that 1994, the International Year of the Family, had ensured that 'families have taken their rightful place at the heart of the social policy agenda' (IYF Agenda for Action 1994). Disagreements over the extent to which this statement represents reality or aspiration, and the motives underpinning social policies means that 'the politics of the family' is a lively and contentious arena to which this book aims to make a fresh contribution. The chapters in this volume investigate, through detailed and up-to-date research, both the nature of the assumptions about the family which drive policy and the impact of policy on families, including relationships between family members.

The 1980s have been characterised by rising economic inequality and insecurity. The gap between rich and poor is at its highest level since the second world war, largely as a consequence of trends in the labour market which have intensified the divisions between those in secure, well-paid employment compared with those in insecure, often low-paid employment and those with no jobs at all (the 40/30/30 society, as Hutton (1995) calls it). These labour market changes have been exacerbated by government policies which have deregulated employment, reduced the rights of collective action and generally rewarded the better-off and penalised the poorest. Thus poverty has been rising steadily. The latest DSS figures show about 14 million people living on incomes of less than half of the average, including about 4.3 million children. One in three children lives in a family with incomes below half the average compared with one in ten in 1979 (DSS 1995). The Joseph Rowntree Foundation, surveying these trends as part of their Inquiry into Income and Wealth, concluded that 'in many areas of the UK the living standards and life opportunities are simply unacceptably low in a society as rich as ours' and argued that this 'is a problem not only for those directly affected, but also damages the social fabric and so affects us all' (Barclay et al 1995, Summary).

Families are themselves also increasingly insecure, with one in three marriages ending in divorce. Indeed, in 1993 the number of marriages reached its lowest level since the second world war (Haskey 1995). In that year there were 332.6 thousand marriages, 177.8 thousand divorces, and 236.4 thousand children born to unmarried mothers (Population Trends 1995). Many of these births outside marriage are to cohabiting couples and rates of cohabitation have risen steeply in recent years (Haskey 1995). Debate about both the causes and consequences of these trends has been intense - much more so than debate about the causes and consequences of family poverty. On the one hand there has been a steady stream of comment, much influenced by new right ideas from America, arguing that government policies are to blame for the 'breakdown' of the family. The right-wing think tank, the Institute for Economic Affairs (IEA), has been at the forefront of these arguments: not only bringing Charles Murray over from the United States to argue that Britain has a growing 'underclass' (Murray et al 1990) as a result of the welfare state, but also publishing home-grown versions of the same argument. Dennis and Erdos (1993), for example, produced a well-publicised tract arguing that, between feminist influence and government policy, men were increasingly marginalised in family life. More recently Patricia Morgan (1995), in a scathing attack on government policies argued that the Conservatives have positively discriminated against married couples and working fathers in favour of lone parents. She sees state support for lone parents as leading to a decline in marriage and the rise of a class of young men whose status is self-defined by predatory sexual behaviour and violence. Morgan, like Dennis and Erdos, claims that children brought up by a single parent are more likely to suffer health and educational problems, and to be delinquent and criminals, even though, she claims, a lone working mother is financially better off than a married couple where the father works and the mother stays at home (Morgan 1995, the *Guardian* 3 January 1995). The IEA has now turned its attention to the proposed divorce reform (Whelan et al 1995), arguing that the marriage contract has been increasingly undermined and that allowing no fault divorce has led people to view marriage as 'just another life style choice' (in the title of another of their publications, Davies 1993).

While the authors writing for the IEA would like to turn the clock back and restore the 'traditional' two-parent family of employed father and mother at home with the children, others have been arguing that the real problem is that government policy has not kept up with changing family patterns. This was a key theme, for example, in the recent report of the Commission on Social Justice (1994). Economic, political and social 'revolutions', they argued, have made the Beveridge welfare state increasingly out of step with the way in which people live now and policies are needed which reflect these changes and are tailored to new needs and circumstances. Amid much controversy, the Board for Social Responsibility of the Church of England put forward a similar argument about changing family patterns in their report *Something to Celebrate* (1995). The proposal that the phrase 'living in sin' was inappropriate to describe cohabiting couples received the most publicity but the report as a whole stressed the 'need to recognise and value the different ways in which people live in families at the end of the twentieth century' (p. 210).

The responses to the Church's report show how contentious are the issues surrounding the family. Notions about what the family is, and what it should be, are highly charged, as can also be seen by the furore over the BBC Panorama programme, *Babies on Benefit* which Sue Slipman, then Director of the National Council for One Parent Families, condemned. The Broadcasting Complaints Commission upheld the criticisms of the programme as unfair and unjust to lone parents, but much of the popular press jumped to the defence of the BBC. This acrimonious debate is symptomatic of the divisions within British society over family issues. These divisions are found within, as well as between, political parties. Tony Blair, in one of his first interviews as leader of the Labour Party, spoke out in favour of the traditional family in a way which has caused consternation to some of his party members who fear that such comments reinforce the stigma attached to those who do not live in traditional families. Some leading members of the Conservative party (notably Michael Howard, Peter Lilley and John Redwood) have frequently condemned the collapse of the traditional family and the rise in lone parenthood. By contrast Virginia Bottomley has dismissed the idea of a golden age of the family as mythical, and has defended working mothers and lone mothers, most of whom she argues provide good care for their children irrespective of poverty, disadvantage and adversity. Similarly, Alistair Burt has argued that the demands of employment are a threat to family life and family stability while Michael Portillo has suggested that people should put their jobs before their families. Moreover, not only are there differences between Cabinet members, but individual ministers also seem to reassess their views. For instance, at the 1992 Conservative Party Conference Peter Lilley adopted a judgmental tone towards lone parents with his 'little list' of benefit scroungers in which lone mothers came near

3

the top; two years later he seemed to have come around to the view that the benefit system and widening wage differentials in the 1980s played a key part in the growth of crime and lone parenthood (the *Guardian* 27 May 1994, 19 November 1994). Even Margaret Thatcher, conviction politician to the end, now seems to regret not having tried to regulate family behaviour more than she did when Prime Minister, and to condemn the social security budget (which sky-rocketed in the 1980s) for encouraging anti-social behaviour, including dependency (Thatcher 1995, p. 544).

Thus, the ways in which governments do, or should, intervene to alter existing family patterns, or behaviour within families, is central to political debate in Britain, and is one of the key themes of this book. As part of the International Year of the Family, Virginia Bottomley, speaking in her capacity as Minister for the family, set out the four essential duties of government in relation to families: first, to acknowledge the privacy of family life - stressing the responsibility of parents and the importance of keeping the state out of private family matters; second, to ensure that the framework of law underpins family life in a changing world; third, to ensure that protection and help is available when family relationships do not provide the support that they should; and finally, to support public agencies, including voluntary bodies, which provide practical help for families (IYF Agenda for Action 1994). This is a highly 'private' view of the relationship between the family and the state, in which the state plays only a very residual role: picking up the pieces when things go wrong but otherwise leaving families to get on with things in their own way. But, alongside an agenda which stresses the 'burden' of public expenditure and the need to cut costs, this has led to policies which have sought to increase the role of families and reduce the role of the state. Two pieces of legislation in particular highlight this, and also highlight the way in which policy implementation, and the power of those affected by policy change, can influence the political response.

The *1990 NHS and Community Care Act* began operating in 1993. This legislation transferred to local authorities the responsibility for assessing and paying for services for the elderly and other vulnerable groups. One consequence of the Act is that an increasing number of elderly people are being expected to fund their own care and, if they have capital assets, to realise these in order to pay for care. Another consequence has been an increased reliance on unpaid carers, usually family members, often elderly themselves but also an increasing number of children (about 10,000 according to one estimate, The *Independent* 9 January 1995). However, although community care policy relies heavily on 'informal' care, those providing such care have few rights and the local authority is not obliged to assess their needs as part of the 'care package'. The Carers (Recognition and Services) Act 1995 gives carers the right to be assessed for services to meet their own needs, such as respite care and help at home. However, in order to ensure some chance of success, the Act empowers, but does not *require*, local authorities to provide services for carers. This Act was introduced by a back-bencher, Malcolm Wicks, as a private members bill, and touches on only one aspect of the community care. Thus, while many families have been affected by policies of community care - both financially and practically - they have generally lacked the political capacity and the power to put the government under real pressure to introduce changes.

This is very different from the situation in relation to child support. Like the community care legislation, the *1991 Child Support Act* also began operating in 1993. This policy set out to increase the financial obligations of 'absent parents' towards their children by introducing a set formula for maintenance payments and enforcing these through the new Child Support Agency. It has been highly controversial from the start with those most affected - separated parents, the vast majority fathers - setting up a storm of protest. Following its first annual report, showing little progress in either assessing or collecting child support, the CSA received extra money and staff and lower targets. Yet the criticisms continued. The Commons Select Committee, the Ombudsman, National Audit Office Report and an independent government inspector all damned the CSA to varying degrees and, in what the *Guardian* headlined as 'U-turn by Lilley on CSA rules', the government announced in January 1995 that it would be making a number of changes which it had previously ruled out. Thus, although it is probably the case that fewer people have been directly affected by the child support legislation than by the community care legislation, the high visibility of this policy, its implementation at national rather than local level, and the vociferous and organised nature of the opposition have together forced policy change and made the development of coherent policy for the support of children in separated families likely to be much more difficult to achieve in the future.

Some of the many issues raised by the community care and the child support legislation are addressed in more detail in chapters here. Of course not all aspects of family life, or of government policy as it affects families, are covered. However, the various chapters in this volume do cover a range of current policy issues while providing a guide through the morass of highly complex and confusing issues surrounding policies which affect families. This complexity is the result of four main factors. First, as discussed above, there is very little consensus over the goals of policy in

5

relation to the family, which often seem unclear or contradictory. In the 1980s, for example, ministers spoke out in favour of the traditional family while whittling away the married man's tax allowance and freezing child benefit. Secondly, there are a whole range of policies which are not drawn up explicitly with the family in mind but which do nevertheless affect family life. For example, many middle-income families have been hard hit as a consequence of housing policies which encouraged owner occupation in the boom years of the 1980s but which failed to help those suffering in the recession years of the 1990s. Thirdly, and related to this, policies that affect the family lack central coordination. The role of minister for the family was undertaken by Virginia Bottomley when she was in the Department of Health, but in this responsibility she was without portfolio and her role was limited. Her recent move leaves responsibility for family policy very unclear. Ministers do meet periodically to examine the impact of government policies as a whole on the family but, especially compared with many other European countries, the institutional framework for family policy is very weak. Fourthly, policies affecting the family are constantly changing, and there is a need, therefore, for research findings which can contribute to the independent monitoring and assessment of policies and make suggestions for improvements.

Ruth Lister's opening chapter illustrates two of our key themes: the contradictions of policy and the way in which policy often seems less concerned with the actual circumstances of families and more concerned with encouraging or discouraging certain attitudes and behaviours. As she points out, 1993 was the year in which the 'breakdown' of the family hit the top of the policy agenda. But, although there was much concern expressed about what was supposedly happening to the family, this did not translate into any clear policy, for example, to provide more support for the increasing numbers of working parents or poor families or lone parents. Rather there was an increased entrenchment of ideological positions around what families *should* be like and *should* do. From there a fairly short step leads to the position that, if families fail to conform to these ideals, the role of government should be to make sure that they do: thus policy initiatives such as 'back to basics' in which the government seeks to define the outlines of appropriate moral behaviour.

The consequence of political change for families is the main theme of Chapter Two, in which Ilona Ostner examines the impact on families, and especially on women, of the reunification of East and West Germany. These two countries formerly had very different stances towards the family. Policy in West Germany was based on an assumption of a 'male breadwinner family' with men in employment and women at home looking

6

after children. The economic security of women and children was thus guaranteed through male wages and wage replacement benefits. By contrast, in East Germany, both parents were expected to work and their standard of living was maintained less through the market wages that their work brought and more through the state provision of services and price subsidies. For those from both East and West, reunification has thus brought major changes and new insecurities: the West German model has been much the most dominant but has also changed. In particular the family is increasingly failing as a source of economic security for women and their earnings are becoming more and more essential to family income. Thus, as in the UK, there are growing divisions between families with and without paid work and an increased 'commodification' of women.

The next chapters return mainly to the UK in order to pursue in some detail recent policy towards lone-parent families - the family type which has been at the heart of the political debate over the family. The issues of insecurity and lack of consensus over policy goals are central to Jane Millar's analysis of the *Child Support Act* in Chapter Three. She contrasts the widespread lack of support for this policy in the UK with the response in Australia to the introduction of a child support scheme there and suggests that this reflected differences in both the structure and objectives of the two schemes. She also argues that current policy is likely to increase, rather than reduce, the financial insecurity of lone mothers and concludes by suggesting that current policy towards lone parents is highly divisive, setting one type of family against another. In the following chapter Sue Morris and Fran Wasoff take this further by considering whether or not the child support legislation could be said to be in the interests of women and at the expense of men: a reading of the legislation which has been popular in the press and among the pressure groups of separated fathers which have sprung up to oppose the legislation. However Morris and Wasoff conclude that the majority of women will gain little or nothing financially from the Act and that many will lose in terms of their independence and relationships. Not that men gain either - the Treasury may be the only gainer although the failure to collect much child support leaves this rather in doubt - but by setting men against women the legislation is a source of further conflict between separating couples.

The differential impact of policy on men and women is also a theme of Chapter Five, in which Peter McCarthy examines the housing consequences of marital breakdown. Again the policy contradictions are highlighted. Men are exhorted to maintain contact with their children after divorce but, unless they can afford the option of owner-occupied housing of a 'family' size, their chances of getting accommodation that would make this feasible are very limited. For both men and women, housing circumstances (as with family income) tend to improve if they re-partner, those who remain alone have difficulty in getting adequate housing. Then, in Chapter Six, Peter Selman unpicks the statistics on teenage motherhood. Just as lone parents are at the heart of political debates over the family, so teenage unmarried mothers are at the heart of the debate over lone motherhood. But, as his analysis shows, teenage birth rates were actually much higher in the 1960s than in the 1980s, but while the most common outcome then was marriage (followed later by divorce?), today the most common outcomes are abortion or a birth outside marriage. Selman argues that limited sex education and difficulties in obtaining contraception coupled with poor economic circumstances mean, not necessarily that the desire for children is strong, but that the motivation to avoid pregnancy is weak.

The following chapters shift the focus somewhat to examine the issue of access to welfare benefits and services. They all, in various ways, suggest that recent policy has made such access more difficult. Ian Law, Carl Hylton, Alyas Karmani and Alan Deacon examine the take-up of benefits among families of non-white ethnic origin. They show that there are significant differences in take-up rates between the ethnic groups in their study and these relate, at least in part, to differences in the construction of family versus state obligations and public versus private boundaries. Thus, for example, older Bangladeshis and Pakistanis sometimes felt that it would be shameful to claim benefits and men more often dealt with the claiming process than women (which may be a contrast to the situation among white families). However, although these cultural differences in attitude are important the authors also stress that the administration of the benefits is central to understanding differential patterns of receipt. Many aspects of the procedure made claiming difficult for the families they interviewed and much poverty, which could have been avoided, was the result. Thus the policy and administrative context is very important in shaping the nature of the possible responses.

Chapter Eight, by Hartley Dean and Di Thompson and Chapter Nine, by John Baldock and Claire Ungerson, both examine the impact of the community care legislation, and also illustrate this point about how policy can act to constrain choices. Dean and Thompson set their analysis within a theoretical context that seeks to explain how the state constructs particular family obligations and gender roles. The community care legislation, they argue, means that the obligation to care is assumed and expected: there is no opting out of providing family care despite a rhetoric which emphasises choice and a 'mixed economy of care' in which carers act in partnership with local authority services. Baldock and Ungerson show how difficult this is in practice: 'consumers of community care' must learn, not only how to negotiate a very unfamiliar map of public and private provision but also they must, in the course of doing so, change their expectations about what will happen and, for some, their beliefs about what should happen. The same is true for the disabled men, and their partners, interviewed by Gillian Reynolds and reported in Chapter Ten. For these men the ideological assumptions about care and dependency on the one hand, and masculinity on the other, create a situation in which they find it difficult to construct an identity and this creates further difficulties in getting access to benefits and services.

Finally, in Chapter Eleven, Janet Finch argues that, precisely because policy is so often ideologically driven and based on assumptions about what families (and the individuals within families) should be doing, so it is especially incumbent on researchers to provide clear evidence on the actual beliefs, attitudes and behaviour of families. She illustrates her point by drawing on her own research into patterns of inheritance within families. Her chapter brings us back, in a sense, to the 'politics' of the family: the varied circumstances and needs of families cannot be reduced to simple or rigid policy responses and policies driven by politics and ideology seem to leave little space for the voices of the men, women and children that make up families to be heard. Re-structuring the welfare state is not simply about restructuring the relationship between state and economy: the relationship between the state and the family is also at the heart of these issues. The question of the balance between state, individual, family, market, and voluntary sectors in welfare provision is fundamental to the future of welfare policy in Britain, and thus to the economic and social security of the whole population.

References

Barclay, P. (chair) (1995), *Report of the Inquiry into Income and Wealth*, Joseph Rowntree Foundation, York.

Board for Social Responsibility of the Church of England (1995), *Something to celebrate: valuing families in church and society*, Church House Publishing, London.

Commission on Social Justice (1994), *Social Justice*, Vintage, London.

Davies, J. (ed) (1993), *The Family: is it just another lifestyle choice?*, Institute for Economic Affairs, London.

Dennis, N. and Erdos, G. (1993), *Families without fatherhood*, Institute for Economic Affairs, London.

Department of Social Security (1995), *Households below average income*, HMSO, London.

Haskey, J. (1995), 'Trends in marriage and cohabitation', *Population Trends* 80, pp. 5-15.

Hutton, W. (1995), *The state we're in*, Jonathan Cape, London.

International Year of the Family Agenda for Action (1994), *Speech by the Rt Hon Virginia Bottomley MP*, Department of Health Press release 94/576, 8 December 1994, London.

Morgan, P. (1995), *Farewell to the Family? Public policy and family breakdown in Britain and the USA*, Institute for Economic Affairs, London.

Murray, C. with Field, F., Brown, J., Walker, A. and Deakin, N. (1990), *The emerging British Underclass*, Institute for Economic Affairs, London.

Population Trends (1995), HMSO, London.

Thatcher, M. (1995), *The Path to Power*, Harper Collins, London.

Whelan, R. (ed) (1995), *Just a piece of paper? Divorce reform and the undermining of marriage*, Institute for Economic Affairs, London.

1 Back to the family: Family policies and politics under the Major government

Ruth Lister

Introduction

The politics of the family have assumed a new significance during the 1990s, providing a touchstone for the ideological positioning of many on the Right. Thus, the Major years have been characterized more by the growing political salience of a discourse around the 'breakdown of the family' than by any coherent policy response to a set of family trends more or less common to Western industrialized societies. This chapter therefore first outlines briefly these trends and the debates surrounding them as well as the dilemmas they raise for a post-Thatcherite Conservative Government, before looking at actual policy developments since 1990.

'The family' does not constitute a discrete area of policy especially in a country, such as the UK, which has neither an explicit policy nor a minister with formal departmental responsibility for families. A wide range of social and economic policies affect the well-being of families. The chapter covers those social policies which have had the most direct impact on families with children and the women in those families.

This focus is not to discount the growing importance for families of the rise in the number of older people and the community care policies directed towards them which are the subject of other chapters in this collection. Nor is it to overlook the fact that men, as well as women, live in and have responsibilities towards families. Indeed the nature of these responsibilities and how well men are - or are not - meeting them have recently begun to be the subject of some public discussion. As such, they are part of a wider, increasingly intense, debate about changing family patterns in general and the perceived threat to civilised society of the onward march of lone parenthood in particular.

Social and economic trends

John Major came to power at the end of a decade in which a number of long-term trends in family and women's employment patterns had accelerated.

In line with most members of the European Union (EU), the number of marriages was down and the rate of cohabitation was up. Although cohabitation remained a prelude to marriage in most cases, for a growing minority it had become an alternative. The proportion of women aged 18 to 49 who were married had fallen from 74 per cent in 1979 to 61 per cent in 1990. Conversely, the proportion of women in this age-group cohabiting had increased from 11 per cent to 22 per cent over the same period. (By 1992, the figures were 59 per cent and 21 per cent respectively.) A rising proportion of second marriages has meant that step-families have become increasingly common.

The proportion of births outside marriage more than doubled during the 1980s to nearly one in three by 1992, of which three-quarters were registered to both parents at the same address. The overall birth rate has been falling and the child-bearing years have become increasingly compressed. Again, despite considerable variations between countries, the trends follow a wider Western European pattern.

Divorce has also been increasing in most European countries although the main increase was during the 1970s. By 1991, for every two marriages in Great Britain there was one divorce - the highest rate in Europe.

One politically sensitive consequence of these trends was the rapid rise in the proportion of families headed by a lone parent (nine out of ten of whom are women) from 12 per cent in 1979 to 21 per cent by 1992. The biggest increase was amongst single, never-married, mothers. The proportion of lone parent families increased in all the main ethnic groups but there remain considerable variations between them. By the end of the 1980s, the UK was estimated to have the highest proportion of lone parent families in the EU (Roll 1992).

1990 marked the first year in which the classic household of married couple plus children was overtaken by single person households as the most common type. By 1992, they represented 24 per cent and 27 per cent of all household types respectively compared with 31 per cent and 23 per cent in 1979. Again, there was considerable variation between ethnic groups.

These changes in family patterns have been parallelled by fundamental labour market trends which have contributed to a revolution in women's labour market participation. Between the end of the 1970s and the beginning of the 1990s, the proportion of married women with children in

Table 1.1
Proportion of families headed by a lone parent

Family type	1979	1990	1992
Lone mother	10	18	19
single	2	6	7
widowed	2	1	1
divorced	4	7	6
separated	3	4	5
Lone father	2	2	2
All lone parents	12	20	21

Source: OPCS, General Household Survey 1992, HMSO, 1994.

paid work rose from 52 to 63 per cent. Among those with children aged under five the increase was from 27 to 47 per cent. However, over the same period the proportion of lone parents in work fell from 47 to 42 per cent. One consequence was a politically sensitive growth in reliance on social assistance from 38 per cent to 70 per cent of all lone parents between 1979 and 1992.

During the 1980s, women's share of total employment rose throughout the EU but the trend has been particularly marked in the UK where women are now set to outnumber men in the labour market. However, it is a labour market which is still segregated along both vertical and horizontal lines and in which the majority of jobs open to women have been low paid and part-time (for a diminishing number of hours). The UK has the second highest proportion of female part-time workers in the EU (though part-time work is much less common among minority ethnic women). It also boasts the highest earnings gap between women and men.

The revolution in women's participation in the labour market has not been matched by any significant change in men's participation in the home and family. The 'new man' remains hard to find. Indeed, Mintel gave up the search and in their report Men 2000 made do with 'Newish Man', wholly or mainly responsible for just one everyday household chore. Nearly one in five met this stringent criterion; more numerous were the 'semi-sharers' who shared responsibility for at least one task and the 'sloths' who left all the main tasks wholly or mainly to someone else (Mintel 1994).

As the International Social Attitudes report noted, despite 'profound objective changes in the structure, composition and functioning of the family throughout Europe and North America...many of the traditional gender roles have remained steadfast' (Scott et al. 1993, p. 24).

Men continue to undertake longer hours in paid work on average than in any other EU state. At the same time, men's full time employment has been diminishing and high unemployment continues to have a damaging impact on family life and living standards. This is part of a broader trend of growing labour market insecurity which is taking its toll on families (see, for instance, Gallie et al. 1994, Wilkinson 1994).

The gap between two earner and no earner families has widened and overall the 1980s were marked by a disastrous growth in family poverty. Between 1979 and 1991-92, the proportion of children in households below average income rose from one in ten to one in three (DSS 1994). Women, as the managers and shock-absorbers of poverty, will have borne the main brunt of this increase in family hardship. The proportion of total household income going to families with children fell from 37 per cent in 1979 to 30 per cent in 1990. Over the same period there was a marked increase in the number of homeless families, although the trend did begin to turn in the early 1990s.

Family politics

Tory preoccupation with 'the family' surfaced at intervals during the 1980s, having been prominent in the run-up to the 1979 Election when the two main parties vied with each other in their claims to be the party of the (traditional) family. However, apart from a leaked document from the government Family Policy Group which suggested various ways of encouraging families to reassume their responsibilities (only some of which were followed up), it was not until towards the end of Mrs Thatcher's reign that she really focused on the issue. Her memoirs revealed her growing belief that strengthening the 'traditional family' was the only way to get to the root of crime and other social problems. She told the 1988 Conservative Women's Conference that 'family breakdown...strikes at the very heart of society therefore policies must be directed at strengthening the family'.

A similar message was being articulated by the right-wing think tanks, most vociferously the IEA Health & Welfare Unit which had as its central project 'to restore the ideal of the two parent family' (Green 1993, p. viii). The IEA's position was summed up in one of a series of papers, *The* our free and reasonably successful society will be able to remain free and stable only when each generation moves into its maturity and its civic responsibilities when it has effectively internalized those values which make for freedom and stability. The only institution which can provide the time, the attention, the love and the care for doing that is not just 'the family', but a stable two-parent mutually complementary nuclear family. The fewer of such families that we have, the less we will have of either freedom or stability (Davies 1993, p.7).

At the same time, the discourse of the 'dependency culture' was shifting its target from the male unemployed to female lone parents, reflecting the influence of U.S. New Right 'underclass' theorists such as Charles Murray, although the debate in the UK has not been racialised in the same way that it has in the US.

The coming to power of the more ideologically pragmatic John Major signalled a softening of this discourse and concern about 'the family' remained relatively low key. The issue continued to rumble in the media but predictions that 'the family' would be a central issue in the 1992 General Election campaign proved unfounded.

This was all to change in 1993 which was widely seen as the year in which 'the breakdown of the family' hit the top of the political agenda. On the one hand, the James Bulger murder and media coverage of a spate of 'home alone' cases raised public concerns about the nation's children and parental responsibility for them. On the other, growing anxieties about crime and incivility, linked by many to lone parenthood, were seized by the Right as a potent weapon in their battle for the direction of the Conservative Government.

Again the IEA Health & Welfare Unit played a pivotal role. It pulled off something of a coup with its publication in 1992 of a paper by two ethical socialists, Norman Dennis and George Erdos, with a foreword by A.H. Halsey, in which many of society's ills were attributed to the impact of lone parenthood on children and, in particular, to the absence of fathers from their lives.

This was taken up by the media and one of the loudest and most persistent apostles of the message has been Melanie Phillips then of the *Guardian* and now the *Observer*. It was also seized upon by politicians, notably Michael Howard who cited the paper at the 1993 Tory Party Conference in a speech linking juvenile crime to lone parenthood.

The 1993 Party Conference proved to be a defining moment, after a Summer in which the political rhetoric around lone parents crescendoed.

Particularly notable was the visit of the Welsh Secretary, John Redwood, to a Welsh housing estate with a high proportion of lone parent families, after which he hit the headlines by urging that absent fathers be forced back into the family home. (This was to the dismay of local police who maintained that it would create more problems than it would solve, given levels of domestic violence.) A junior minister then called for a more judgemental attitude towards lone parent families and laid part of the blame for the growth in their numbers on the feminist movement.

At the Conference, Ministers vied with each other in their moralising attribution of a range of social ills to lone parent families despite, it emerged later, to some embarrassment, their possession of a Cabinet briefing paper which challenged their arguments. The briefing paper also revealed the objectives for a review of provision for lone parent families being undertaken at Cabinet level: to tackle incentives to become and remain a lone parent; to strengthen incentives for lone parents to support themselves through work and child maintenance and, most controversially, to increase the responsibility of young lone parents' own parents to provide support.

The tone of ministerial speeches contrasted with that at the 1990 Conference. Then, despite a highly charged debate, under the Conference banner of 'Working to keep the family together', Angela Rumbold, Minister at the Home Office with responsibility for women's issues, responded by warning against moralising and attempting to turn the clock back.

By the 1992 Conference though, Peter Lilley was beginning to set out his stall with his proclamation that 'we Conservatives believe in the family. It is the most important institution in society...The family is under threat from the left. They hate it because it is a bastion against the dominant state'. He also developed what was becoming an increasingly familiar theme, that of the duties of parents, especially absent fathers. This echoed a widely-publicised speech by Margaret Thatcher, back in January 1990. In this speech, billed by the media as a moral crusade, Mrs Thatcher warned that 'seeing life without fathers not as the exception but as the rule...is a new kind of threat to our whole way of life, the long-term implications of which we can barely grasp'. Looking forward to the subsequent White Paper on maintenance, she declared that 'no father should be able to escape from his responsibilities'.

Major did not himself join in the orgy of lone parent-bashing at the 1993 Conference and later in the year was reported to have reined back his Cabinet colleagues when it became apparent that their vilification of lone parents had not struck the expected chord with the electorate. Nevertheless his end-of-conference 'Back to Basics' rallying cry was widely interpreted as a victory for the Right and was welcomed by his predecessor as signalling that 'Thatcherism is alive and well'. Stuart Hall suggested that Major fell back on Thatcherite themes in an attempt to mobilise political support because he lacks an authentic language of his own (Hall 1993).

His subsequent attempts to disassociate 'Back to Basics' from moralising about the family, in the face of a series of embarrassing lapses from family values amongst his colleagues, were not wholly credible given that family respect and responsibility figured prominently in his original articulation of 'Back to Basics'. The whole tone had been to counterpose family-based common sense against the supposed 'politically-correct' orthodoxies seeded in the permissive sixties. The right-wing MP, Edward Leigh (1994), commented later that, in order to survive the conference, in Back to Basics Major gave his right wing ministers carte blanche to open up a new front against the state-funded permissive society, as briefings around his speech made clear.

During the summer of 1994, Peter Lilley was once again in the headlines with a speech which called attention to the 'serious social and personal problems arising from the disruption of family life. We cannot ignore them. Nor should we' he argued. However, he also challenged the idea that government had much power to prevent family breakdown. 'The idea that Government could impose family values by edict or exhortation is authoritarian and impractical. Likewise, the idea that the state can strengthen the family by undertaking most of its functions is equally objectionable. It amounts to nationalising parental responsibility, making fathers redundant and mothers dependent.' (Lilley 1994)

Lilley's speech was contrasted by the press with a speech the previous month by Virginia Bottomley in which she distanced herself from 'the family pessimist view [which] relies heavily on the [misguided] notion that there was once a golden age of the family'. She also emphasised the need for support from the wider community for families.

A further intervention by Lilley, at the end of 1994, marked a distinct softening of the moralistic tone he had adopted at the 1992 party conference, as he shifted his focus to the impact on families of labour market changes, an issue he had begun to explore in his earlier speech. In it, he identified widening earnings differentials and the declining earning power of unskilled young men and women as a key factor in the break-up of families, the growth of lone parenthood, and increased reliance on benefits. Although he still looked to free-market solutions, Lilley's diagnosis was widely interpreted as signalling a possible significant change in government thinking on 'the family'.

It remains to be seen whether this is the case and whether the interventions by Bottomley and Lilley presage a new period of debate within the Conservative Party about family trends and their policy implications. The position of the Labour Party has also come under some scrutiny as its new leader Tony Blair identified himself with a more traditional approach to 'the family', expressing his disapproval of 'the small group of women' who choose to raise children on their own. The turn of the year saw the publication of a number of contributions to the ongoing debate including reports marking the end of the International Year of the Family and a new report from the IEA. The latter, by Patricia Morgan (1995), attributed the breakdown of the traditional family largely to government policies which, it is argued, have favoured lone parent families at the expense of two parent one earner families.

Lone parent families have also figured prominently in one of the most politically sensitive policy areas of the 1990s: the Child Support Act (CSA) (see Chapters 3 and 4). The impact of the Act and the problems with its implementation have dominated the media headlines to an extent rarely seen in the social policy field, with absent fathers portrayed as the oppressed victims of a punitive state out to fleece them for every last penny (Lister 1994).

Less prominent, were the beginnings of a debate about men's behaviour, as fathers, partners and the main perpetrators of crime, and about the implications for men's role and identity of the demise of unskilled full-time 'male' jobs. Feminist commentators such as Beatrix Campbell, Angela Phillips, Anna Coote and Patricia Hewitt have been asking questions about men's absence from the family and what their presence entails. More thoughtful Conservative MPs such as David Willetts (1993) have noted that

> a pattern is beginning to emerge of women reaching out for new opportunities but no compensating change in behaviour by men. Many men like to see themselves as breadwinners with the big wide world as their domain while they see women as pre-eminently responsible for domestic work. But increasingly economic reality is coming to conflict with this picture. And there is a further twist. Not only has there been little change in men's perceptions of their role, there has been at the same time a decrease in their ability to fulfil it (pp. 8-9).

It is the usurping of men's patriarchal role which is worrying many of those crusading to save the traditional family. Back in 1987, the Conservative Family Campaign, backed by a number of Tory MPs, made this explicit with its declaration that

The Conservative Family Campaign aims to put the father back at the

18

head of the family table, he should be the breadwinner, he should be responsible for his children's actions. He should be respected by those who teach his children. He should be upheld by social workers, doctors, and others who professionally come into contact with his children. Years of militant feminism, and harmful legislation like the Equal Opportunities Act have undermined the clear biblical concept of the father (quoted by Loney 1987).

It is the supposedly harmful effects of the absence of fathers on children's development that is also Norman Dennis' central thesis (although he was quoted in the *Independent* [20 November 1993] as saying that this is only speculation and that he has no actual evidence to support it).

At the end of the day, though, it was primarily women - and in particular lone mothers - who figured as the main butt of the ideological crusade to reassert the primacy of the traditional two parent family, although the gender implications of this crusade are becoming more complex. As Andrew Marr, political columnist of the *Independent* noted

So, a man problem, acknowledged in most of the serious work done on family policy, from leftish think-tanks to Tory MPs. And what is the political response? It is pretty difficult to stand in front of the Conservative Party conference and talk about a 'profound crisis of maleness'. It is rather easier to go for gym-slip mums (5 November 1993).

The family crusade was not without its dilemmas and contradictions for the Conservative Party. As Margaret Thatcher recognised in her memoirs, there is a difficulty in squaring an ideological commitment to reducing the influence of the state with intervention in the 'private' sphere of the family. Peter Lilley's speech in which, as noted above, he combined concern about the problems arising from family breakdown with a laissez-faire attitude towards their resolution, can perhaps be read as an attempt to sidestep this particular dilemma.

A growing tension has also emerged between the Tory commitment to a free enterprise society and growing concerns amongst some on the Right about the impact of such a society on families and communities. This has been articulated by commentators such as David Willetts MP, David Green of the IEA and, in particular, apostate John Gray, previous IEA contributor and author of a Social Market Foundation pamphlet in which he stated that 'the fragmentation of family life which contemporary conservatives bemoan is, in very large part, a product of the culture of choice, and the economy of unfettered mobility, which they themselves celebrate' (Gray 1994, p. 39). He developed the theme further in a series of Guardian articles

The dilemmas of the Conservatives is that they inherit a simplistic neo-liberal ideology utterly at odds with the spirit of the '90s...Efforts to buttress neo-liberal policies on the economy and welfare with a rhetoric of religious and family values, of the sort made recently by Michael Portillo, are not electorally credible (4 October 1993).

The core institution of any stable society, the family, has [after a decade and a half of neo-liberal policies] been subjected to all the stresses of unchannelled economic change, leaving it fractured and resourceless in communities themselves rendered fragile and impotent by a form of public policy in which social life is reduced to a series of market exchanges (9 June 1994).

A particular dilemma for the Conservatives has concerned the proper place of mothers and, in particular, lone mothers. On the one hand, traditional Conservative thinking accorded primacy to mothers' place in the home and community care policies were predicated on assumptions about the availability of, primarily female, carers. On the other, the 1990s had been hailed by Sir Norman Fowler and others (including the Ministerial Group on Women's Issues), as the 'decade of the working woman' as employers looked to women to supply their labour needs.

The resolution of this dilemma lay in an official stance of neutrality. This was summed up by Major when, as Chancellor of the Exchequer, he stated in the 1990 Budget speech that 'it is not for the Government to encourage or discourage women with children to go out to work. That is rightly a decision for them to take, and one in which the Government would be wise not to interfere'.

The fact that this attitude was maintained for lone mothers as well as mothers in two parent families, despite the burgeoning social security bill as the former's labour market participation collapsed during the '80s, was perhaps testimony to the continued strength of traditional Conservative values with their emphasis on mothers' place in the home. The most the Government felt able to do was to encourage lone mothers to take paid work by means of a combination of the Child Support Act and a parallel set of minor social security reforms (see below). In the case of lone mothers, any contemporary dilemma also reflects a historical ambiguity as to whether lone mothers were to be regarded primarily as mothers or workers (Lewis 1992).

20

Family policies

Employment, women and families

Whilst the neutral stance remains, under Mr Major's premiership there has been something of a shift away from Mrs Thatcher's antipathy towards the working mother. After his initial faux-pas of an all-male Cabinet, he emphasised his support for women's promotion in the workplace through the encouragement of women to senior public appointments and his public backing for Opportunity 2000, an employer-led initiative to help women break through the 'glass ceiling'. After the 1992 Election, Gillian Shepherd, then Employment Secretary, established a top-level working group, to advise her on how to address the difficulties encountered by working women. The Women's Issues Working Group, whose membership includes ministers, business representatives, one member of the voluntary sector, and the chairwomen of the Equal Opportunities Commissions for Britain and Northern Ireland, has continued in existence under Mrs Shepherd's successor, Michael Portillo, although it meets only infrequently.

The difficulties facing working women were, however, exacerbated by the Major Government's continued commitment to labour market deregulation symbolized by its final abolition of the wages councils, highlighted by Mr Major himself as an example of how his Government surpassed Mrs Thatcher's in its radicalism. Four-fifths of workers covered by the Councils were women. The Equal Opportunities Commission predicted a consequent 'unacceptable' widening of the wages gap between women and men in the context of evidence of the harmful impact of other deregulatory policies and labour market trends, such as competitive tendering, casualisation, performance-related pay and decentralised and fragmented wage-bargaining, on women's pay and conditions (Equal Opportunities Commission 1993).

The EOC's calls for new, stronger, clearer and more accessible, legislation on equal pay and sex discrimination continued to be rebuffed on the grounds that the Government believed that voluntarism was the best approach so as not to burden employers and threaten competitiveness.[4] (The limits of such an approach were, however, implicitly acknowledged in the second report of Opportunity 2000 which recorded a distinct lack of progress, in the face of recession and employer resistance.)

Voluntarism has also continued to be the hallmark of the Government's approach to resolution of the difficulties faced by mothers trying to juggle paid work and family responsibilities. A review of social policies affecting women in Europe concluded that 'the British government is distinguished by refusing to take any responsibility for addressing' this issue (Lewis 1993, p. 5). As a result, the UK continues to lag behind most other countries in the EU in the support provided for working parents (see e.g. Bradshaw et al 1993, Clasen 1994) and to resist European Commission attempts to regulate in this area.

The 1992 Manifesto summed up the Government's child care policy: 'We shall continue to encourage the development of child care arrangements in the voluntary and independent sectors'; local authorities would be asked to ensure that the standards for which they are now responsible under the Children Act would be 'applied sensibly'. Building on the approach taken by the Thatcher Government, though with greater emphasis on the needs of working mothers, funds have been made available to promote the provision of pre-school and after-school care by the voluntary sector and employers have been exhorted to make more provision. For their part, a group of major employers, under the banner of Employers for Child Care, called upon the Government to increase funding for child care and to set a national framework and standards.

John Major made the issue of pre-school provision his own when, at the end of 1993, he declared that he wanted 'over time to move to universal nursery education'. This followed growing media coverage of the US evidence of the positive impact of quality nursery education on the later development and propensity to criminal behaviour of children and young people, prompted partly by the espousal of universal nursery education by the National Commission on Education which reported in 1993. However, by Easter 1994, there appeared to be some back-tracking and a year after the commitment was made, it is still not clear what will be its practical outcome.

A minor, but politically significant, initiative has been the introduction of a child care allowance, worth up to £28 a week, for certain parents claiming family credit and related benefits. This measure was explicitly designed to make it easier for lone parents and other low income mothers to take full time paid work (defined for this purpose as 16 hours or more a week).

The development of accessible child care services is one of the provisions contained in the Recommendation on Child Care adopted by the Council of Ministers in 1992 to enable women and men to fulfil their work and family obligations. Another is the promotion of flexible leave arrangements. Like the Thatcher Government before it, the Major Government has resisted attempts by Brussels to place obligations on member states in this area. It managed to water down the Directive on The

Protection of Pregnant Women at Work so as to minimise the improvement it had to make to maternity leave and pay. In the event, it introduced more generous reforms under the Directive than expected, although they still leave the UK with the worst maternity provision in the EU.

The Major Government also blocked an attempt to reactivate a Directive on parental leave originally obstructed by its predecessor. A new directive will now be brought forward under the Maastricht proposal, thereby triggering the first British opt-out. The British Government took a similarly negative stance on the Working Time Directive (despite the public recognition by one junior minister, Alistair Burt, that the demands of employers are often incompatible with meeting responsibilities in the family). The same applied to attempts to introduce Directives to regulate the employment of part-time and temporary workers and to extend to them employment and social security rights. Again these will now be reintroduced under the Maastricht Social Protocol. However, under European law, the Government has been forced to accept, grudgingly, the extension to part-time workers of employment rights with regard to unfair dismissal and redundancy, following a House of Lords ruling in 1994.

Thus it has been the same old story of hostility to any form of regulation of employers and an abdication of any governmental responsibility for measures which would ease the lives of those trying to combine paid employment and unpaid care work. Individual parents and carers are deemed to be responsible for finding their own solutions.

Income maintenance

'Accepting responsibility for yourself and your family and not shuffling it off to the state' was one of the 'basics' extolled by Mr Major at Tory Party Conference.

Malcolm Dean of the *Guardian* (11 September 1993) has suggested that 'the redefining of the boundary between public and private provision' marks 'the third stage of the Thatcher revolution', heralded by Portillo's major public spending review announced in February 1993. However, while we may now be witnessing an acceleration in the process, it has been at, the very least, an undercurrent in social security policy throughout most of the Conservatives' time in office. From the mid-1980s onwards the need to promote self reliance as opposed to 'dependency' upon the state has been a central theme of policy. Finch and Mason (1993) note that

> it can be shown that, in periods when governments are trying to keep down the cost of public expenditure, there is an incentive to encourage families to provide as much as possible. One such period, it can be

23

argued, was the 1980s when the British and many other Western governments tried to re-draw the boundary between state responsibilities and family responsibilities to place more in the realm of the family (p. 177).

One of the clearest examples of the attempt to shift the boundary between public state and private family responsibility for income maintenance is afforded by the CSA. The CSA was very much Mrs Thatcher's baby but Mr Major's Government was responsible for its parliamentary passage and enactment and for defending it against an onslaught of criticism.

Described by the Social Security Select Committee as 'the most far-reaching social reform to be made for 40 years' (Social Security Committee 1993, pv.), the Act effectively shifted a significant proportion of the bill for maintaining lone parent families from the state to absent fathers, since for lone parents on income support (the majority) any maintenance payment is simply offset against their benefit. Most of the controversy around the CSA has centred not on the underlying principle of the financial responsibility of absent fathers for their children but on the impact of the rigid formula devised to make effective that responsibility and its effect on previous settlements (see Chapters 3 and 4). The fact that that formula also, in effect, includes an allowance for the maintenance of the caring parent, thereby reinforcing women's economic dependence upon the fathers of their children, has been insufficiently addressed (Lister 1994).

The CSA was supported by a number of social security changes designed to encourage lone mothers into full time paid work. A further, Cabinet level, review of the position of lone parent families, designed to reduce their reliance on the state still further, has not, as yet, produced the cutbacks in social security some had feared.

Instead, an early product of Lilley's social security review was the proposal to replace unemployment benefit, paid for twelve months, by a job-seekers' allowance, paid on a contributory basis for only six and at a lower rate to those aged under 25. The proposal was attacked during the Second Reading debate by one of the government's own backbenchers, Alan Howarth MP, as 'prejudicial to families...[and] particularly prejudicial to young families' (House of Commons Debates 1995).

The reduction in entitlement for young people was but the latest in a long line of cutbacks during the 1980s designed to increase young people's dependency on their families. In a review of social security for young people during the 1980s, Neville Harris (1989) concludes that the chief characteristic of the period was 'much reduced independent entitlement, with unemployed under-25 year olds facing more and more obstacles to independent household formation' (p. 103).

The job-seekers allowance also represents a further erosion of married women's right to an independent benefit (see Lister 1992), for only a minority of them will qualify for income support instead.[5] At the same time the equalization of the pension age at 65 was finally announced. A substantial cutback in help with mortgage interest for income support claimants, announced at the time of the 1994 Budget, is likely to mean considerable hardship for many low income families and to put home ownership out of the reach of many others. The particular implications for those home owners who have to claim income support because of marriage break up are not yet clear.

The one main policy reversal executed by Major concerned child benefit where his personal commitment to the benefit contrasted with his predecessor's hostility. Frozen since 1987, child benefit's future beyond a further Election, when the Government would not be hamstrung by the binding thread of a comma in a Manifesto pledge, looked distinctly tenuous. Already as Chancellor, Major had partially broken the freeze and, once Prime Minister, not only was a further increase announced but also the index-linking of the benefit. This was the first time such a commitment had ever been made. The 1992 Manifesto promised that 'child benefit will remain the cornerstone of our policy for all families with children. Its value will increase each year in line with prices...[It] will continue to be paid to all families, normally to the mother, and in respect of all children'. However, a series of leaks has suggested that child benefit's longer term future is once again uncertain as the Right's influence over social policy has strengthened.

Another change of direction has been the effective phasing out of the married couple's tax allowance in contravention of the earlier principle that the tax system should pay 'regard to the special relationship and responsibilities that exist within marriage' (HM Treasury 1986, para 3.14). (The abolition of the married couple's, previously married man's, tax allowance has long been called for by feminists and poverty pressure groups who have seen it as a potential source of funds to finance an increase in child benefit. There is a danger that this is one of a number of 'pots of gold' which will have been exhausted by the time an alternative government comes to power.) The demise of the allowance is, however, consistent with a more general trend in fiscal policy documented by Hilary Land (1993). Since the late 1970s, recognition of family responsibilities through the tax system has been increasingly eroded, the latest example being the phased reduction in tax relief on maintenance announced in the November 1993 Budget.

Family policies and policies affecting families

John Major marked the International Year of the Family by appointing Virginia Bottomley, the Health Secretary, to coordinate family policies. Without a Cabinet Committee to chair, however, the appointment was seen as carrying little weight.

The contrast between Government preoccupation with 'the family' and the failure to institutionalize a family policy is not new. On the one hand family values and parental responsibilities are invoked in support of a range of policy initiatives; on the other no attempt is made to assess the impact of policies on families through the kind of family impact statements the Conservatives promised when in Opposition. Criminal justice and education policy provide examples of the former; policies on homelessness, travellers and immigration exemplify the need for the latter.

The Criminal Justice Act 1991, which imposed new responsibilities on the parents of children before the courts, including for fines imposed on them, is being strengthened by the Criminal Justice and Public Order Act 1994 which, in turn, includes further powers to fine or even ultimately jail the parents of young offenders who fail to comply with court orders. Parental responsibility was also a theme of the Parent's Charter (echoing Mr Major's own reference to parental responsibilities as citizens in his Foreword to the Citizen's Charter) which was supposed to have been sent to every parent.

Similarly, new guidelines on sex education in schools, which has been made voluntary, advised that the emphasis should not be on explicit sex education but on 'the value of family life', to the dismay of the Department of Health.

A White Paper on adoption law placed strong emphasis on the married couple as the ideal family unit for adoption; it also gave rise to some confusion as to whether homosexual couples would be allowed to adopt - the answer appeared to be no, although single homosexuals would be considered. With regard to homosexuality more generally, Mr Major made an important symbolic gesture in meeting Sir Ian McKellan of Stonewall but then voted against the equalisation of the age of consent.

Pro-family members of the Conservative Party (and, it has been reported, of the Cabinet) have opposed the Green Paper proposals for the reform of divorce law which would allow divorce after a year, after mediation, on the main grounds of irretrievable breakdown rather than fault. This approach was seen by them as inconsistent with the Government's family values stance. These proposals were published in the White Paper of April 1995 (Lord Chancellor's Office 1995).

26

Inconsistencies have also been highlighted, from outside the Conservative Party, between the emphasis on prevention in the Children Act 1989, which provides the framework for Government policy on children, and the impact on children of many of its policies.

Of particular concern have been the likely implications of proposals to reform homelessness legislation which currently primarily protects families with children. The genesis of the proposals lay in the Right's mythology that young women get pregnant in order to acquire council accommodation. Although the lone parent factor was played down in the consultation document which finally emerged, lone parent families, who it has been estimated are eight times as likely to be homeless as other households, will be disproportionately affected. Fears have been raised of a return to the situation exemplified by Cathy Come Home, with homeless families unable to find permanent accommodation; of an increase in the number of children defined as 'in need' under the Children Act; and that women will find it harder to escape domestic violence. At the time of writing, there have been suggestions in the press that the Government might be back-peddling on these proposals in the face of overwhelming opposition, including from some Conservative councillors. Certainly, they were not included in the 1994 Queen's Speech.

Similarly, Save the Children and other children's charities have warned of the impact on children of the provisions in the Criminal Justice and Public Order Act to repeal the Caravan Sites Act 1968 (following an, ultimately unsuccessful, attempt by the House of Lords to delay the repeal for five years). A prospect of frequent moves and insecurity will, it has been argued, damage children's health and education.

A disregard for the family life of minority groups has also been a feature of immigration policy under the Conservatives, the latest example being the Asylum and Immigration Appeals Act 1993. Similarly, the introduction, in 1994, of a new 'habitual residency' test into the benefits system has hit families where the claimant has travelled abroad or entered the country in the previous five years. Some families, left penniless, have had to turn to social service departments for support. The Children's Rights Development Unit (1994) has documented the ways in which British immigration law and policy have contravened Articles 9 and 10 of the UN Convention on the Rights of the Child which uphold the child's right to family life and family reunion.

This is but one of a long list of examples of how, it is argued, the UK is failing to comply with the Convention (Children's Rights Development Unit, 1994). The Government's first progress report to the UN has been criticised as complacent and misleading and has been compared with the more honest and self-critical reports submitted by some other governments. The Government's refusal to appoint a statutory Children's Rights Commissioner has also been contrasted with initiatives taken in other countries in response to the Declaration.

Conclusion

The politics of the family during the 1990s have represented both a response to a set of underlying trends, far from unique to the UK, and a staking out of the ideological terrain by the Right in what has come to be characterised as the era of post-Thatcherism.

As the Right reasserted its power in the Government, they increasingly made the running in the promotion of a discourse of traditional family values. Although Mr Major restrained ministers' attacks on lone parent families, his Back to Basics credo was essentially supportive of their stance. However, by the end of 1994, some commentators were detecting a possible shift in the Government's attitude, even amongst its more right-wing members who had previously overshadowed ministers more sympathetic to families' needs. Reflecting back on the International Year of the Family, the Director of the Family Policy Studies Centre has suggested that 'the government has moved from moralising about lone mothers to a recognition of the social and economic changes that are undermining family life' (Roberts 1994, p. 1).

It remains to be seen whether this optimistic reading of the Government's position is justified. Certainly, it has not yet been translated into a more positive policy stance. Thus, for instance, the enthusiastic embrace by the Major Government of Thatcherite deregulation policies and the antipathy of some Conservative politicians towards European integration have ensured a hostile response to EU attempts to strengthen policies to help working families and part-time workers.

The rehabilitation of child benefit represents the one unambiguous example of John Major's personal stamp on policy, although whether or not it will hold remains to be seen. For a time it looked as if a commitment to universal nursery education might provide another, but it would now appear that that personal commitment could go the same way as the similar one made by Mrs Thatcher back in 1972, in the face of fears about its public spending implications.

Overall, the Major Government has worked within the context of the agenda set it by the Thatcher Government, sometimes extending it, occasionally softening it. It is more likely to be remembered for the 'moral panic' about the breakdown of the 'family' and the backlash against lone parent families that it helped to unleash, together with the legacy it inherited in the form of the Child Support Act, than for any distinctive policies of its own directed towards families and women. It is thus family politics rather than family policies that have thrived during the first half of the 1990s.

Notes

1. This chapter expands on an earlier chapter in Kavanagh, D. and Seldon, A. (eds.), *The Major Effect*, Macmillan, 1994. The author is grateful to the editors for permission to reproduce the material.

2. This point is not invalidated by the allocation to the Health Secretary of responsibility for the coordination of family policies, discussed later.

3. Dennis, N. and Erdos, G. (1992), *Families without Fatherhood*, Foreword by A.H. Halsey, IEA Health & Welfare Unit. The paper was published in a second edition in October 1993 at the same time as a further paper by Dennis, *Rising Crime and the Dismembered Family: How Conformist Intellectuals Have Campaigned Against Common Sense.*

4. Newspaper reports at the end of 1994 have suggested that the EOC is now under pressure to modify its critical stance towards government policies and that a possible merger with the Commission for Racial Equality is under discussion.

5. It is officially estimated that 70 per cent of men, but only 43 per cent of women, who lost entitlement to unemployment benefit would qualify for income support. House of Commons Hansard, 2.12.93.

References

Bradshaw, J., Ditch, J., Holmes, H. and Whiteford, P. (1993), *Support for Children. A Comparison of Arrangements in Fifteen Countries*, DSS/HMSO, London.

Children's Rights Development Unit (1994), *UK Agenda for Children*, CRDU, London.

Clasen, J. (1994), 'Supporting families with children in the European

Union', *Benefits*, No. 11, Autumn.

Davies, J. (1993), *The Family: Is it Just Another Lifestyle Choice?*, IEA Health and Welfare Unit, London.

DSS (1994), *Households Below Average Income. A Statistical Analysis 1979-1991/92*, HMSO, London.

Equal Opportunities Commission (1993), Annual Report 1992, HMSO, London.

Finch, J. and Mason, J. (1993), *Negotiating Family Responsibilities*, Routledge, London.

Gallie, D., Marsh, C. and Vogler, C. (1994), *Social Change and The Experience of Unemployment*, Oxford University Press, Oxford.

Gray, J. (1994), *The Undoing of Conservatism*, Social Market Foundation, London.

Green, D. (1993), 'Foreword' to Dennis, N., *Rising Crime and the Dismembered Family*, Institute of Economic Affairs Health and Welfare Unit, London.

Hall, S. (1993), *Moving On...*, Democratic Left, London.

Harris, N. (1989), *Social Security for Young People*, Avebury, Aldershot.

House of Commons Debates (1995), 10 January, col. 77.

HM Treasury (1986), *The Reform of Personal Taxation*, HMSO, London.

Land, H. (1993), *The Domestic Basis of National Welfare*, paper given at ESRC personal welfare programme seminar, London.

Leigh, E. (1994), The *Independent*, 14 January.

Lewis, J. (1992), *Women in Britain since 1945*, Basil Blackwell, Oxford.

Lewis, J. (1993), *Women and Social Policies in Europe*, Edward Elgar, Aldershot.

Lilley, P. (1994), Speech at Birmingham Cathedral, 20 June.

Lister, R. (1992), *Women's Economic Dependency and Social Security*, Equal Opportunities Commission, Manchester.

Lister, R. (1994), 'The Child Support Act: Shifting family financial obligations in the UK', *Social Politics*, Summer.

Loney, M. (1987), 'A War on Poverty or on the Poor?', in Walker, A. and Walker, C. (eds), *The Growing Divide*, CPAG, London.

Lord Chancellor's Office (1995), *Looking to the Future: Mediation and the Grounds for Divorce : The Government's Proposals*, HMSO, London.

Mintel (1994), *Men 2000*, Mintel Lifestyle Report, London.

Morgan, P. (1995), *Farewell to the Family?*, IEA, London.

Roberts, C. (1994), 'Consensus grows on families' needs', *Family Policy Bulletin*, December.

Roll, J. (1992), *Lone Parent Families in the European Community*, Family Policy Studies Centre, London.

Scott, J., Braun, M. and Alwin, D. (1993), 'The Family Way', in Jowell, R., Brook, L. and Dowds, L. (eds), *International Social Attitudes: The 10th British Social Attitudes Report*, Aldershot, SCPR/Dartmouth Publishing.

Social Security Committee (1993), *The Operation of the Child Support Act*, HMSO, London.

Wilkinson, R. (1994), *Unfair Shares*, Barnardos, London.

Willetts, D. (1993), *The Family*, W.H. Smith Contemporary Papers, London.

2 Families and family policies in transition: The case of post-unification Germany

Ilona Ostner

Introduction

What might be expected from families in eastern Germany after unification? To what extent have they moved towards the contemporary (West) German model? Are they shifting towards a family model with 'strong' male breadwinner husbands and equally strong, supportive wives and mothers who are, in the main, discontinuously employed? Finally, how do they perceive and handle western values and provisions?

For the time being, it is difficult to answer these questions. However, unification has certainly fuelled the restructuring of the social-conservative German welfare regime towards a more liberal one. Liberal values, such as individual responsibility, work performance or dependence on the family not the state, are to be strengthened at the expense of security provided by state welfare. Women and men in both Germanies have to learn new lessons, the rules of an unknown game: in the market, and at work they are confronted with ambiguous principles such as efficiency, which aims for speed as well as high quality results; in the household they are taught the supposed advantages of complementary gender roles.

Since unification, money has also gained a new meaning and importance for east German households, their neighbourhood and the wider community; money is replacing previous forms of *Gemeinschaft*, which was, however, an artificially created community solidarity, which grew out of socialism's failure to satisfy consumer needs (Gebhardt and Kamphausen 1994). Money is an important driving force for individualism, on the one hand, and for modern familism on the other (Millman 1991, Zelizer 1994). As incomes increase, so people may opt out of state welfare services; and the boundary between state and household (marriage and family based) provision of welfare may be redrawn.

To give an example: at first, east German skilled industrial workers complain about the west German remuneration system which honours the group's effort, not the individual's. They resent a group premium system which aims to decentralize power, to increase the group's responsibility for the quality of each worker's contribution and thereby to decrease inefficient competition within the assembly line group. This system, they argue, punishes those who are more skilled and more disciplined, in effect the higher achievers; to them it (as under socialism) unduly levels individual achievement and, now under capitalism, it reduces individual purchasing power, one of the treats capitalism has to offer.

Just as East Germany's political system has changed, so too have work, marriage, the family and the monetary system. Spouses, children and parents now have to rely on each other and negotiate their relationships in ways unknown to former East Germans. The 'intimate dynamics of families and money' (Millman) have yet to be investigated. Germans in the new *Länder* (states) have had to modify their attitudes towards the changed institutions in their life. Work, money and the family have different meanings under capitalism and under socialism because each system produces different choices and constraints. New trade-offs between work, love, and family, work and money, and love and money are emerging. Stripped of the providential state, forced to rely either on continuous employment or on unemployment benefits or pension (public welfare), or on families' and breadwinners' solidary, women (and men) will experience new vulnerabilities and painful realities, even though the majority of east German men are winners under the new system. This is to a lesser extent, true for women too.

The move towards a market economy increases social differentiation: different cohorts are differently affected by the change. Surprisingly for instance, lone mothers are not generally the main losers. As Eva Maedje and Claudia Neusuess (1994, p. 140) argue, for quite a lot of women being on social assistance offers a desirable alternative to paid work or marriage, because for east Germans it is seen as a structural phenomenon rather than an individual failure and problem.

A social market economy

West Germany is said to be a *social market economy* (for details see Mueller-Armack 1956, Preston 1991, p. 67). A 'social market economy' relies on principles such as undistorted competition buffered and complemented by social elements. Undistorted competition primarily aims to create the sovereignty of suppliers and consumers: access to resources is governed by the ability and willingness to pay for goods or services; income derives from individual market performance. Collective labour law strengthens the ongoing dialogue between the two social partner, employers and employees. The wider community or state intervenes only subsidiary. Subsidiarity - the primacy of the smaller unity, eg. the family before the wider community or state - is safeguarded by custom and law; state intervention in families or the market is, therefore, restricted (Nell-Breuning 1957). These liberal tenets prevail in Germany, with a stronger focus on relations and status than on individuals. Society's solidarity is designed to support continuously these relations - be it husband-wife, parents-children, worker-employer - to reach their full potential.

West German social policies have consequently promoted mobility outside, and stability inside, the home (Moeller 1993, Ostner 1994). They have favoured middle-class men returning home after a stressful working day; that is until recently they have backed the male wage based entirely on work/job performance (*Leistungslohn*) and sufficient to provide for a family with two-parents and two-children. Additionally, in cases of the average workers' risks eg. invalidity or unemployment, the former status was widely guaranteed. West Germany merged principles of a social market economy with others, such as status maintenance or subsidiarity of marriage and family as worthy institutions of their own intrinsic value. Until now, tax, and other allowances and benefits enabled (married) women to undertake less paid work while their children were small, and to stay at home as housewives. In West Germany women's employment patterns and work careers during their life course matched these principles.

The (West) German strong male breadwinner regime can be shown by indicators, such as the extent of mothers' employment, individual or 'derived' social security entitlements as well as the extent of public child care provisions. It decommodifies - giving exit options from paid work - to those skilfully and continuously employed while familiarizing those (mainly mothers) who do not fit that norm. Consequently, mothers' labour market participation is relatively low and predominantly part-time while children are young; there are virtually no child care facilities for children under the age of three; existing facilities only take children on a part-time basis and so do not support women's full-time employment. Not surprisingly, most women still depend heavily for an income on marriage and family based social security.

At the same time, decommodifying male labour the German welfare regime pursues a status maintenance strategy: for average employees' risks civil servants are entitled to income replacement rates between 75 and 100 per cent; and standard (mainly male) workers are entitled to rates between 60 and 100 per cent, sometimes unlimited and usually without any means testing. The principle of status maintenance also guides marriage, family and divorce law. Thus, divorced partners (or children) are entitled to share the former partner's (or parent's) standard of living.

Since unification ideas of a social market economy have been back on the agenda. Profiting in part from the end of socialism, but mainly, from rapidly growing public borrowing and spending, as well as economic recession, the ruling Christian Democrats and Liberals have moved towards a modernized or purer version of a social market economy with less status maintenance, and maybe non in the future? The likely shifts, fiercely debated now, can be described as moving from wage replacement to wage supplements, from paying-off risks to incentives to take any paid work; from unconditional widows' pension to pensions based on caring periods out of employment. They stress the importance of self-reliance for both men and women, for example, by softly forcing them to accept lower wages and less security, on the one hand, and by targeting those 'proved' to be in need, on the other. From this perspective, male work will become 're'-commodified or less 'de'-commodified; while, women's life in contrast will be 'de'-familized. The two processes, however, are occurring at a time of declining workers' rights and worsening labour market conditions.

In the course of this creeping purification of the German social security state, family policies have become a special target. They aim to increase social insurance contributions while decreasing the number of those who profit from the schemes without having contributed to them. Brave working families whose members make every possible joint effort to make a living and raise their children properly are now a matter of great concern. As it is widely argued, childless couples, especially two-earners, or 'swinging singles' should no longer be advantaged by tax and social security rules. At the moment, Germany seems to be coming closer to traditional liberal values, such as individual autonomy and responsibility and socio-economic independence through waged work, the family and local community.

Many observers of the socio-economic transformation in unified Germany foretell a peculiar dialectic: while eastern Germans strive (or are more or less forced) to adopt the West German model, this model is changing in its essence. Therefore, what East Germans aspire to (i.e., equal living and working conditions) has become a moving target, with a changing German welfare regime. With the end of the socialist alternative all Germans may experience a 'race to the bottom', towards minimalist welfare. What then will happen to the breadwinner norm and reality? Before answering this question, the next section summarizes the main features of the GDR system.

Socialist welfare

Rebuilding East Germany after 1945 necessitated the full-time employment of all women. During the fifties and early sixties, demand outstripped the availability of child care facilities: grandmothers took care of their grandchildren, in order to help their daughters earn a living, as many women now remember. Ideological competition between the socialist German nation and the West German social market economy and economic necessity merged the idea of economic independence with emancipation. In the 1960s policies oriented towards mothers and children (e.g., day care with meals provided, and maternity leave) emerged gradually. Every woman had the right to one day off per month for household responsibilities (*Hausarbeitstag*). She could also claim paid maternity leave for the first year after the birth of a child. Pronatalist policies privileged mothers with more than two children by granting an extended maternity leave and a reduction of working years required before retirement (Bast and Ostner 1992). A far greater number of women worked throughout their lives in East Germany rather than in West Germany and spent most of their daily life apart from their families. The Socialist party or the firm regularly organized pastime and (very cheap) school holiday activities for children. East German working mothers often exploited themselves and became estranged from their children, who were often apart from their mothers ten or twelve hours per day. Children had few choices and were kept on strict schedules. The state - not the parent- decided about children's future: for instance, schooling and vocational training, job placement, and job location. It is well known that after the wall came down several thousands of children were abandoned by their parents who moved to the west - some were left with the institutions which had taken care of them during the week. A recent comparative study on child development based on thematic perception tests emphasizes the extent to which ten year old East German children voiced fears of being left on their own, while their West German counterparts most feared their parents' conflicts, and not matching their parents expectations for them (Leuzinger-Bohleber and Garlichs 1993, see also Zwiener 1994).

In 1950 East Germany formally abolished women's economic dependence and, thus, the idea of the male-breadwinner-headed household, although in reality it never completely disappeared. In addition, the notion of a full-time homemaker and wife faded away. Yet, despite the same training, women seldom enjoyed the same work opportunities and earnings as men; most households needed a two-earner's income and relied on benefits in kind directed at families (e.g., free daycare, subsidized clothes and food for children). Additional income was needed in order to make ends meet and to afford household appliances and expensive extras. Women in East Germany had higher rates of marriage; they married and had more children than West German women earlier in their lives. Early marriage and parenthood is often taken as one sign of a lack of choice which in turn partly explains the recent decline in marriage and birth rates.

From a sociological perspective one could argue that East Germany resembled a traditional society, especially after the wall was erected in 1961: a socialist *Gemeinschaft* based on group similarities rather than diversity and individuality, with social rights tied to everyone in the quasi kin network. The providential socialist state and the firm became the providers of child care, and arranged care for older persons. Public institutions and workers regularly looked after retired employees.

As with traditional *Gemeinschaft*-like societies, East Germany continued the traditional gender segregation of work and duties. While the gendered division of care work has been repeatedly questioned in most western societies, socialist East Germany, like other eastern bloc European societies, expected women to divide the work of care among themselves. Not until the late 1980s were fathers entitled to claim parental leave, provided they could offer good reasons. I argue that socialism also tendentially prevented the development of partners' and parents' roles which are fundamental to western societies.

Women barely questioned the gender division of work. A feminist movement as known in Western societies did not exist. Christiane Lemke (1991) discusses the 1980s East German womens' 'movement' in terms of a 'literary feminism' which, more generally deplored a 'quality of life' under socialism. As Gebhardt and Kamphausen (1994), Lemke also reveals common ground - similar mentalities - between east and west Germans, eg. the 1980s GDR citizens' movement's concern with 'life', peace and ecology, issues.

East German abortion practice discloses the extent to which men had been freed from responsibilities as partners and fathers. Abortion was supported by the state as a common form of contraception along with other contraceptives, such as the free pill. In both cases, the burden fell on the woman. In my view, abortion is janusheaded and not easily talked of as emancipating. As with the pill, when the state readily bears the costs, men are freed from responsible intercourse. Unsurprisingly, *Pflichtberatung* (mandatory counselling which has to precede abortion) - the new regulation - is differently perceived - even by east German feminists. As one east German feminist explained, many east German women understand this measure positively as an obligation on the state to offer counselling in order to enable the woman - and the unborn's father - to make better choices about abortion - something women did not have under the communist regime. West German women on the other hand perceive the counselling as coercive and patronizing (quoted in Lemke 1994, p. 282, footnote 20). In my view, contraceptive and abortion rules and practices reveal the extent to which a woman and a man have become a couple in the modern sense - constructing their own peculiar reality based on shared meanings - and will become parents for their children on the basis of these meanings.

Women were in many ways married to the state. Therefore there was little need to develop high profile parents' - that is mothers' and fathers' - roles. As one woman told me: In GDR times, as a lone mother one was more secure. One knew that what ever did happen there was a creche for the baby, child care for pre-school and school children after the lessons, as well as money. And everything was foreseeable and calculable. Another woman reports: As a lone mother of three children I was *Kinderreich* (literally childrich) - considered to have a large family. I didn't fare badly. The children had free meals during the day, the older ones free holidays organized by the firm and I got money from the community every now and then. By using the old fashioned term '*Kinderreich*', this woman alludes implicitly to the opposite: in west Germany, a single mother who has more than one child is seen as irresponsible; she also risks poverty. While children positively affected the living standard or did not cost much extra, east German lone mothers are now in many ways at risk of poverty. The majority of lone mothers agree (Hanesch et al. 1994, p. 302): under socialism they didn't need to marry; and they could easily cope without a father for the children (or partner for themselves).

Women and men who shared a household were better off, since women earned up to 40 per cent of the household income (compared to often only 15-20 per cent in West Germany). However, money did not matter that much, if one considers the scarcity of goods and the need to patch together an income. Therefore, it mattered less than the opportunities to utilize Gemeinschaft-based forms of generalized reciprocity: exchanging scarce goods; getting help and device - opportunities provided by the partner's network.

It is still unknown whether and how money was shared between the couple, although one can assume separate financial obligations. Records from interviews support this assumption (Hanesch et al. 1994). In some cases couples separated because the employed partner did not want to maintain the jobless one: the old hidden contract surfaced and broke. In other cases conflicts arose over who should pay for the children's extras, be it clothes or holidays. (Remember that many families consisted of non-biological fathers - *'soziale Väter'*; that costs of children were born by the state.)

In my view, the East German social and political system prevented a public/private dichotomy fundamental to western democratic market economies. It hindered what Habermas sees as crucial for any modern democratic society: a separation between 'system' and *'Lebenswelt'* (social world), the development of the separate roles of the citizen, the worker and the private household member. Instead it indirectly created an 'all in the home' culture. The boundaries between the workplace, home, party and state were blurred; occupational and private roles overlapped. Altogether, and sociologically speaking, socialist Germany was apparently less differentiated and rather homogenous (*Gemeinschaft*-like) and did not promote or tolerate much diversity, but instead a great deal of mechanic solidarity. The other side of socialist security and egalitarianism was a highly standardized life course characterized by a lack of choice in consumption, occupation and travel.

The East German 'plan' or 'command' economy and society has been transformed into a social market economy. This process implies several major shifts towards the above mentioned liberal characteristics. It offers a move from no, or little, choice as to what to buy, what to do, or where to go. Now, choices have to be made and opportunities grasped. Obligatory choice contributes to feeling insecure. In this context money gains an unforeseen power and a new meaning, while the idea as well as the reality of *Gemeinschaft* is fading. As one lone mother complains: Formerly all of us planned how to spend time together. Nowadays, my friends talk about three topics only: cars, travelling and how to earn money. I am much poorer and with my three children, I am stigmatized and unwanted.

Ongoing social differentiation, resulting differences in income and wealth as well as envy resulting from these differences (*Sozialneid*) - resulting from differences in individual achievement and aspirations which can flourish in a market economy - contribute to the destruction of *Gemeinschaft*. Interviewees, often the losers or non-winners, stress the extent to which *Gemeinschaft* was built on scarcity and austerity - solidarity was based on necessity: all were in the same boat; there was little chance to excel or rip-off others. Help and advice was naturally given and reciprocated. Today, those with money call the tune and pay labour. Socialist reciprocity has collapsed, and a new one has to emerge yet. Those still in work complain about a lack of time, e.g. to reciprocate. Both the speed and quality of work have changed. The household can hardly bear two hard working people exhausted by the new regime. This is especially true for commuters. They are the most individualized and the first to live the breadwinner-husband model.

Empirical shifts

Since unification east German households have had to take some crucial turns: the most obvious is that from two-earner to one-earner households, that is, to male-breadwinner households. Recent data based on the German Socioeconomic Panel (1990-93) reveal this trend (for the following: Berger and Schulz 1994).

Panel data offers a surprise. One would expect a high proportion of households to be unemployed. However, two thirds, or 6.5 million, employed persons managed to stay in employment, about half of these continuously, and a third again with the same employer. This is more likely to be the case for men than for women, and for the younger than for workers over the age of forty. Although two-earner couples still make up the majority of two parents with children households, their proportion fell from 80 to 57 per cent between 1990 and 1992; it decreased from 53 to 24 per cent for two persons households without, or without living-in, children. The latter group mainly consists of older couples. Many of them took early retirement. 74 per cent of the 33 per cent non-working women who lived in two parents/with children households were unemployed in 1992 (59 per cent in 1990). Lone mothers make up six per cent of all households in the 1990 and 1992 panel (two parents with children: 38 per cent; two persons/no children: 25 per cent; one person households: 26 per cent, the majority of these, 59 per cent, retired persons' households; other: 5 per cent). Lone mothers' labour market participation rate fell from 84 to 61 per cent between 1990-1992; in 1992 about 20 per cent were on social assistance. In couple households with children male employment decreased from 97 to 88 per cent.

Despite deindustrialization and stable unemployment, most east German households now have more money. This is also true for households dependent on public transfers. Male wages in particular are much higher now than under socialism. Unsurprisingly, contentedness with the living standard is highest when both partners are still employed, and in each case

41

higher for men than for women. However, male contentedness decreases when the female partner is unemployed. Thus, one can surely distinguish non-winners, losers, short-term winners and winners. The losers are the longterm unemployed, those forced to take early retirement or those who agreed to retraining but remained unemployed. However, as argued above, recent research on German - east and west - mentalities reveals more similarities than differences. Both Germanies stress the ideology of *Gemeinschaft*; during the 1980s both parts developed ideas of a better - more ecologically sensitive - quality of life; east German literary feminism rejected the socialist idea of emancipation which gave little space to women to develop femininity. In 1988, before the wall came down, more than fifty per cent of East German women and nearly two thirds of men believed that where there were small children the woman should lower her work expectations (Winkler 1990, p. 274).

In 1988 - before the wall came down - East German employees gave higher priority to their families than West German workers. This was due to East Germany's secure employment and the obligation of all citizens to work full-time, compared to West Germans who have been sensitive to the labour market as the most important system of allocating money, status, and opportunities. East German women not only wanted but had to work in order to make ends meet. With few choices, and forced into dead-end (female) occupations, despite vocational and other efforts at training, women placed an ambiguous value on employment. The less attractive a job, the more readily women opt out of the labour market, or reduce their working hours. Given the West German family model of men with sufficient income, many women will willingly work shorter hours (or even interrupt employment), although the labour force participation rate for women will continue to remain higher in eastern Germany. Its socialist policies did not abolish the gender division of household tasks and as the West German employment system is highly demanding of its workers (i.e., in time commitment, the (male) breadwinner will need support from his family.

Survey data foretell a process of growing acceptance of West German norms, especially with regard to family norms. To date, most mothers of small children in eastern Germany prefer part-time to full-time employment - as do mothers in western Germany. Opinions, however, differ in relation to a woman's professional status and qualification. The majority of male and female respondents maintain that in times of high unemployment women, whose partners could support them should leave their jobs. On the other hand, almost all eastern German women and men (compared to just over a half of the western German respondents) claim that both partners should contribute to the household income. This position seems inconsistent. The paradox can be solved, however, by assuming that household members have been less familiar with paying for each other from one purse, which is the west German norm, especially for their children.

Conclusion

Women and men will slowly move towards first the West German family model, though towards its modernized version (senior-junior-partners). West and east German women will meet in the middle: both are expected to earn their own living, at least part-time, if there are no children or elderly persons in need of care. Households in both parts - even more than before - need a secondary income to bridge shortcomings in times of increasing economic uncertainty. Considering the growth in unemployment and the scarcity of jobs, those with both paid work and a family are well off.

Family policies will increasingly support poor working families. Social policies, in general, are moving towards temporary assistance: provisions will be to a much lesser extent linked to status, thereby fixing it, than to status passages; continuous mobility between various status will thereby be enhanced - entries, exits and reentries - and together with it individual choices - however restricted.

References

Bast, Kerstin and Ostner, Ilona (1992), 'Ehe und Familie in der Sozialpolitik der DDR und BRD' in Winfried Schmaehl (ed.), *Sozialpolitik im Prozeß der deutschen Vereinigung*, Campus, Frankfurt, pp. 228-270.

Berger, Horst and Schulz, Annett (1994), 'Veränderung der Erwerbssituation in ostdeutschen Privathaushalten und Befindlichkeit der Menschen' in *Aus Politik und Zeitgeschichte*, B 16/94, pp. 3-15.

Gebhardt, Winfried and Kamphausen, Georg (1994), *Zwei Dörfer in Deutschland. Mentalitätsunterschiede nach der Wiedervereinigung*, Leske and Budrich, Opladen.

Hanesch, Walter et al. (1994), *Armut in Deutschland*, Rowohlt, Reinbek.

Lemke, Christiane (1991), *Die Ursachen des Umbruchs. Politische Sozialisation in der ehemaligen DDR*, Westdeutscher Verlag, Opladen.

Lemke, Christiane (1994), 'Women and Politics, The New Federal Republic of Germany' in Barbara J. Nelson and Najma Chowdhury, (eds.), *Women and Politics Worldwide*, Yale University Press, New Haven and London, pp. 261-284.

Leuzinger-Bohleber, Marianne and Garlichs, Ariane (1993), *Früherziehung West-Ost. Zukunftserwartungen, Autonomieentwicklung und Beziehungsfähigkeit von Kindern und Jugendlichen*, Juventa, Weinheim and München.

Maedje, Eva and Neusuess, Claudia (1994), 'Alleinerziehende Sozialhilfeempfängerinnen zwischen sozialpolitischem Anspruch und gesellschaftlicher Realität' in Michael Zwick (ed.) *Einmal arm, immer arm? Neue Befunde zur Armut in Deutschland*, Campus, Frankfurt, pp. 134-155.

Millman, Marcia (1991), *Warm Hearts and Cold Cash: The Intimate Dynamics of Families and Money*, Free Press, New York.

Moeller, Robert G. (1993), *Protecting Motherhood: Women and the Family in the Politics of Postwar Germany*, Berkeley University Press, Berkeley.

Müller-Armack, Alfred (1956), 'Soziale Marktwirtschaft' in *Handwörterbuch der Sozialwissenschaften*, Vol. 9, Stuttgart, pp. 390-392.

Nell-Breuning, Oswald von (1957), 'Solidarität und Subsidarität im Raume von Sozialpolitik und Sozialreform' in Erik Boettcher (ed.) *Sozialpolitik und Sozialreform*, Mohr, Tübingen, pp. 213-226.

Ostner, Ilona (1994), 'Back to the Fifties: Gender and Welfare in Unified Germany' in *Social Politics*, 1, (1), pp. 32-59.

Preston, Ronald H. (1991), *Religion and the Ambiguities of Capitalism*, SCM Press, London.

Winkler, Gunnar (ed.) (1990), *Sozialreport '90. Daten und Fakten zur sozialen Lage in der DDR*, Verlag Die Wirtschaft, Berlin (GDR).

Zelizer, Viviana A. (1994), *The Social Meaning of Money*, Basic Books, New York.

Zwiener, Karl (1994), Kinderkrippen in der DDR. Materialien zum 5. *Familienbericht*, Vol. 5, Deutsches Jugendinstitut, München.

3 Poor mothers and absent fathers: Support for lone parents in comparative perspective

Jane Millar

Poverty among lone-parent families has risen substantially in recent years and especially in the 1980s. This rise in poverty has also affected couples with children, and families - whether with one or two parents - are the now increasingly found at the bottom of the income distribution (Goodman and Webb 1994, Jenkins 1994). At the same time social security policy has focused on two main strategies - more 'targeting' of benefits so that they go only to those most in need and greater personal responsibility in order to reduce dependency on the state. These aims were central to the social security review of the mid-1980s and are even more to the fore in the current reviews. As Peter Lilley put it in his MAIS lecture in 1993 'any effective structural reform must involve either better targeting, or more self-provision, or both'.

These ideas have played an important part in the development of policy for the financial support of lone parents. Currently almost 1 million lone parents are in receipt of income support and this is projected to rise to 1.4 million by the turn of the century at a cost of almost £5,000 million in 1993/4 prices. Reducing this 'dependency' on social security, and the associated costs, are thus central to government policy towards lone parents. As the Cabinet Briefing paper on lone parents, leaked to The *Guardian* in September 1994, put it:

> We have assumed that the primary objective of any measures taken will be to reduce the burden on public expenditure caused by lone-parent families, and that measures should be therefore directed towards discouraging lone parenthood and other ways of reducing public expenditure which do not harm the interests of the children of lone parents.

The phrase that 'measures should be therefore directed towards discouraging lone parenthood' reflects the way in which recent debate has focused almost entirely on a negative view of lone mothers, and their 'feckless' partners, and their 'delinquent' children. There is a strong view in some quarters that state support for lone parents has gone too far, creating perverse incentives in favour of lone parenthood and against marriage (Morgan 1995). The Cabinet Briefing Paper, while pointing out that there is no evidence to support these claims, goes on to set out various proposals to try and discourage lone parenthood and encourage self-support among existing lone parents.

However, in introducing the 1991 Child Support Act the government was keen to claim that this is not explicitly intended to discourage lone parenthood. It is stated in the Foreword to Children Come First (DSS 1990) that 'governments cannot ensure that families stay together' and that the aim of policy is therefore simply to ensure that parents honour their financial obligations to their children if they do, for whatever reason, separate. Nevertheless the Child Support Act is very much about changing attitudes and behaviour among both separated fathers and lone mothers. There are two main objectives to the Act: first, getting more separated (or 'absent' in the language of the White Paper) fathers to pay significantly more child support for their children and second, encouraging more lone mothers to take paid employment. Both are controversial since neither rest on a clear consensus that these are the most appropriate goals for policy.

The debate about the obligations of absent parents is very fierce, as we know from the responses to the child support legislation. Although the principle that parents should be financially responsible for their children seems clear cut and is quite widely supported by popular opinion (Kiernan 1992) backing for this simple principle become much more ambivalent when faced with the actual circumstances of families. Goode (1993, p. 338) expresses this well:

> While public opinion favours supporting one's children, we all know of individual cases in which someone has been ordered to pay an amount that seems excessive or unduly harsh, and we "understand" his efforts to thwart or escape the court order. The tendency to individualise suggests that there are no clear-cut social norms or customs, and neither is there a consensus about what is appropriate behaviour - that is, what *should* happen - nor a common understanding about what *will* happen (emphases in original).

This ambivalence means that the child support legislation has to both establish new rules for the payment of maintenance when parents separate

46

and gain legitimacy for those new rules. It seems that the UK government has failed to do this with an almost overwhelmingly hostile response to the Child Support Act that has forced significant changes to be announced after just over one year of operation (DSS 1995a). However in Australia what looks like a very similar scheme for child support has also been introduced in recent years and that scheme has apparently been able to gain quite widespread support and acceptance. The first section of the chapter compares the UK and Australian experiences of introducing child support legislation.

Whether or not mothers should go out to work or stay at home and care for their children is an issue of longstanding debate. The post-war UK social security system was predicated on the idea that women with children should be mothers first and foremost - staying at home to care for their children and only taking paid employment if this could be made compatible with their child care role. In the immediate post-war period this was usually taken to mean that mothers should not be employed outside the home at all. Now, however, part-time work is usually considered to be compatible with motherhood, especially among those with older children. Nevertheless this employment is seen as a personal choice for mothers and not the concern or responsibility of the government. Thus the government continues to define child care as an issue of private choice and not public policy - if parents (mothers) want to work they must make their own arrangements to do so.

In relation to lone mothers this 'neutrality' has been the stated policy for some time. Lone mothers should decide for themselves whether or not they want to be employed and the state should neither help nor hinder in this decision. However the consequence seems to have been an increasing proportion of non-employed lone mothers, with currently about 39 per cent of lone mothers in employment compared with about 62 of married mothers (Sly 1994). Should lone mothers be allowed to continue to make this 'choice' when more and more married mothers are 'choosing' work? And especially when that choice is so costly in terms of social security benefits.

The 'underclass' debate also throws up ambivalent attitudes towards employment among lone mothers. On the one hand, getting off benefit and into employment is seen as moving from dependency to independence and lone mothers who work are thus providing their children with appropriate role models, teaching them 'a more positive attitude to work and independence' (DSS 1990, p. 41). On the other hand, employed lone mothers are not putting their children first, not providing them with the care and attention they need, and thus possibly creating the delinquents of the future.

Given the conflicting views about whether or not policy should discourage, encourage, or even compel, employment among lone mothers the government seeks to hold onto a neutral stance. Lone mothers should choose for themselves whether or not to work but policy should be adapted to tip the balance more in favour of part-time employment among lone mothers. The second main section of the chapter considers this policy in the light of what we know about labour supply among lone mothers.

Child support - getting absent fathers to pay

Getting the majority of separated fathers to pay regular child maintenance, at a level above a few pounds per week, requires a major change. Only about one in three lone parents receive any maintenance payments and, among those who have not been married, this falls to one in seven. In 1989 the median amount received was about £20 per week (Bradshaw and Millar 1991).

The reasons for the payment or non-payment of maintenance have not really been investigated in any depth in this country, and whether non-payment stems from lack of capacity or from lack of willingness to pay is not clear. The rather limited research reported in *Children Come First* suggest that absent parents are more likely than men in general to be unemployed and to have lower earnings than average in work (DSS 1990, vol. 2). The lone parents in our survey, where they had some knowledge of their former partners' circumstances, mostly thought they could not afford to pay, or to increase their payments (Bradshaw and Millar 1991). Against this, however, studies in other countries (the USA and Australia in particular) suggest that separated men usually see their incomes increase on divorce and that many could certainly pay more than they currently do (McDonald 1986, Goode 1993).

As regards attitudes to paying maintenance, our in-depth interviews with separated men suggested that factors such as contact with children, perceptions of current circumstances of the lone parent, perceived obligations to second families, and views about the relationship form a complex set of attitudes towards this obligation. Child support is not seen as unconditional but rather as contingent upon various other factors (Burgoyne and Millar 1994). In their recent research following divorcing couples through the legal process, Davis, Cretney and Collins (1994) highlight the way in which perceptions of fairness (who contributed what to the marriage, who was to blame for what happened) and ownership (who earned the money) affected how people felt about their obligations and rights. They also found that the people felt that the divorce process ignored their views and this left both parties with a continued sense of grievance, rather than a feeling of settlement.

Of course it could be argued that the reasons why separated fathers do not pay maintenance are largely irrelevant and that what is important is the existence of adequate enforcement procedures to compel payment, where payment can be made. This is the route followed by several states in the USA, which use some very strong enforcement measures. These include attachments of earnings and of tax refunds, use of tax records to trace absent parent, use of credit and debt collection agencies, and the posters and television advertisements naming the 'deadbeat dads' who owe child support. Nevertheless compliance rates with child support orders are rarely above 40 - 45 per cent (CSEAG 1992). At the end of 1989 it was estimated that more than $18 billion in unpaid child support was owed to about 16 million children in the US (Goode 1993).

Thus, unless very draconian measures of enforcement are accepted, it is important that separated fathers do accept an obligation to pay child support and are thus willing to cooperate in making payments. However, as Ros Hepplewhite, the first Chief Executive of the Child Support Agency, put it, this requires 'a major cultural change. Many people in the past have not seen paying maintenance as an ordinary financial obligation, but as it were to some extent optional' (quoted in The *Observer* 17 October 1993). The challenge, she argued, is to get separated fathers to give paying child support priority above other ways of spending their money. The government minister responsible for child support policy, Alistair Burt, made the same point: 'Persuading people that parents should pay for their own children is a slow process. Child support agencies around the world face the same challenge of changing attitudes to the provision of support for children' (The *Observer* 3 July 1994).

Looking round the world, to Australia, the Australian Department of Social Security has recently reviewed the working of their child support scheme, introduced about five years ago. They conclude that 'by any tests of international benchmarking, or measures of outcome against stated objectives, the Australian child support scheme is a success' (DSS 1993, p. 124) and that it 'represents a major shift in attitudes and a major re-balancing between public (taxpayer) provision of child support and private (parental) provision' (ibid p. 7).

The statistics indicate the degree of change: the proportion of sole parent pensioners with maintenance rose from about 34 per cent pre-Scheme to 46 per cent for stage 1 and 42 per cent for stage 2; the average amount of child support awarded is much higher (A$46 per child compared with A$26 per child); most of the money collected goes to lone parents (about 70 per cent); nevertheless the net savings to the government have risen threefold since 1989, up to A$36 million in 1992/3; and finally about 73 per cent of maintenance awards are collected (slightly more if the payment is made directly). The scheme has certainly brought a significant improvement in the numbers paying child support and the amounts that they pay.

However there has been somewhat less success in ensuring that payments are made regularly, are of the correct amount, and are paid on time. Thus three in ten lone parents with a child support award have received no payments and only about half the child support collected by the Agency is paid in time (DSS 1993). Among lone parents receiving their child support direct from the absent parent, 29 per cent reported that they received less than the agreed amount and 44 per cent reported that payments were not made regularly (CSEAG 1992, vol. 2). Whatever the success of the Australian scheme, ensuring the reliability of child support remains a major problem (a point returned to later).

As regards attitude change it seems that this has been primarily at the level of views towards child support obligations among the population in general and among the organisations and groups concerned with policy and provision for families with children, rather than necessarily among the absent parents themselves. Thus, the Child Support Evaluation Advisory Group (1992, p. 4), conclude:

> The most significant circumstance is that there has been a marked change in the public debate relating to child support...when these reforms were first proposed...controversy centred around questions of the extent to which parents should support their own children compared with the responsibility of the community to do so through social welfare ...The debate now...is entirely different. Almost without exception the submissions to us acknowledged that it is the primary responsibility of parents to support their own children...A major effect of the Scheme is a change in the community ethos so that support by parents is seen as a necessary consequence of their separation rather than as an exception (CSEAG 1992, p. iv).

The widespread support for the child support scheme can be seen in recent submissions to a Parliamentary Select Committee from a variety of groups (e.g. the Brotherhood of St Laurence 1993, the Combined Community Legal Centres Group 1993, Sisters-in-Law 1993, the Council for Single Mothers and their Children 1993). All these groups fully support the legislation (a 'long overdue political and philosophical recognition that non-custodial parents...have a responsibility to financially support their children', according to the Council of Single Mothers and their Children). The criticisms from these groups focus mainly on certain aspects of the administration but the general tone is extremely supportive of both the aims of the policy and the means used to achieve these. Not that there is 100 per cent support. Certainly absent parents continue to feel aggrieved and rather unjustly treated. About 80 per cent think they are paying too much child support and have been very unhappy about their dealings with the Child Support Agency (CSEAG 1992, vol. 2). However it seems that the widespread acceptance of, and support for, this legislation has largely been able to sideline their objections. Getting community support may be thus a necessary pre-requisite for getting absent parents to accept child support as a legitimate obligation that cannot be ignored or evaded.

That consensus of support is badly missing in the UK context, as has been seen in the reactions published to mark the first anniversary of the implementation of the legislation. Although only the Campaign Against the Child Support Act (Wages for Housework and Payday Men's Network 1993) has argued explicitly for abolition of the legislation, other groups have been heavily critical. The Child Poverty Action Group (Garnham and Knights 1994, p. 120-121) argue that 'from nearly ever angle the CSA is flawed...The question now is how to change the law, not whether it should change.' NACAB (1994, p. 3) similarly concludes that the evidence from the first year 'gives a strong warning to the government that major changes are urgently needed if the scheme is to succeed'. Even the National Council for One-Parent Families (1994, p. 5), which has been a staunch supporter, finds that 'the CSA is failing to deliver to those that it was meant to help'. Two reports from the Social Security Select Committee (1993, 1994) have also criticised the workings of the scheme and proposed quite substantial changes, some of which have been taken up by the government (DSS 1995a).

Why is it that the Australian scheme apparently commands widespread support while the UK scheme has generated almost nothing but criticism? Of course the Australians have had longer to accept their scheme - five years of operation to our one - but nevertheless the reactions seem entirely different. The legitimacy and acceptability of the Australian scheme seem to rest on two main factors largely missing in the UK. First there is the way in which the scheme was developed and has been subsequently evaluated and monitored. The Australian scheme did not come out of the blue in the way the UK scheme seemed to, and has been subject to close, and public, evaluation ever since. The Australian Scheme was first mooted in 1980 but not introduced until 1988. During those eight years a number of further consultative documents were published and the Australian Institute for Family Studies produced a number of reports examining the financial consequences of divorce for both custodial and non-custodial parents. By contrast in the UK an inter-departmental committee was established in 1989, the White Paper published in 1990 and the Act passed in 1991. The new policy was thus adopted a mere two years after the idea was first seriously considered, with very little opportunity for public debate of the issues and very little research evidence to support the proposed changes.

In Australia there have been five major evaluations of the Scheme in the five years of operation and this weight of evidence has been important in promoting the Scheme and in countering some of the objections, especially from absent parents. By contrast government sponsored evaluation is just starting here and the only study that has attempted to monitor directly the Act (Clarke, Craig and Glendinning 1994) was funded by a consortium of five charities. The British government has apparently felt little need to gain support for this major policy change, which has meant that those against the scheme have easily been able to put their case and have gained much media support for this. Headlines such as 'Cruel Sadistic Agency' (*The Daily Star* 4 April 1994) and 'Fleecing the fathers' (*The Times* 27 October 1994) with stories of poverty, failures of second marriages, and even suicide have dominated media coverage, further alienating support for the Act.

The second factor leading to the different responses lies in the very different way the two schemes are structured. And this, in turn, relates to the objectives of the schemes. Saving money appears to be the most important factor in the UK while in Australia, although there has been a concern with saving money, there is also a much clearer commitment to improving the incomes of lone parents and their children. This is apparent in three main ways. First, although the child support liabilities produced in the two countries are similar, the way in which this is done is very different. The Australian formula was set by reference to the costs of supporting children and varies directly with family size (18 per cent for one child, 27 per cent for two and so on). The UK formula was set by reference to income support rates and includes in this the personal allowance for the lone mother. For families with one or two children this part produces the largest component so it appears that much of the child support is actually support for the mother. Secondly, in Australia much more of the child support paid goes to the lone parent. Millar and Whiteford (1993) calculated that, in 1992, at average male earnings the child support liability for a two-child family would be about £65 in the UK and £58 in Australia. The lone mother on income support in the UK would gain nothing from this; the lone mother on supporting parents pension in Australia would retain £34, or about 59 per cent. Thirdly, the targets for benefit savings have also been significantly higher in the UK than in Australia and have led to accusations that the CSA has unfairly pursued the 'responsible' fathers, already paying something, rather than the feckless fathers who pay nothing (Social Security Select Committee 1993).

Finally, and perhaps most importantly, there is no retrospection in Australia. The scheme only applies to those who separated after it came into effect and so, as Whiteford (1994, p. 2) points out:

> This means that many of the thorniest issues affecting child support in the UK are simply not relevant in Australia. Past property settlements are generally not affected, and the effect on second families will not appear for some years, and even then it will be the case that liable parents will be forming new relationships with the knowledge that they are paying for earlier children.

Thus both the structure of the scheme and the way it was introduced have been important in gaining support for this policy in Australia. The attitudes of the absent parents may not have changed much but widespread support for the scheme seems effectively to have defused this opposition. In the UK the attitude change which would get child support accepted as a legitimate obligation of all parents, whatever their circumstances, still seems a long way away. The issue still facing the government is how to gain acceptance and legitimacy for this policy. Can it be made more acceptable? What sort of changes would be needed to achieve this? The two main reforms that would probably do the most to gain legitimacy would be the introduction of a child support disregard for those on income support and getting rid of the retrospective element. The latter may be happening in practice to some extent, given the announcement in December 1994 that the CSA would not pursue certain pre-1993 cases. The former is still resisted and indeed the changes recently announced seem to be most concerned with deflecting the criticisms of absent parents than with improving the outcomes for lone mothers (DSS 1995a).

Getting lone mothers into work - income packaging

As far as changing behaviour goes, the objective of encouraging more lone mothers into employment at least starts with more of an open door than the objective of getting more absent fathers to pay child support. All the evidence shows that many non-employed lone mothers would very much like to get into work (e.g. Bradshaw and Millar 1991, McKay and Marsh 1994) so here the policy goal is to find ways to allow them to achieve this aim. The main method which has been chosen to achieve this goal is to manipulate financial incentives so that work, especially part-time work, becomes more financially attractive to lone mothers.

This has been done in three main ways. First eligibility for family credit has been extended to those working 16 or more hours per week, thus opening up the benefit to part-time workers. Second, the first £15 of child support is disregarded when calculating in-work benefits such as family credit and housing benefit. Thus lone mothers on income support gain nothing from receipt of child support but if they get into work there is a financial gain. Third, family credit claimants who are paying for professional child care for children aged under 11 can offset up to £40 of the child-care costs against their earnings when claiming the benefit. Because of the way the means test works this gives a maximum gain of £28 per week.

In theory, this package will mean a significant improvement in the financial gains from working, as McKay and Marsh (1994, p. 62) put it, 'the new treatment of maintenance under Family Credit rules and, if it is achieved, a greater flow of maintenance to this group, will make a combination of maintenance, earnings and family credit a viable, even attractive, income package for many lone parents'. The potential gains can be seen in Figure 3.1, which shows the impact of child support on total income for a lone mother with two children aged four and six, receiving about £50 child support (the amount from a man on median male manual earnings living alone, paying the average housing cost for a single householder). The income gain amounts to between £27 and £30, increasing for higher earners who do not get family credit.

In practice, however, this income package might not be quite so attractive as it appears on paper. This is because it is so heavily reliant upon means testing and this gives rise to two major problems: complexity and insecurity. In order for lone mothers to be able to take paid work, and to achieve an adequate regular income, it is necessary for them to claim everything and do so in the right order. The child-care disregard is only of any value to those who are paying for professional child care, thus excluding many lone mothers who use informal systems of child care. Although housing benefit has high take-up rates, about 66 per cent of those eligible to be entitled to family credit are receiving it (DSS 1995b) and so there are a significant number of eligible non-claimants. In addition take-up tends to be lower when entitlement is lower, so if receipt of child

Figure 3.1 Effect of child support on net income

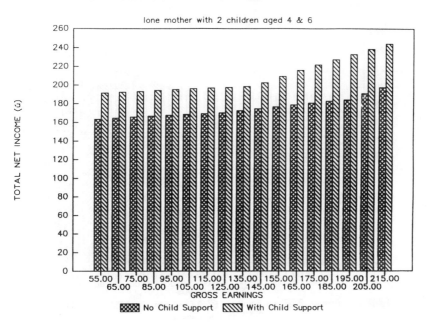

Source: derived from DSS (1993) Tax Benefit Table, April 1993.

Absent parent assumed to have gross earnings of £256.60 and housing costs of £42.69.

support leads to reductions to the amount of benefit to be received, this might in turn lead to still lower take-up rates. The whole process requires lone parents not only to deal with the Child Support Agency but also to make a number of separate benefit claims and getting these in the right order can make a difference to the final outcome. In addition there are interactions with other benefits such as the disability benefits, and complications when the child, or children, live sometimes with one parent and sometimes with the other.

   The insecurity in the package comes partly from the way in which almost everything interacts - for example, if child support or wages go up the amount of family credit goes down - and partly from the fact that receipt of the various components is not guaranteed on a week to week basis. The interactions are apparent in Figure 3.2, which shows the level and composition of total income, including child support as above and assuming

Figure 3.2 Level and composition of total net income

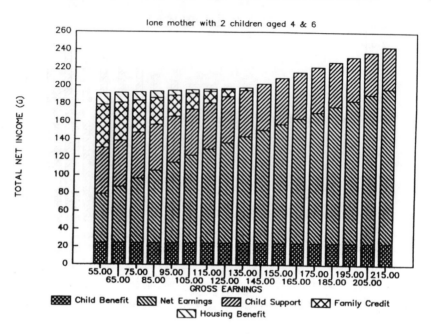

lone mother with 2 children aged 4 & 6

Child Benefit   Net Earnings   Child Support   Family Credit   Housing Benefit

Source: derived from DSS (1993) Tax Benefit Tables, April 1993.

full take-up of all benefits. The level of income remains fairly flat at the lower end of the earnings distribution, where the part-time workers are likely to be found. After about £145 per week gross, income starts to rise because the family is no longer eligible for means-tested benefits and the total value of child support is now added to earnings. However at about £185 per week the earnings of lone mother are high enough to affect the child support liability of the absent parent, which falls slightly.

At the lower earnings levels income is very complex. For a lone mother on fairly typical part-time earnings of about £65 gross per week, total income is made up almost equally of the three main sources: net earnings (33 per cent), child support (27 per cent) and family credit (22 per cent) with child benefit contributing 13 per cent and housing benefit about six per cent. So if any one of these either goes unclaimed or is for some reason unpaid, this will leave a large gap in total income. But the only thing guaranteed is child benefit and the others are all out of the control of the lone mother. Getting regular child support, of the correct amount and paid on time, is not an easy goal to achieve, as the Australian experience shows. Furthermore the amount of child support due will change if the absent parent has a change in his circumstances but family credit is not immediately reassessed if this happens. There is some evidence that these interactions are already causing problems for lone mothers, who find their family credit reduced because of child support entitlements which are not actually forthcoming (Garnham and Knights 1994, NACAB 1994).

Jobs are also potentially insecure, especially the sort of low-paid jobs that this policy is intended to encourage. Thus, as McKay and Marsh (1994, p. 19) point out, lone mothers are very reluctant to take jobs that may only be temporary because:

> Getting into work, paying set-up and travel costs...rebudgeting to cope with a differently structured income, all present difficulties and uncertainties. The likelihood of making such an adjustment only to be flung back onto income support after a few weeks is a threat...It is a threat that people know about, and it is a major disincentive to work.

The central reliance on means testing for almost every component of income in this package means that lone parents are expected to derive their incomes from a variety of sources over which they have little or no control, and to cope with continuing uncertainty as to what the income will actually be each week. These are precisely the circumstances that give rise to debt. Under these conditions, employment for lone mothers will not mean an increase in financial independence, far from it - their dependency will be significantly increased. The lone mothers interviewed by Clarke, Craig and Glendinning (1993) were concerned that receipt of child support would make them more dependent on their former partners, enmeshing 'them in the very same patterns of obligation and control from which they had tried to escape in the course of rebuilding their lives as single parents' (ibid. p. 73). The overall effect of this approach will make it far harder for lone mothers to become financially independent, from either their former partners or the state.

The fact that these issues of security and control have been given so little importance in policy-making follows from the very narrow way in which labour supply has often been conceptualised and analysed. The key assumption underlying much of the research seeking to explain employment decisions has been that incentives to work can be expressed in purely financial terms and can be measured by comparing levels of income in and out of work. If income out of work is higher people will choose to stay at home, if income in work is higher people will choose to take jobs. This simple model has, however, been increasingly questioned in recent years, not least as a result of in-depth studies which suggest that factors such as security and reliability of income are important factors that people also take into account (Bryson and McKay 1994, McLaughlin 1994). The idea that financial incentives are the only, or even the most important, factor determining lone mothers' employment decisions seems particularly inadequate. Research evidence suggests that what is important to lone mothers are: their perceptions of the needs of their children; their access to reliable child-care, preferably with someone they know and can trust; jobs which are stable but flexible enough to fit with their domestic responsibilities; and incomes that are secure as well as adequate for family needs. None of these are well captured in the economic models of labour supply. Nor are they supported by current policy, in which means testing looms so large.

Would it be possible to add some income security to this package? Child benefit is, as noted above, the one source of income that is received by all lone mothers whatever their circumstances. For the lone parents in our survey child benefit and one-parent benefit contributed, on average, about 18 per cent of disposable income (Bradshaw and Millar 1991). Child benefit is also deducted from income support so, although it is received both in and out of work, it is additional to earnings but not benefits. However, the main drawback of increasing child benefit is, of course, the cost.

Guaranteeing child support would be another possibility. Schemes of guaranteed, or advanced, child maintenance do exist in a number of other countries: in all the Scandinavian countries plus, in a more restricted form, Belgium, France and Germany. The ways in which the schemes work - their coverage, eligibility criteria, duration, level of support given and so on - differ from country to country. However what they have in common is that the state undertakes to pay child maintenance at a standard amount and then seeks to recoup as much of the cost as possible from the absent parent. In Sweden (which has one of the most comprehensive schemes) about 15 per cent of all children receive a maintenance advance, and about one in three of single men aged 35 to 44 are paying something (Gustafsson and Klevmarken 1994, p. 104). In 1992 about 30 per cent of the costs were recouped from the absent parents but some families receive the maintenance advance even where there is no liability for the absent parent to pay. Excluding these cases then about 80 per cent of costs are recouped. Thus the scheme in effect provides lone parents with an additional flat-rate benefit for their children. This is likely to be a much more effective wage supplement than the variable and insecure payments that non-guaranteed child support offers.

Guaranteeing an income for the children of lone parents was also the goal of the Finer Committee's recommendations twenty years ago (Finer 1974). The proposed 'guaranteed maintenance allowance' was divided into two parts: the adult allowance, which was to be means tested and taper out slowly as earnings rose; and the child allowance, which was to be non-means tested and thus payable for all children in lone-parent families. Maintenance itself would be assessed according to a standard formula and used to offset the costs of the GMA. Thus lone parents would have received a benefit in which the child component was secured and their earnings would have been added to this. In many ways the Finer proposals seem to offer the solution to achieving security and adequacy without institutionalising dependency on former partners. 'Back to Beveridge' is often proposed in reforms of social security but, as far as lone parents are concerned, 'Back to Finer' might be far better!

Conclusion

Two main points can be drawn in conclusion. First, the Australian experience suggests that it is possible to devise a scheme of child support that can command general support and can ensure that more absent fathers pay maintenance for their children. But the limitations of child support should not be ignored. The amount of money that can be raised in this way is always going to be limited and to be variable and irregular. It could be argued that the changes in family structure and in employment are making the idea of the 'family wage', which is what the idea of child support depends upon, obsolete. Inequalities in male wages have widened significantly in the 1980s and those at the bottom of the earnings distribution have seen their wages fall in real terms (Gosling, Machin and Meghir 1994). Alongside high levels of unemployment, this means that there are an increasing number of men who cannot support one family on their wages, let alone two. Although some lone mothers, separated from well-paid husbands, would benefit from better enforcement of child support for the majority the financial gains are small and the emotional costs are high. Recognising that child support is only of limited value for most lone mothers does not, however, mean that we should forget all about it. There may be other reasons why we should expect absent fathers to pay child support, in particular in order to discharge the moral obligation that they owe to their children. But it might be useful to separate out more clearly the different possible objectives of policy in this area rather than, as at the moment, rolling these together.

59

Secondly, the income package of low wages, means-tested benefits, and private transfers may represent the future for many families at the bottom of the labour market. Means-tested benefits, family credit in particular, to supplement low wages are central to government policy more generally. The picture is much more complex for lone parents than for married couples because there are more sources of income involved, but the broad strategy is the same. We have already moved a long way from the Beveridge model of social security benefits as wage replacements to an increasing reliance on benefits as wage supplements. Lone mothers may be the spearhead here, they are already used to juggling different income sources and are less likely to see themselves as 'breadwinners' than unemployed men, many of whom remain reluctant to take low-paid and part-time jobs which do not satisfy the breadwinner ideal. The 'Campaign Against the Child Support Act' is against this policy for precisely these reasons. It argues that the aim is to get more women into low-paid and insecure jobs and to reduce their entitlement to support for the work of bringing up children, while at the same time child support payments reduce those in second families to the poverty line. There seems to be some justification in this criticism, especially in light of the extent of means-testing involved. But if jobs are becoming more insecure and wages less able to meet family needs it may be that directly supplementing *individual* wages is not the most useful approach. The social wage - the services that benefit everyone - may be, as Land (1992) has argued, more of the answer.

Finally, current policy towards the financial support of families is very divisive. It sets men against women, lone parents against couples, first families against second families, and those with jobs against those without. However it is universal measures - policies to help all families - that are most likely to help the most vulnerable families. Recognising the needs that families have in common is an important part of reversing the trends towards child poverty that have been such a feature of recent years.

Note

Thanks to Helen Brownlee and Marilyn McHugh for pointing me to sources of information on Australia and to Heather McCallum for producing the graphs.

References

Australian Institute of Family Studies (1993), Submission to the Joint Select Committee on Family Law, AIFS, Melbourne, Australia.

Bradshaw, J. and Millar, J. (1991), *Lone parent families in the UK*, HMSO, London.

Brotherhood of St Laurence (1993), Submission to the Joint Select Committee on Family Law Issues about the operations of the Child Support Scheme, BSL, Melbourne, Australia.

Bryson, A. and McKay, S. (eds.) (1994), *Is it worth working?*, Policy Studies Institute, London.

Burgoyne, C. and Millar, J. (1994), 'Enforcing child support obligations: the views of separated fathers', *Policy and Politics*, 22, 2, 95-104.

Child Support Evaluation Advisory Group (1992), *Child Support in Australia: final report of the evaluation*, Vols. 1 and 2, Commonwealth of Australia, Canberra, Australia.

Child Support Agency (1994), Statistical Information 5th April 1993-31st March 1994, CSA, London.

Clarke, K., Craig, G. and Glendinning, C. (1993), *Children Come First? The Child Support Act and Lone Parent Families*, Barnardos, The Children's Society, NCH, NSPCC and SCF, London.

Clarke, K., Craig, G. and Glendinning, C. (1994), *Losing out: children and the child support act*, The Children's Society, London.

Combined Community Legal Centres Group (1993), Submission to the Joint Select Committee on Family Law, CCLCG New South Wales, Australia.

Council for Single Mothers and their Children (1993), Submission to the Joint Select Committee on Family Law, CSMC, Victoria, Australia.

Davis, G., Cretney, S. and Collins, J. (1994), *Simple quarrels: negotiating money and property disputes on divorce*, Clarendon Press, Oxford.

Department of Social Security Australia (1993), Child Support Scheme: DSS submission to the Joint Select Committee on Certain Family Law Issues, DSS, Canberra, Australia.

Department of Social Security (1990), *Children come first: the government's proposals on the maintenance of children*, Vols. 1 and 2, CM 1263, HMSO, London.

Department of Social Security (1995a), *Improving child support*, HMSO, London.

Department of Social Security (1995b), *Income related benefits: estimates of take-up in 1992*, HMSO, London.

Finer, M. (1974), Report of the Committee on One-Parent Families,

HMSO, London.

Garnham, A. and Knights, E. (1994), *Putting the Treasury first: the truth about child support*, Child Poverty Action Group, London.

Goode, W. (1993), *World changes in divorce patterns*, Yale University Press, New Haven and London.

Goodman, A. and Webb, S. (1994), *For richer, for poorer: the changing distributions of income in the UK, 1961-1991*, Institute for Fiscal Studies, London.

Gosling A, Machin, S. and Meghir, C. (1994), *The changing distribution of wages in the UK 1966-1992*, Institute of Fiscal Studies, London.

Gustafsson, B. and Klevmarken, N.A. (1994), 'Taxes and transfers in Sweden: incentive effects on labour supply' in Atkinson, A.B. and Mogensen, G.V. (eds) *Welfare and Work Incentives: a North European perspective*, Clarendon Press, Oxford.

Harrison, M., Snider, G., Merlo, R. and Lucchesi, V. (1991), *Paying for the children*, The Australian Institute of Family Studies, Melbourne, Australia.

Jenkins, S. (1994), *Winners and losers: a portrait of the UK income distribution during the 1980s*, Department of Economics Discussion Paper, Swansea University.

Kiernan, K. (1992), 'Men and women at work and at home' in Jowell, R. (ed) *British Social Attitudes Ninth Report*, SCPR, London.

Land, H. (1992), 'Whatever happened to the "social wage"?' in Glendinning, C. and Millar, J. (eds) *Women and Poverty in Britain: the 1990s*, Wheatsheaf, Hemel Hempstead.

McDonald, P. (1986), *Settling up: property and income distribution on divorce in Australia*, Australian Institute of Family Studies, Melbourne, Australia.

McLaughlin, E. (1994), *Flexibility in work and benefits*, Commission on Social Justice, Institute for Public Policy Research, London.

McKay, S. and Marsh, A. (1994) *Lone parents and work*, HMSO, London.

Millar, J. and Whiteford, P. (1993), 'Child support in lone-parent families: policies in Australia and the UK', *Policy and Politics*, Vol. 21, No. 1, pp. 59-72.

Morgan, P. (1995), *Farewell to the family? Public policy and family breakdown in Britain and the USA*, Institute for Economic Affairs, London.

National Association of Citizens Advice Bureaux (1994), *Child Support: one year on*, NACAB, London.

National Council for One-Parent Families (1994), *The child support agency's first year: the lone parent case*, NCOPF, London.

Sisters-in-Law (1993), Submission to the Joint Select Committee on Family Law, SIL, Australia.

Sly, F. (1994), 'Mothers in the labour market', *Employment Gazette*, November, 403-13.

Social Security Select Committee (1993), *The Operation of the Child Support Act*, HMSO, London.

Social Security Select Committee (1994), *The operation of the child support act: proposals for change*, HMSO, London.

Wages for Housework Campaign and Payday Men's Network (1993), *Against re-distributing poverty*, WHIC, London.

Whiteford, P. (1994), *Child support - lessons from Australia*, Social Policy Research Unit, University of York.

4 The Child Support Act: A victory for women?

Fran Wasoff and Sue Morris

Introduction

The Child Support Act 1991 (CSA) is often portrayed as a victory for women and a defeat for men in a gender war. For example Sue Slipman, former Director of the National Council for One Parent Families (NCOPF) has publicly supported the CSA (The *Guardian*, 12 May 1994). Gingerbread, too, have been public supporters of the Child Support Act as a means to help lone parents financially. In a Commons debate in February 1994 about the Child Support Act, all parties: Labour, the Liberal Democrats and the Conservatives were agreed that the fundamental principles of the child support reforms were right although tinkering with its implementation was seen by some to be necessary (The *Guardian*, 11 February 1994). Polly Toynbee, writing about the reforms in February 1994 in the Guardian, asked if

> the silent battalions of divorced and single mothers who stand to gain so much from the CSA will have to get themselves organised quickly to do battle with the swelling ranks of angry men. For the silence of women has been conspicuous. Already 90,000 have benefited, yet it's hard to find many who will hymn its praises in public. Privately they admit their lives will be transformed: for the first time they have a chance of getting off social security and going to work.
>
> For the CSA is delivering an average of £50 per week to women. Some have said this is meaningless as it is simply deducted from their benefit. But that misses an important point. If and when they want to go out to work, which most of them do, they will have that £50 and the Child Benefit in their pocket...But where are the women to raise the banner for the biggest redistribution of wealth in their favour since the

Married Women's Property Act of 1882 gave them power over their own money? They risk losing it...The Government may have to cave in again, and retreat from its unfamiliar role as champion of women's rights (The *Guardian*, 2 February 1994).

It is our contention that such a portrayal is misleading since there are far more women who are losers than winners under the new child support legislation. The Act's benefits are poorly targeted, leaving very few women better off and many worse off than before. The Act itself needs to be viewed in a wider context of trends in the means-tested social security system that is placing greater emphasis on in-work benefits as well as changes increasing private obligations of support and in further residualising of the role of income support and women's independent entitlement to benefit. In elaborating this argument, we begin by outlining the reasons most commonly given by Government, the media and lone parent pressure groups in support of the view that the Child Support Act benefits women.

Why the Child Support Act is seen as a benefit for women

Children Come First, the 1991 White Paper that preceded the Act sets out some of the benefits to mothers the Act was meant to bring. Firstly, the Child Support Agency was set up to ensure that more non-custodial parents paid maintenance for their children and that therefore more lone mothers received child support. The Agency is also supposed to ensure more realistic levels of maintenance, linked to the costs of caring for a child. Furthermore, the formula-based approach to determining the amount of child support gives greater consistency than a discretionary and negotiated settlement (DSS 1990, p. 5, Wasoff 1992).

Secondly, the legislation aims to 'enable caring parents who wish to work to do so as soon as they feel ready and able to do so' (DSS 1990, p. 5). This is because child support does not cease if the parent with care comes off benefit, either Income Support or Family Credit. This will provide women with a transportable and flexible source of income. It has been claimed that this provision not only benefits women who want to work but also allows women unable to work at present to plan for employment since they know how much they will be entitled to if they enter the labour market.

Thirdly, the assessing of child support separately from custody or access issues and also from other financial or property arrangements on divorce or separation has also been presented as an improvement in resource

66

distribution after family breakdown and as a way to reduce the scope for conflict between parents (DSS 1990, p. 5).

Finally, the collection and enforcement of child support under the previous court based system was seen to be costly, ineffective and inefficient and the Child Support Agency, with its specialist remit, was meant to overcome this to provide a speedy and effective enforcement mechanism that would get money from the wallets of absent parents in the purses of parents with care.

Underlying these aims and objectives, the Child Support Act provides a strong moral message through its underlying principle that children are the economic responsibility of both parents and the financial demands this makes on the non-custodial parent should be both a high priority and for a substantial amount. It is also claimed by some commentators that children benefit from the knowledge that their fathers are contributing to their maintenance although they do not live with them. This moral message is strengthened by the fact that there is no significant reduction of child support in the event of the parent with care remarrying.

For all these reasons, the Child Support Act 1991 has been hailed by its supporters as a victory for women as mothers. This has included not only the Government but also the Opposition, the media and some groups who represent the interests of women.

Assessing gainers and losers

Our view is that the purported benefits to women from child support legislation arise only when viewed in narrow focus. In the foregoing analysis of its 'benefits', little account is taken of how child support interacts with other social security benefits as well as housing and property issues on divorce (Wasoff and Morris 1993). Also, no distinction is drawn between lone parents' aspirations for employment and the reality of their labour market participation. Apart from any practical considerations involved for lone mothers entering the labour force, employment at even very modest wage levels is not simply there for the asking (McKay and Marsh 1994 and see Jane Millar's chapter here).

Furthermore, it is mistaken to consider women as a unified group with homogeneous experiences and interests. Whilst all absent parents may well be 'losers' in financial terms, it does not therefore follow that the corresponding parents with care are 'winners'. Rather than seeing the Act as significant for only parents who live apart, it is more accurate to see it as a game with 3 or even 4 players: absent parents, parents with care, the

Treasury/Department of Social Security and the Child Support Agency itself.

It is important too that the Act is not seen in isolation from other issues that arise in divorce. Assessing gainers and losers cannot ignore the interactive effects between the new legislation, the benefits system, the housing market and other forms of family property redistributed (or not) on separation. In this chapter, economic prospects are the main focus of assessment, but other issues, for example, custody, access and the potential for clean break settlements are also likely to arise as a result of the Child Support Act. We also concentrate here on three groups of lone mothers but the Act potentially affects other women's lives by the constraints it may introduce on social, economic and reproductive choices, for example, women who are partners of absent parents or single women who may wish to have a child without living with its father. In order to understand the impact of the Child Support Act in its wider context, we first review some key characteristics of lone parents and their reliance on means-tested benefits.

The context for child support: lone parenthood

The demography of lone parenthood is well documented (FPSC 1990, Ermisch 1991, Bradshaw and Millar 1991, Holtermann 1993, Haskey 1994). Most parents with care are mothers and most absent parents are fathers. About 19 per cent of families with dependent children are headed by a lone parent (1,243,000 families) (OPCS 1993a, Table L89), 95 per cent of whom are women (OPCS 1993b, p. 25).

Lone parent families as a group are highly dependent for their income on means tested social security benefits. About three-quarters of lone mothers (933,000) are receiving Income Support (IS), 190,100 (15 per cent) receive Family Credit (FC) and less than 300 (<.1 per cent) are in receipt of Disability Working Allowance (DWA) (DSS 1994a, pp. 3-5, pp. 15-18). Though some lone parents may be in receipt of both benefits at different times in the year, these figures show that only a small minority of all lone parents during any given year are not in receipt of any of the three relevant means-tested benefits.

Lone parent families also predominate in the number of families on benefit. As a proportion of all families on IS, lone parents predominate, although they comprise only one in five of the population of families with dependent children. Out of a total of 1,623,000 families on Income Support with a qualifying child in terms of the Child Support Act 1991, 65 per cent are lone parents (CPAG 1994, p. 18). Lone mothers comprise 40 per cent of all families on FC (DSS 1994a, p. 3). They predominate even more amongst families on benefit with qualifying children. Of the 1,305,331 families on a relevant benefit with a qualifying child, 95 per cent are lone parents (CPAG 1994, p. 18).

These data all show that the great majority of the population of lone parents likely to be affected by the Child Support Act are lone mothers on benefit and primarily those on Income Support. We can see that the number of lone parents who are not in receipt of any of these benefits is a relatively small proportion of the population of lone parents.

In the following sections, we consider in greater detail how the child support reforms will affect the three groups of lone mothers – those on Income Support, those on Family Credit (and Disability Working Allowance) and those who are not currently in receipt of any relevant benefit. We view the child support legislation in terms of three dimensions – principles, formal provisions, and implementation and interaction with other social security provisions and family law. Briefly, there are two broad principles or objectives for the legislation, one overt and one semi-covert: firstly, the idea that parents should contribute substantially to their children's support, whether they live with them or not and secondly, that public expenditure on lone parents should be reduced. By formal provision, we mean the detailed content of the Child Support Act and its associated regulations that translated these objectives into substantive legislation. Implementation refers to the administrative machinery put in place to assess, collect and enforce the provisions of the Act.

We argue that the effects of the legislation can be seen in relation to each of these dimensions. In our view, most women will not be gainers, not because of the nature of the principles underlying the Act, but because of the way that these principles have been translated into formal provision. Where women do stand to gain from the formal provision of the legislation, many will become losers as a result of the implementation process and the interactive effects of the legislation with the wider means-tested social security, housing and family law systems.

Women on Income Support

Income Support is available to lone mothers without their having to be available for paid work. The effect of any child support is to substitute for that amount of benefit, so that Income Support is effectively 'taxed' at a marginal rate of 100 per cent for every pound of child support paid. This is the case unless the level of child support is high enough to float a parent with care off Income Support entirely (see below). Thus in terms of its formal provision the Child Support legislation simply substitutes the income source without changing the amount, and thus in formal terms the effect on income level is neutral, thus ensuring mothers remaining on Income Support will not be gainers (though they will not be losers either).

For parents with care on Income Support, all of the child support collected from absent parents is transferred to the Department of Social Security, but only part of that sum will result in public expenditure savings, since the recovery costs of the Child Support Agency will absorb a high proportion of the amount collected (see below). But this substitution may have informal economic and social costs. For women remaining on Income Support these may entail, on the one hand, increased demands from an absent parent who sees child support as attached to increased rights of access and control, or, on the other, the loss of benefits in kind or access visits from an absent parent who can no longer afford the costs of such involvement, as some early evidence indicates (Clarke, Craig and Glendinning 1994, NACAB 1994). So what might at first seem a financially neutral effect will for many become a substantial cost. Measuring that cost is likely to be highly complicated, not least because some of these costs are not readily quantifiable in monetary terms. We consider below what additional costs may arise as an inescapable child support obligation is reflected in divorce and separation settlements, including housing redistribution.

For women who are lifted off Income Support by child support (because the level of child support exceeds the amount of benefit), it might first appear that they will be better off, at least to the extent by which child support exceeds their benefit. However, there may be a net loss in income if child support does not exceed the Income Support sum *plus* the value of passported benefits,[1] thus making such a parent with care worse off than she would have been without child support.

In addition, since there is no housing benefit for owner-occupiers unless they are in receipt of Income Support, for women floated off Income Support by child support, the housing penalty may be very great. It is not yet known what proportion of women are likely to get child support at these levels, but the numbers are certain to be very small. But even for women floated off Income Support through high child support payments without these financial penalties, any economic benefits may still be outweighed by the informal economic and social costs mentioned above.

At present, some lone mothers dependent on Income Support who are also owner occupiers have achieved a degree of housing security because they secured a greater share in the former matrimonial home by conceding future claims to maintenance for their children. But this is no longer possible, since lone mothers on Income Support are obliged to cooperate with the Child Support Agency in pursuing child support at formula levels. Therefore, further costs may arise for parents with care who will be in receipt of Income Support in the future since as the legislation becomes more established, absent parents might no longer be prepared to concede housing resources when making arrangements after family breakdown, knowing there will be no prospect for 'clean break agreements' that substitute additional housing resources for reduced maintenance. Thus a future cost of the Child Support Act is likely to be reduced housing security for parents with care and their children.

One objective of the legislation was to provide an incentive for lone mothers on Income Support to move from this benefit into paid employment, with or without the help of Family Credit. We now turn to look at the gainers and losers in this group.

Women on Family Credit

Family Credit (FC) is a means-tested benefit available to families where a parent works for 16 hours or more per week and whose income from employment is low. There is a £15 disregard of child support in the assessment of Family Credit, that is the first £15 of child support assessed is ignored for the purpose of calculating Family Credit entitlement and amount. For every £1 of child support in excess of this disregard there is a corresponding £1 reduction in the level of Family Credit due, in effect a marginal rate of 'taxation' of 100 per cent over the £15 threshold. Thus, unless the level of child support is sufficient to make a parent with care ineligible for Family Credit, £15 per week is the maximum possible benefit from child support for parents with care on Family Credit, representing an additional in-work benefit which supplements their existing income. In addition they may also be eligible to receive another in-work benefit: a childcare 'disregard' of up to £28 net for 'allowable' childcare costs, introduced in October 1994, intended to enhance further the package of in-work benefits to lone parents.

Women eligible for Family Credit therefore can be identified as possible gainers from the formal provisions of the Act, although the gain will be limited. Nevertheless, this may satisfy one of the objectives of the legislation which was to provide a work incentive for parents with care by enhancing their package of in-work benefits. Even so, for many lone mothers making the transition from IS to FC, any gain will be offset, to greater or lesser extents, by interactive effects with the wider social security system, such as the loss of passported benefits; loss of housing benefit (if an owner occupier) and the effect of housing benefit tapers (if a tenant) (see Jane Millar's chapter here). In addition the possible gains to some lone mothers on Family Credit may also be offset by the social costs such as the lack of job security and regularity of payment of child support itself as well as the possibly unwelcome intrusion in their lives of a former partner. Finally the childcare allowance, whose rules are complex, will not help the lowest paid who are already receiving the maximum level of Family Credit. This group includes 28 per cent of all lone parents on Family Credit (SCSP 1994).

It is important to establish how much of a work incentive this will prove to be in practice and to what extent it will encourage lone mothers to seek employment + Family Credit rather than Income Support. While the *Guardian* (24/3/94) reported that 7000 lone mothers receiving maintenance applied for Family Credit in the CSA's first 3 months of operation, how many of those did so *because of* child support is not known. Bingley et al. (1994, p. 83) have estimated the work incentive effect of the Child Support Act. Although their assumptions about the Act upon which the estimate is based may well exaggerate the incentive effects, their estimate is nevertheless modest: only 40,000 lone mothers (under 5 per cent of those currently on IS) will join the labour force as a result of Child Support Act 1991. An additional pointer as to the work incentive effect of this level of maintenance disregard can be seen in the work of Marsh and McKay (1993) who report that the employment incentive of a £15 *earnings* disregard for lone parents on IS is minimal, being used by only one in six lone parents on IS.

For parents with care considering a transition from Income Support to Family Credit, there may be further disincentives. These include the costs of employment itself (travel to work, childcare etc) as well as concerns about the reliability of income from child support and from possibly insecure employment. Whilst there is a £15 disregard for child support, this relates to the assessed sum and not to the amount actually received. Some of these disincentives may be partially offset by changes proposed by Peter Lilley, Secretary of State for Social Security in January 1995 when he announced the Government's intention to introduce a limited maintenance credit for parents with care coming off Income Support to take a job. In these circumstances, she will be entitled to receive a bonus of up to £1000 consisting of the accumulation of £5 per week of maintenance collected while she was in receipt of Income Support (DSS 1995). This change will make some parents with care leaving Income Support limited gainers.

Since child support is 'guaranteed' for parents with care on Income Support, but not for those on Family Credit, there may be a significant shortfall in income if child support is not paid regularly. In the National Client Survey of the Child Support Agency (DSS 1994b, p. 112) only 52 per cent of absent parents interviewed stated they never missed a payment (see also Jane Millar in this volume who stresses the importance to lone parents of certainty of income). The inefficient enforcement of child support by the Child Support Agency is itself a disincentive for women to make the transition. Furthermore, since Family Credit is assessed for a six month period, any reassessment downwards of child support will not result in a corresponding reassessment of Family Credit. More detailed work is required in order to quantify the extent to which formal gains are offset by losses arising from these interactive effects and to estimate the resultant number of net gainers in this group.

Further interactive effects between child support and the family law system may emerge in future. These will relate to housing and property settlements that may be made on separation and divorce, since absent parents cannot 'trade' housing assets on divorce for reduced obligations of child support post-divorce. The effect may well be to produce less advantageous housing settlements for parents with care, with a resulting loss of housing security for them and their children.

In the light of the formal legislation and its interaction with the social security and family law systems, it is evident that not only most lone mothers on Income Support are unlikely to gain from the Act, but also that many, and possibly most, lone mothers on Family Credit will be, at best, limited gainers. As far as the formal provisions of the Child Support Act are concerned, though, lone mothers who are not in receipt of means-tested benefit stand to gain rather more. How far this is likely in practice will depends crucially on the implementation of the legislation through the work of the Child Support Agency.

Women not on benefit/in paid work

The Child Support Act has the potential to be of substantial benefit to women who are not in receipt of means-tested benefits at all – either because they are economically inactive and maintained by a new partner, or because they are in paid employment, at an income sufficient to take them over Family Credit level. For this group, there is neither an obligation to pursue child support nor a direct benefit penalty from the receipt of child support. Where both parents are in employment, the child support assessment is divided in proportion to the size of parents' respective assessable incomes. Thus, women on high earnings will be expected to make some financial contribution themselves towards the maintenance assessment.

For parents with care for whom there was no legally binding maintenance agreement when the Act came into force, maintenance assessments are likely to be at substantially higher levels than could be expected under the previous system. Thus in terms of the formal provision of the Child Support Act, such women are likely to see the greatest benefit from the Act. For them, there are no interactive effects from the means tested social security system to reduce the gain from child support. However, their actual benefit will also depend on effective implementation. Given the substantial operational difficulties reported by the Child Support Agency in its first year (DSS 1994b and Social Security Committee 1994), the sums actually transferred were well below those assessed. In addition, because the Child Support Agency also targeted 'benefit' cases, there was relative neglect of these 'non-benefit' cases, and many parents with care not on means tested benefit had great difficulty in even obtaining a maintenance assessment. Insofar as the Agency's agenda is about cutting the cost of public expenditure on child support, securing maintenance for this group of lone mothers will remain a low priority. Eekelaar (1994) reported that delays of up to 3 months to produce assessments are common, and collection and enforcement give further cause for concern. More recent data from the Child Support Agency's Annual Report suggests even this figure may be optimistic: much longer delays are reported as well as an inability to deal with some claims at all. In effect, the Child Support Act has provided this group of women with a potentially valuable social right without an effective means of pursuing it. For this group of women, questions of due process arise in as much as they have a legal, but an unenforceable 'right'. Even if the operational difficulties of the Child Support Agency are eased and the potential benefits to this group become realised, there is a danger that the benefit from the formal provision will be reduced because of political concessions made to absent parents.

The amendments made in February 1994 to the Child Support regulations have further reduced income redistribution between parents away from this group of lone mothers. Virtually all of these amendments addressed the interests of absent parents. Briefly, they have resulted in more protected income for absent parents; more exempt income in making child support assessments; more phasing-in arrangements for absent parents with pre-

74

existing child maintenance agreements; lower levels of adult carer's allowance for parents with care; and a reduced formula demand on the incomes of wealthier absent parents. This of course means less income to be transferred to the parent with care. These concessions to absent parents may not stop there. The proposals made in January 1995 by the Government make further concessions to absent parents, due to take effect in April 1995. These include introducing a ceiling of 30 per cent of net income that can be collected for maintenance and reducing the additional element of maintenance to be paid by wealthy absent parents. In addition, changes to the assessment formula will be made to allow further expenses, such as travel to work costs, costs of access visits, caring for stepchildren and full housing costs for stepfamilies to be taken into account (DSS 1995). These concessions will reduce the amount of child support transferred from absent parents to parents with care not on a relevant benefit.

For parents with care not in receipt of means tested benefit who already had a legally binding maintenance agreement when the Act came into force, there is a transitional period until 1996/97, during which the court retains jurisdiction. These women will not be eligible to apply to the Agency for child support assessments in this period and their child support arrangements remain governed by the old, discretionary court-based system, unless they begin to claim a relevant benefit. They are formally unaffected by the Act in the meantime. In the White Paper, *Improving Child Support* (DSS 1995), the Government announced that it would defer indefinitely the length of the transitional period, as a concession to criticisms by absent parents that the Child Support Act was unjust, retrospective legislation. (It is significant that this concession applies only to pre 1993 'clean break' agreements, and not to agreements made subsequently.)

In future, there may be costs in terms of housing security for this group in future as ex-partners are likely to be advised not to enter into substitution or 'clean break' agreements. Parents with care, even those not in receipt of a relevant benefit, cannot guarantee they will *not* seek child support in future. This is because they cannot guarantee they will not be in receipt of a relevant benefit in future and the 1991 Act makes seeking child support virtually compulsory for all mothers in receipt of state benefits. But even if they do not claim a relevant benefit, agreements about not seeking child support are no longer legally enforceable.

Portrait of the CSA gainer

It appears, therefore, that the number of women gaining from the Child Support Act is likely to be smaller than claimed and for many of them, any gains are also likely to be marginal. Existing gainers among those lone mothers on Income Support include the few immediately lifted off benefit by a margin above the value of the loss of passported benefits and who have reasonable relationships with ex-partners.

Future beneficiaries from this group include those planning to return to paid employment where they would join the category of limited gainers among those on Family Credit and gainers who are independent of the benefit system. Further gainers from this group include those who are able to find work and whose economic obstacles to obtaining reasonable employment are overcome within the margin of the Family Credit maintenance disregard plus any benefit from childcare allowances.

Gainers among lone mothers *already* on Family Credit are those who will get to keep up to the first £15 per week maintenance paid. For them, the costs of employment (eg child care, transport and loss of passported benefits) have already been incurred. Their gain from child support is limited to £15 per week as long as they qualify for Family Credit - they are, at best, limited gainers. Their gain can only exceed £15 if the amount of maintenance collected exceeds their entitlement to Family Credit and takes them off benefit altogether and places them in the next category. However this gain from the Child Support Act may be substantially off-set by loss of housing security, unwelcome contact from an ex-partner, and non-receipt of the assessed child support through inefficiencies in the collection system itself. The first two are also true for lone mothers on Income Support.

Those mostly likely to gain from the formal provisions of the 1991 Act are lone mothers earning enough to lift them out of the benefit system and whose child support will add to their income without any reductions of benefits in cash or in kind and mothers who live with a new partner and who are not in paid work whose child support will add to their income without penalty.

Summarising all this, we can construct a portrait of the gainer. She is a lone parent in reasonably paid and reasonably secure work, either not in receipt of Family Credit, or receiving a small amount of Family Credit (and getting the maximum of £15 maintenance disregard and also getting the maximum £28 childcare allowance - available only to those who are least dependent on Family Credit already). Alternatively, the gainer is a mother who has repartnered and whose new partner is earning (and whose previous partner is well-heeled and in regular employment). These women already belong to the most advantaged group within the pool of those potentially affected by the Child Support Act 1991. This portrait of the gainer does not look like the great majority of the population. Thus one effect of the Child Support Act might be to intensify the divisions between parents with care, leaving those at the bottom end at best no better off (and many worse off) and those at the top end possibly better off if the implementation of the legislation can be made more effective, but with perhaps a future cost of reduced housing security.

The portrait of the gainer is the image of lone parents painted by Sue Slipman of NCOPF and Polly Toynbee, and is also the government's ideal and the aspiration if not the reality for most lone parents (Bradshaw and Millar 1991, McKay and Marsh 1994). Perhaps this idealised imagery is the reason that the Child Support reforms have attracted the support of these otherwise champions of women's rights. This picture is also part of a feminist agenda for social change. However, while the Child Support Act has been sold by the politics of aspiration, it does very little to get the bulk of lone mothers closer to achieving those aspirations in reality.

What appears to be the case is that child support as presently constituted is an upside down benefit that benefits least of all (for many, not at all) the great majority of parents with care on the lowest incomes, which benefits those on low earnings to a very limited extent and even those benefits are offset by interactive effects elsewhere in the social security, family law and housing systems. It potentially benefits most those who are out of the means-tested social security system entirely, although for them also the gain is offset by losses from the family law and housing systems. This group are also suffering from the Agency's implementation of the legislation itself. On the experience of the Agency's first year, it appears to be no better at speeding up assessment and collection of maintenance than the system it was designed to replace. Potential gains accruing to this group have been reduced through the changes introduced in the regulations early in 1994 which almost entirely benefited absent parents at their expense (Child Support [Miscellaneous Amendments and Transitional Provisions] Regulations 1994).

Conclusion

In thinking about the impact of the Child Support Act, less attention needs to be paid to the details of the formula than to how child support interacts with the wider means-tested social security system. It is not the overt principle underlying the Child Support Act that makes women losers: the principle that non-custodial parents should contribute to their children's economic support attracts a wide consensus. What makes women losers is the Treasury-driven use of the legislation to make public expenditure savings on lone parents, the covert principle underpinning the Act. The Child Support Act reduces women's access to the social security safety net by transferring women's dependence to both the labour market and men, without corresponding policies to strengthen either the capacity of the labour market or the willingness and ability of men to provide income support.

What would be needed to make more women gainers is to relax the requirement for public expenditure savings, without necessarily eliminating it entirely. This might involve introducing changes such as, for example: a maintenance disregard for women on Income Support, possibly in the form of a disregard plus taper as in the Australian system (on which ironically the UK legislation claims to be based); a more generous disregard and/or taper for women on Family Credit, which takes more realistic account of the costs of working, including child care, loss of other passported benefits and loss of housing benefit for owner occupiers. A guaranteed maintenance advance for women on Family Credit would help reduce the uncertainty of income from child support. Such reforms may not represent such a great 'cost' to the Treasury, since many absent parents might be more prepared to contribute and co-operate if they saw their own children deriving some direct benefit. Thus some of these 'costs' could be met through efficiency savings by reducing problems and costs of assessment, collection and enforcement and could provide the Child Support Agency with a political constituency that has an interest in defending its existence.

There is also a division in the population of lone mothers between those with and without choices. At the bottom end of the income scale, there is no choice about pursuing child support, except with a considerable benefit penalty, whereas at the top end some choice still exists. For women on Income Support with little prospect of raising their incomes above Income Support level, whether in or out of work, the Child Support Act represents an erosion of their (limited) rights of citizenship as lone mothers, inasmuch as their entitlement to independent income support via public benefit has become conditional on the obligation to be financially dependent on the father of their children and to cooperate with the state in pursuing him, even where there is no benefit to herself or her children.

Nor can the shift that the Child Support Act entails in the dependency relationships between private and public support for lone mothers be ignored. There is a real danger that the Child Support Act will result in a revival of women's difficulties in leaving a bad relationship because of their dependency on partners to support them in caring for children. The Income Support safety net which allows many women to leave unsatisfactory relationships has been severely weakened by the Act. Even women in paid work and in receipt of Family Credit or in well-paid work are in a vulnerable position both because they have dependants and because of uncertainties in the labour market. As a social policy measure to help children from families in greatest need, the Child Support Act cannot be deemed a success.

Thus, the 1991 Act is not a victory for women. On the contrary, most women are being legally, and not only morally, obliged to remain dependent on men with whom they once had a relationship. Those concerned with the rights and wrongs of women need to address the long-term implications of the Child Support Act for the position of women in the UK. It is thus misleading when groups claiming to represent the interests of women or lone parents portray the Child Support Act as a victory for lone mothers when it is not clear that it promotes independence for women, when it is only an economic gain for a few and only for as long as they retain their advantaged position.

Note

1. Passported benefits for those on Income Support but not for those on Family Credit include: free school meals, free milk. Help with NHS costs, such as free prescriptions, dental treatment, etc. are available to families in receipt of both benefits.

References

Bingley, P., Symons, E., and Walker, I. (1994), 'Child Support, Income Support and Lone Mothers', *Fiscal Studies*, 15(1), pp. 81-98.
Bradshaw, Jonathan and Millar, Jane (1991), *Lone Parent Families in the UK*, HMSO, London.
Burghes, Louie (1993), *One Parent Families: Policy options for the 1990s*, Joseph Rowntree Foundation, York.
Child Support Agency (1994), *Child Support Agency: the first two years*, Department of Social Security, London.
Child Poverty Action Group (1994), *Putting the Treasury First*, CPAG,

London.

Clarke, K., Craig, G., and Glenndinning, C. (1993), *Children Come First?*, Barnardo's, National Childrens Homes et al, London.

Clarke, K., Craig, G., and Glenndinning, C. (1994), *Losing Support,* Barnardo's, National Childrens Homes et al, London.

Department of Social Security (1990), *Children Come First, The Government's Proposals on the maintenance of children*, HMSO, London.

Department of Social Security (1995), *Improving Child Support,* HMSO, London.

Department of Social Security (1994a), *Social Security Statistics 1993*, HMSO, London.

Department of Social Security (1994b), *Child Support Agency National Client Survey*, HMSO, London.

Department of Social Security and the Treasury (1994c), *Government's Expenditure Plans 1994-95 to 1996-97,* Cm2513, HMSO, London.

Eekelaar, John (1994), 'Third thoughts on Child Support', *Family Law*, February, pp. 99-102.

Ermisch, John (1991), *Lone Parenthood: an Economic Analysis,* Cambridge University Press, Cambridge.

Family Policy Studies Centre (1990), *One Parent Families*, Family Policy Studies Centre, London.

Haskey, J. (1994), 'Estimated numbers of one-parent families and their prevalence in Great Britain in 1991', *Population Trends*, 78, Winter, pp. 5-19.

Holtermann, Sally, (1993), *Becoming a Breadwinner*, Daycare Trust, London.

Marsh, A., and McKay, S., (1993), *Families, Work and Benefits*, Policy Studies Institute, London.

McKay, S and Marsh, A. (1994), *Lone Parents and Work,* London: HMSO.

Millar, Jane (1992), 'Lone Mothers and Poverty', in Caroline Glendinning and Jane Millar (eds.), *Women and Poverty in Britain the 1990s*, pp. 149-161, Wheatsheaf, Brighton.

National Association of Citizens Advice Bureaux (1994), *Child Support: one year on*, NACAB, London.

OPCS (1993a), *Census of Population 1991*, HMSO, London.

OPCS (1993b), *General Household Survey 1991*, HMSO, London.

Roll, Jo (1992), *Lone Parent Families in the European Community*, European Family and Social Policy Unit, London.

Scottish Council for Single Parents (1994), *Childcare Allowance*

Information Sheet, SCSP, Edinburgh.

Social Security Committee (1994), *Fifth Report: The Operation of the Child Support Act: Proposals for Change*, HMSO, London.

Statutory Instruments 1994 No. 227 *Family Law Child Support The Child Support (Miscellaneous Amendments and Transitional Provisions) Regulations* 1994.

Wasoff, F. and Morris, S. (1993), 'The Child Support Act 1991 and family and civil law in Scotland', *Journal of the Law Society of Scotland*, (December).

Wasoff, Fran (1992), 'The New Child Support Formula: Algebra for Lawyers?', *Scots Law Times*, Vol. 40, pp. 389-392.

The *Guardian*, 5 July 1994

The *Guardian*, 12 May 1994

The *Guardian*, 11 February 1994

The *Guardian*, 2 February 1994

5 Housing and post-divorce parenting

Peter McCarthy

Introduction

In England and Wales there are currently more than 160,000 divorces per annum and 37 per cent of new marriages are expected to end in divorce (OPCS 1994a). During the last thirty years the rate of dissolution has increased from 2.1 to 13.5 per thousand marriages (OPCS 1994b). The result is a divorce rate which has risen to become the second highest in the European Union, though still lagging behind some other countries such as the United States where around half of all new marriages end in divorce. Approximately 60 per cent of divorces involve couples with children and it has been estimated that one in four British children will experience the divorce of their parents before they reach the age of sixteen (Haskey 1991).

Of course, divorce reveals only part of the story of the breakdown of nuclear family units. The rate at which relationships between non-married (or cohabiting) couples break down is not known but, leaving that aside, it is clear that the rate at which marriages are ended by divorce has in itself got important implications for the provision of housing. In terms of housing, marriage and divorce may be regarded as a game of snakes and ladders. Newly married couples who want separate accommodation are increasingly dependent on their ability to enter owner occupation. Over the last decade or so there have been a series of inducements to encourage such couples to become owner-occupiers. They have been prime targets in the drive towards creation of a nation of home owners, a drive which even government ministers are beginning to accept has gone too far in that it has drawn in couples who have been unable to afford it. This has led to financial pressures which have placed strains on relationships and which may themselves be a factor in marital breakdown.

83

Marriage may be regarded then as a point of entry to climbing the housing ladder: currently 78 per cent of married couples are home owners compared with 50 per cent of households headed by a single man and 42 per cent of those headed by a single woman (OPCS 1992). For many couples, divorce can be the head of the slippery snake down.

This chapter examines the impact of divorce on housing circumstances, particularly those of non-resident parents. Although the discussion concentrates on fathers, the points raised seem likely to be as relevant for non-resident mothers. The data were drawn from several related studies involving surveys and face-to-face interviews with a sample of people who were divorced during 1986. The sample was initially selected for the purpose of studying the costs and effectiveness of family mediation services (Conciliation Project Unit 1989). At that time, mediation was only available in connection with issues about children and it became apparent during that study that housing issues were crucial in determining how decisions about child-care arrangements were made. Consequently, we recommended that mediation ought to be able in principle to deal with all issues connected with marital breakdown, including the crucial decision about the marital home. In addition, we re-contacted the sample of divorced people for a specific study of the housing consequences of divorce. The housing study primarily concerned analysis of questionnaires completed by 642 divorced parents and in-depth interviews with 33 survey respondents. The questionnaires were completed in January 1990 and the interviews were conducted during the following six months (for more details see McCarthy and Simpson 1991). So the data at this stage were collected between three and four years after divorce.

Subsequent studies with the same sample of divorced people have been concerned with the long term effects of mediation (Family and Community Dispute Research Centre 1991) and with fathering after divorce (FCDRC 1993).[1] The latter study in particular has had an important influence on our analysis of the housing and divorce findings.

Making the break

As a part of the housing study, we examined more than 4,000 petitions concerning divorces initiated in various parts of England and Wales during 1986. This revealed that one in six couples shared the same address at the time that one of them thought that the marriage had deteriorated sufficiently to warrant divorce proceedings. This may not mean that these couples were actually living together. In some instances, one party may have

84

simply used the marital home as a convenient postal address. In other cases, living together during divorce proceedings might not have been a problem. However, information provided by divorced people during interviews, and in questionnaires, suggests that for the majority of these families cohabitation at this stage of relationship breakdown presented very real problems. The main reason couples were still living together, despite the fact that one party had taken decisive action to terminate the relationship, was that neither partner would make the equally decisive decision to leave. This was primarily due to the feeling that they had nowhere else to go: they were unable to find alternative accommodation.

For those couples who found themselves involved in a negative relationship, kept together by little else than co-residence, by the inability to find alternatives and by the length of time it takes to get a divorce, the consequences were often drastic. Even though both parties might have had the best of intentions, staying together in such circumstances tended to exacerbate domestic conflict. Tensions were apt to 'boil over' and cause deep and sustained stress for all members of the family. In such circumstances it can be difficult to predict what the outcome will be. For instance, during interviews one man said:

> She just said "I want you out". I said "where do you want me to go? Do you want me to sleep in the gutter?" She says "go to your parents". I says "don't be daft, you know I don't speak to them". She says "go to your Nan's". I said "they're in their seventies, how can I go to them? They don't want me in their seventies". I says "I've got nowhere to go!" So I went to my solicitor and my solicitor says "don't go anywhere, don't listen to her, no matter what kind of pressure she puts on you, don't go anywhere".

However, the result of not going anywhere was that the conflict between this man and his wife got worse and eventually led to an outbreak of violence. As a result, his wife went to court and was awarded an injunction which excluded him from the home. Consequently, he did move in with his grandparents although one might question whether this was an outcome which was fair on them.

The following case also involved violence but the housing outcome was radically different. A female interviewee described how:

> We were living in the same house but the social security was paid separately and we'd buy separate foods. We were basically living separate lives in the same house. It just was really awkward. I was buying food for me and the kids and he was just taking the food and there was nothing I could do to stop him...she [solicitor] was just saying

wait till we get to court and this will go against him but in the meantime it was me who was having to live through the situation.

However, these tensions blew up long before the couple ever got to court. The woman was assaulted by her husband but rather than taking out an injunction she left the marital home, taking the children with her, and moved back into the home of her parents. Thus, despite the legal advice to stay put, she was unable to live in the same house as her husband and did not feel able to cope with the difficult legal process of having him removed. As a consequence, she lost the home and had great difficulty persuading her local council that she was homeless because, as far as they were concerned, she was adequately housed in the home of her parents.

In both of the above cases, the advice given by solicitors was to stay put no matter how difficult things got. In the legal sense this may have been good advice, but 'staying put' can be a difficult and sometimes dangerous strategy for women, and men, to follow. They are required to endure circumstances in which there is likely to be a high degree of stress and conflict about the very basics of daily living. In some cases this is made worse by divorce court judges who concoct elaborate, but unworkable arrangements, which supposedly allow couples to continue to live under the same roof. We came across one case where the arrangements devised by the divorce court included times when the parties were allowed to use the toilet.

Where couples are forced together in such circumstances, violence is seldom far from the surface and at times can become serious enough to precipitate emergency action which might be inadvisable in the long term. One in four of the 101 mothers responding to our survey who left the marital home and took children with them said they did so because they could no longer take the violence. They were forced out of the home, and in some cases gave up their rights to it, because they felt it was not safe for them to stay.

When both parties, for their own reasons, refuse to make the decisive move housing authorities face the difficult problem of how to define the point at which someone should be regarded as homeless and under what circumstances homelessness can be considered intentional. When the couple are joint tenants of a council house it is particularly difficult, given that the Housing Act 1980 (since incorporated into Housing Act 1985) guarantees security of tenure to both parties to a joint tenancy. One solution is to have a secure tenancy terminated via the court under the Matrimonial Homes Act 1983, or the Matrimonial Causes Act 1973. However, this only becomes possible when a divorce has been finalised and this itself can take a long time. The average length of time between divorce petition and decree absolute is nine months; and this time is very easily extended when one party chooses to be obstructive. Consequently, it is an action which would appear to be seldom used: during 1989 only 33 such orders were made in England and Wales (Lord Chancellor's Department 1989).

A solution adopted by some housing authorities was provided by a Court of Appeal judgement concerning the case of London Borough of Greenwich v McGrady (1982) where it was ruled that there were sufficient grounds for a joint tenancy to be revoked if one party gave the landlord notice to quit. The landlord is then free to grant sole tenancy to one of the previous joint tenants. This means that a wife who wanted a husband removed would simply need to give notice to quit thus terminating the joint tenancy, at which point the housing authority could award her the sole tenancy. The husband would therefore become an illegal occupant and could be evicted. However, this solution has drawbacks for the women involved in that it puts them at the centre of attempts to make the husband homeless with consequent risks of retaliation. Furthermore, it would seem that an evicted husband could bring legal action for damages on the grounds of breach of trust (Williams 1988). Nevertheless, it is a solution frequently adopted by housing managers in some authorities (Bull 1993) and one suggested to several women in our study, although in practice it was often impractical. As one mother told us:

> I'd got to wait for the divorce first, then I'd got to hand the notice in my name only, wait for the notice to be served, then they would give me the house back and I'd have to get the police to evict him - which I thought was a lot of aggravation really. And as it was the divorce took about three years anyway, so I would've still been there waiting now. I just assumed that as he hadn't got custody it was automatic that I'd get the house but it wasn't that way at all...there was so much aggravation, in the end I'd just had enough. He was getting a bit heavy handed and that.

Clearly, the time scale upon which 'official' strategies operate may not be commensurate with those relevant to divorcing couples. Part of the problem has been that housing is simply one of the issues that tend not to be sorted out until divorce has been finalised. Divorce is the trigger which leads to negotiation about related issues - children, property and financial arrangements - and there is no timescale within which such arrangements should be made. The proposed divorce law reform aims to change that. The green paper 'Looking to the future: mediation and the ground for divorce' (Lord Chancellor's Department 1993) proposes that all ancillary issues be sorted out within twelve months of a divorce application and that the divorce will not be finalised until this is done. This may serve to shorten the time that incompatible couples are forced to live together but, if it is introduced, it seems likely to increase the demands on local housing authorities as people become conscious of the need to find quick solutions to the housing issue.

Whatever divorce legislation is in place the process of separation would be easier if housing authorities were able to offer alternative housing to one of the parties. As this can be seen as providing two houses for what, prior to the finalising of divorce, some might regard as a single household, it is an option which many authorities are reluctant to pursue. Others might wish to do so but be unable to because they do not have enough housing available. Nevertheless, it would be possible if the supply of available housing were to increase.

One has to accept that the current supply of council housing means that there are unlikely to be quick fixes to the needs of any particular group. It is difficult to argue that divorced families should be given higher priority than other families on council waiting lists. Nevertheless, in situations where both parties stubbornly continue to occupy the same dwelling, or where the struggle for rights to occupation or ownership of a dwelling continue after the breakdown of a marriage, the solution in the long term generally involves one of the parties obtaining appropriate alternative housing. Thus, concentrating on housing allocation for non-resident parents can be an appropriate strategy for easing the burdens on mothers and resident children. It is likely to be a more satisfactory solution for them than one which pushes women in this situation into legal actions which result in making husbands homeless and puts themselves at risk.

Who stays? Who goes?

In any decision over which partner should move out of the marital home after separation, and which (if either) should stay, there are a number of factors which would appear to be crucial. These include: gender; child care arrangements; duration of the marriage; number of children; the amount of time a home has been occupied; the tenure of that home and the amount of equity tied up in the home. In our study we examined the impact of each of these factors but only two turned out to be significantly related to the eventual decision as to who stayed in the home: these were gender and child care arrangements. Women and parents with care of the children were most likely to stay.

Care of children was by far the most important consideration. Women were more likely to remain in the marital home but only because they were more likely to have custody of children. Mothers remained in the marital home only if the children stayed there with them. In contrast, approximately one in eight fathers without resident children remained in the marital home and were still there three years after divorce.

The parent who retains primary responsibility for child care is most likely to remain in the marital home immediately after separation. As this is usually the mother, this means that in the first instance it is generally fathers who are in need of re-housing. However, the real issue concerning post-divorce housing is not staying in the home but keeping it. Keeping the home can be a particularly difficult prospect for women left in owner-occupied housing. The demands of paying a mortgage, perhaps augmented by a second mortgage, whilst on reduced income; or of resisting pressures from an ex-husband to sell in order to release capital to enable him to purchase housing; or basic harassment from a dissatisfied ex-husband and his relatives, may prove to be overwhelming. The end result is often that neither party can stay in the marital home. One in three of those mothers with care of the children who initially stayed in the marital home moved out of it within three years of their divorce.

Where do non-resident parents move to?

The two most important issues regarding the housing movements of divorcing people are where they move to initially and where they finish up after all the arrangements connected with the divorce have been sorted out. Table 5.1 illustrates such moves as made by non-resident fathers.

Non-resident fathers who move out tend to move first of all into the homes of relatives or friends or into privately rented housing. The majority of those who make such moves return to their original tenure albeit into homes which are smaller than those which they occupied during marriage and often after several interim moves: in the three years following divorce around one in five non-custodial fathers had moved house on four or more occasions. In many cases the unsatisfactory nature of interim housing arrangements led to loss of contact with children which proved difficult to re-establish.

Moving in with others

The main first move of non-resident fathers is into the home of others, usually their parents (see also Sullivan 1986). This option is most likely to be used by those who move from social-rented housing. It is a move which is not without its problems. It can lead to overcrowding, for example, especially if this home becomes a base for staying access visits. Nevertheless, it is an arrangement which can be a good one in terms of the father's ongoing relationship with the children in as much as it allows access to take place in what is likely to be an acceptable environment, namely the home of the child's paternal grandparents.

Table 5.1

Housing movements of non-resident fathers by tenure of marital home

Tenure of marital home

	owner occupied %	council rented %	other rented %	all tenures %
FIRST MOVE				
no move	13	22	10	14
owner-occupied	19	4	10	16
council	2	9	14	4
housing association	3	0	5	3
other rented	29	13	38	28
bed and breakfast	1	9	0	2
shared	32	43	24	33
total	136	23	21	180
CURRENT TENURE				
owner-occupied	78	17	19	63
council	7	52	24	15
housing association	2	0	10	3
other rented	9	13	38	13
shared	4	17	10	6
total	136	23	21	180

This may carry benefits not only for the child but also for the grandparents in that it provides them with extra contact with their grandchildren: a relationship which is often threatened, if not completely terminated, when sons divorce (McCarthy and Simpson 1990). When the initial move was into the home of friends, the effect on the relationship was likely to be less positive. Friendships were apt to sour as friends given help in times of need outstayed their welcome. If the host household was in receipt of welfare benefits this process was likely to be accelerated as they found themselves at risk of having benefits deducted because of a lodger's assumed rent. One man, who was bitter at having been moved on from two households for this very reason, commented: 'it all boils down to Maggie Thatcher [who was Prime Minister at the time] and her team taking money off people for trying to help someone'.

Privately-rented housing

The privately rented sector plays a crucial role in enabling couples to separate. It was the first destination for around one in three non-resident parents. For most of those who made this move it was regarded as a temporary measure. However, temporary measures can last a long time. Most of those who used the privately-rented sector did eventually return to their original tenures but on average they remained in privately-rented housing for eighteen months. The privately-rented housing they moved into fulfilled immediate needs but was seldom regarded as satisfactory. This is partly due to the poor condition of much of the privately-rented stock, but for those who have recently separated there is another important factor. Regulations which operated within the private sector necessitated divorced men behaving as if they were single because they felt children hindered their access to housing, even if they only visited occasionally. One man who found himself in privately-rented accommodation along with a mixture of students and young single men who were working temporary contracts in the area, described the accommodation as follows:

> All I've got for the money I pay is one room, it's got a bed in it, a wardrobe, a chest of drawers, a television, a video and the rest is downstairs and shared with the others. You never know what kind of people they're going to bring back so you're never at ease in the shared part...can't have friends to stay, I can't have the kids to stop. She doesn't like it anyway, the landlady...even if you're desperate she doesn't like anybody stopping.

At the time of the interview this man had been separated for seven years and the longest he had stayed in one place during that time was the three years he stayed with his mother immediately after the separation. The home of his mother provided some continuity for his children, as this was the place where contact usually took place. However, apart from this, his two children had not experienced any home life with their father for a significant part of their lives.

Local authority housing

Very few fathers who do not have children living with them on a permanent basis gain access to council housing. Those non-resident fathers who moved into public housing tended to do so because they moved in with new partners who were already council tenants. Just as divorced women seem to get access to owner-occupation through men, divorced men would appear to get access to council housing through women. Thus, it seemed that re-marriage (or re-partnering) was, for both men and women, a solution to housing problems: though not necessarily a prime reason for the action.

One in four of the fathers in our study did make enquiries at their local housing departments. Those who felt they were making an altruistic gesture in deciding to move for the benefit of their wives and children tended to be optimistic about their chances of being re-housed, at least on a temporary basis, but their optimism was usually misplaced. In practice, they had little chance of housing and were usually informed that there was no point in applying. As one father put it, 'single man, no kids, not pregnant, I owe them points'.

The most likely outcome for those who did apply was to be placed on a waiting list, usually with a lengthy and lengthening queue in front of them. In some cases this was reluctantly accepted, and one man said:

> At the town hall they say there's a thirteen year waiting list and I've sat with somebody at a desk and I've said well right, I'll wait thirteen years. But after thirteen years waiting here for a house, that's going to make me about fifty, but I'll 'ave one, even if I'm a fifty year old I'll still 'ave one.

But usually when immediate housing was not forthcoming it caused considerable annoyance, especially if fathers felt that the breakdown of the marriage was not their fault. One father who had been refused council accommodation was particularly annoyed when a housing official told him that if his wife had applied she would have been given council accommodation within two or three days.

Fathers were also annoyed when they were assessed as single people even though they were trying to create a home in which children could stay on a regular basis. As one said:

> Even though I had stay over access with my three children they could not, or would not, give me extra points to get accommodation and just treated me as a single person.

Those few fathers who did receive offers of help were offered housing which they regarded as inappropriate in the sense of being unsuitable for their children. However, some felt that they had no option other than to accept although extremely dissatisfied that their status as fathers had not been given consideration. As one father who did have regular contact with his children said:

> I don't want to live in a high rise flat I never have but the council have told me, being single, I won't get anywhere else so according to them I am set here for life. This is unfair as I have access to my children who I now see approximately three days and nights. Why on that basis aren't I allowed a house? I would love a garden for the kids. That's what I have always wanted.

A Court of Appeal decision made during 1990 had potentially important ramifications for men in these kind of circumstances. The Court ruled that the definition of 'priority need' in the Housing and Homeless Persons Act does not necessarily require that a parent has custody of a child or that the child should live with that parent permanently. In reaching this ruling the Court overturned a decision taken by the London Borough of Lambeth that a father who looked after his children for half the week was not in priority need of housing (Knaffler 1990). So it would seem that rights to housing may be established by making arrangements for shared caring, although this might prove a difficult right to establish in practice.

Slipping out of owner-occupation

One effect of divorce is that many people are unable to maintain their status of home owner. Nevertheless, the majority of owner-occupiers either stay in that sector after divorce or eventually return to it. In our study, we found that all but 21 per cent of people who had moved out of owner-occupied marital homes were in owner-occupied housing three years after divorce. For women in particular, remarriage is the step that gets them back on to the housing ladder. All of the women in our study who left owner-occupation after divorce and subsequently returned had achieved this return through re-partnering.

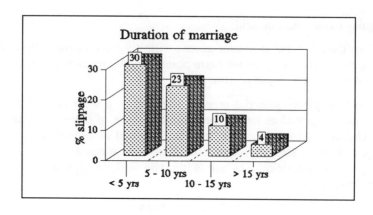

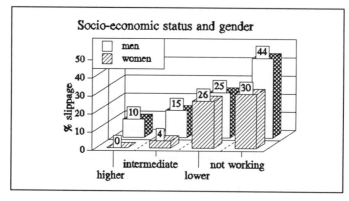

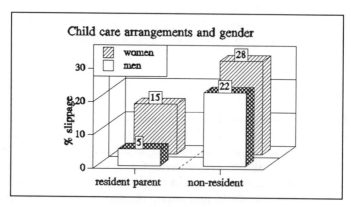

Figure 5.1 Per cent slipping out of owner occupation following divorce: couples divorcing in 1986

94

Although the majority of those who leave owner-occupation as a result of divorce do eventually return to that sector, divorced people are one of the few groups for whom the trend is one of movement out of owner-occupation into rented housing, rather than in the other direction. Moreover, those who move within owner occupation tend to move into worse housing circumstances. Out of 300 previous owner-occupiers in our study, 43 per cent said they were in worse housing three years after divorce, 52 per cent were in dwellings with fewer rooms, 31 per cent were in more densely occupied dwellings and 23 per cent said they were not settled in their current homes. The drift out of owner-occupation is affected by several factors, as shown in figure 5.1. It is more likely to be experienced by people who were in shorter marriages; from lower socio-economic groups and by non-resident parents. It is also more likely to be experienced by men but this is due to men being less likely to be resident parents.

Housing absent parents

A recent publication from the Institute of Housing (1991) proposed the following framework for classifying household types.

- Single person aged under 18 yrs

- Single person 18-59

- Single person over 60

- Elderly couple (at least one over 60)

- Non-elderly couple

- Single parent - pregnant or with children

- Couple - pregnant or with children

- Other households (eg three adults)

It was suggested that this classification would facilitate identification of households requiring different types of accommodation and also assist in the assessment of the effectiveness and equity of housing services for

95

different types of households. However, it is a list which begs the question as to where non-resident parents who have not re-partnered fit in: are they single parents or single persons?

It is reckoned that around one in three non-resident parents - who are usually fathers - totally lose contact with children after divorce (Millar and Bradshaw 1993). However, the converse of this is that a greater number - two out of three - do continue to have contact. Our research suggests that, although many divorced couples are unable to reach amicable agreements about child care, most of them take the notion of joint parenting seriously and make extensive efforts to make it work (FCDRC 1993). The parent with whom the children do not normally live often hopes to maintain regular contact with them, including, in many cases, caring for them during overnight stays. This form of contact is advocated by many who have written on the management of child care arrangements after divorce (e.g. Ricci 1980, Burrett 1993) but obviously the notion of 'dad's house - mom's house' (Ricci 1980) is dependent upon both parents being in housing circumstances in which children are able to live. If joint parenting is to happen, the need is for two family homes. The way housing authorities view this is indicated by the negative responses which fathers in our study tended to get from them and by the practice of defining situations where one parent has remained in a house after the other parent and children have moved out as an 'underoccupation problem' (Bull 1993).

In practice, there would appear to be a contradiction between housing policies and policies in other areas. As far as housing policy is concerned non-resident parents tend to be regarded as single persons. However, the assumption of an ongoing responsibility of absent parents to their children is central to the Child Support Act 1991 which aims to ensure that 'absent fathers' do not neglect their financial obligations regarding their children. The contradiction is further in evidence as a result of the Children Act 1989, which specifically sees divorced couples continuing to share parental responsibilities after divorce. These responsibilities go well beyond the narrow financial considerations of the Child Support Act 1991. The Children Act states that:

> Where a child's father and mother were married to each other at the time of his [sic] birth, they shall each have parental responsibility for the child (part 1: sec 2.1)

In terms of the act, parental responsibility is defined as:

> all rights, duties, powers, responsibilities and authority which by law a parent of a child has in relation to the child and his property. (part 1: sec. 3.1)

96

This position on parenting stems from increasing concerns in family law about representation of 'the best interests of the children'. In the context of divorce, this principle puts emphasis on the notion of joint parenting which is expected to continue beyond separation. It is a position which evolved to some extent from studies of divorced families in which mothers had care and control of the children. These studies indicated that children living with their mothers coped better after parental divorce if they had continuing contact with their fathers (Hetherington et al. 1982, Wallerstein and Kelly 1980). Although this view has been challenged (see Furstenberg et al. 1987, Smart and Sevenhuijsen 1989) it nevertheless forms a central tenet of the pro-contact ideology which currently prevails among the judiciary, court welfare officers, social workers and family mediators. In terms of housing, representing the 'best interests of the children' usually means avoiding disruption to the continuity of their residence. Thus, it is usually thought best if the parent who has the day to day care of the children remains in the marital home. The issue of how to enable the children to maintain a relationship with the other parent tends to be ignored. However, our research suggests that housing circumstances after separation are a major reason, though far from the only reason, why a significant number of fathers lose contact with children. Unless they are able to purchase housing in their own right, absent parents are likely to spend considerable periods in housing circumstances which are unsuitable for staying access. Moreover, their ability to purchase may depend on being able to persuade their ex-partners to give up the marital home so that it can be sold, releasing capital which enables them to purchase. This may have negative consequences for wives and children who have to move from environments which are close to friends, schools, etcetera, and which therefore offer them a degree of continuity and support. The consequences may be that children gain continuing contact with fathers but lose out in other important ways.

Post-divorce housing: supply and demand

When couples divorce it does not necessarily mean creation of two households out of one. Some divorcing people join already existing households, primarily by moving in with relatives or new partners. It has been estimated that for every hundred marriages dissolved, 153 household units seeking separate accommodation are created (Holmans et al. 1987). At the current rate of divorce, this implies a divorce related demand for more than 80,000 extra dwellings per annum, a substantial proportion of the annual increase in the number of dwellings. Moreover, divorce is associated with changes from owner-occupation to tenancies (Holmans 1990, McCarthy and Simpson 1991) and constitutes a significant determinant of the demand for housing to rent. Much of this demand relates to the privately rented sector but around 30,000 council tenancies per year are likely to be allocated as a direct result of couples getting divorced. But, since 1979, 'right to buy' and virtual stoppage of new building has led to substantial restrictions in the availability of council housing. Thus, as Table 5.2 shows, divorce accounts for a significant proportion of housing demand across all tenures, but especially in the rented sectors, where housing supply is falling. The allocation of local authority housing to divorcing families currently takes up a significant proportion of the 250,000 or so new lettings per year (OPCS 1994b).

At the current level of divorce and with the decline of the public housing sector, some local authorities face a scenario where they will be unable to house anyone other than divorcing families. This would present a grim outlook for other households on council waiting lists. For instance, newly married couples would have little chance of housing because of being pushed to the back of the queue by the newly divorced. The privately rented sector, which is also in a state of decline, offers little consolation. On the other hand, provision by housing associations has increased but does not provide sufficient dwellings to come anywhere near to bridging the gap. Thus, the most important issue in any discussion of housing and divorce is that of housing supply.

Of course it is possible that, in this context, housing shortages may be regarded as functional in that they shore up the family by making splitting-up difficult and thereby serve to stem the flow of couples out of marriage and into divorce. However, if the priority is one of minimising the harmful effects of marital breakdown, provision of more choice in housing becomes a priority.

On the surface it would seem that the owner-occupied sector, which continues to grow, is not a problem. However, it would seem that much of the growth in this sector is of housing types which are not particularly appropriate. The type of housing for which supply increases most rapidly (see Table 5.3) are one bedroomed, which are not appropriate for divorced fathers who wish to maintain contact with children, or those with four or more bedrooms which are likely to be larger than needed and possibly too expensive for couples attempting to run two homes on the same amount of money with which they ran one. Given the national diversity in house prices - on average twice as high in Greater London than in the East Midlands (Nationwide 1994) - in some parts of the country mortgage

Table 5.2
Average annual change in supply of various tenures (1979-1989)
and estimates of annual demand due to divorce

	Owner occupied	Private rented	Housing association	Council rented
Average change in supply	+337,000	-75,000	+19,000	-106,000
Divorce related demand	+35,000		+23,000	+30,000

Source: Holmans (1990) and Department of the Environment (1990)

repayments on larger houses are likely to be well beyond what would be regarded as reasonable costs in assessment of child support.

In the divorce context rented housing is important. The fact that its availability has been falling at the same time the divorce rate has been increasing has led to extreme difficulties. Rented housing at least enables people to split up when relationships in every real sense have ended. Although the majority of people do return to their pre-divorce tenure, rented housing provides an important respite.

Table 5.3
Private sector house-building completions

	1976 %	1981 %	1986 %	1991 %
1 bedroom	4	7	12	14
2 bedroom	23	23	28	30
3 bedroom	58	50	40	32
4 or more bedrooms	15	21	20	24
number of dwellings	138,000	104,000	152,000	136,000

Source: OPCS 1994b

Privately rented housing is particularly important. It is the housing sector into which fathers without resident children are most likely to gain access after divorce. However, the accommodation they get is often an inappropriate base for spending time with children. Nevertheless, increased supply of this form of housing would make it easier for people to exit from unsatisfactory marriages and thereby serve to reduce the stresses and strains of living together during periods of outright hostility which often precede the final act of separation. In lieu of such an increase much of the demand created by the needs of divorcing families will continue to fall on local authorities. However, a survey carried out on behalf of the Department of the Environment (Bull 1993) found that less than half of these authorities had developed appropriate policy guidelines.

In terms of access to housing and its allocation, the main objective should be one of ensuring that lone-parents, whether resident with their children or not, are relieved of the discrimination which results from being defined as 'single'. In the first instance this means ensuring that where a couple are local authority tenants both are offered suitable tenancies at the time of separation. In addition, points systems regarding council tenancies ought to take into consideration the fact that non-resident parents are likely to have children staying with them at some time and often for quite long periods.

In putting forward a housing case for non-resident fathers it is difficult to argue that they ought to have priority over other groups: resident mothers in particular. However, if the state expects fathers to continue with parental responsibilities after divorce it needs to provide the supportive structures which would enable them to do so. Otherwise, the philosophy behind the Children Act 1989 begins to look like rhetoric to those who do not have substantial means. At the very least, the particular requirements of non-resident parents ought to be taken into consideration when planning to meet future housing need. As stated by one of the fathers involved in our study of post-divorce fathering 'a house makes the difference between being a father and being a bachelor uncle'.

Note

1. The study of the long term effects of mediation was funded by the Fund for Research on Dispute Resolution, the housing and divorce study was funded by the Joseph Rowntree Foundation and the study of post-divorce fathering was funded by the Nuffield Foundation.

References

Bull, J. (1993), *Housing Consequences of Relationship Breakdown*, HMSO, London.

Burrett, J. (1993), *To and Fro Children: Cooperative Parenting After Divorce*, Thorson, London.

Conciliation Project Unit (1989), *Report to the Lord Chancellor on the Costs and Effectiveness of Conciliation in England and Wales*, Lord Chancellor's Department, London.

Department of the Environment (1990), *Housing and Construction Statistics 1979-89*, HMSO, London.

Family and Community Dispute Research Centre (1991), *Longitudinal Study of the Impact of Different Dispute Resolution Processes on Post-Divorce Relationships between Parents and Children*, Report to the Fund for Research on Dispute Resolution, New York.

Family and Community Dispute Research Centre (1993), *Post-Divorce Fathering: Making it work*, Report to the Nuffield Foundation.

Furstenberg, F.F., Morgan, S.P. and Allison, P.D. (1987), 'Paternal participation and children's well-being after marital dissolution', *American Sociological Review*, 52, pp. 695-701.

Haskey, J. (1991), 'Estimated numbers and demographic characteristics of one-parent families in Great Britain', *Population Trends*, 65, pp. 35-47.

Hetherington, E.M., Cox, M. and Cox, R. (1982), 'Effects of Divorce on Parents and Children', in Lamb, M. (ed.), *Non-traditional Families: Parenting and Child Development*, Laurence Erlbaum Associates, New Jersey.

Holmans, A.E., Nandy, S. and Brown, A.C. (1987), 'Household formation and dissolution and housing tenure: A longitudinal perspective', *Social Trends*, 17, pp. 20-28.

Holmans, A.E. (1990), 'Housing Demand and Need Generated by Divorce', in Symon, P. (ed.), *Housing and Divorce: Studies in Housing No. 4*, Centre for Housing Research, University of Glasgow.

Institute of Housing (1991), *Housing Services for Homeless People*, Institute of Housing, London.

Knaffler S. (1990), 'The shared child and priority housing', *Housing*, August, pp. 6-8.

Lord Chancellor's Department (1989), *Judicial Statistics*, HMSO, London.

Lord Chancellor's Department (1994), *Looking to the Future: Mediation and the Ground for Divorce* (Cmn. 2424), HMSO, London.

McCarthy, P. and Simpson, B. (1990), 'Grandparents and family conflict: Another view', *Family Law*, 20, pp. 480-482.

101

McCarthy, P. and Simpson, B. (1991), *Issues in Post-Divorce Housing: Family Policy or Housing Policy,* Avebury, London.

Millar, J. and Bradshaw, J. (1993), 'The circumstances of lone parent families', *Social Security Research Yearbook 1991-92,* HMSO, London.

Nationwide (1994), *House Prices in the UK,* Nationwide Building Society, July 1994.

Office of Population Censuses and Surveys (1992), *General Household Survey 1992,* HMSO, London.

Office of Population Censuses and Surveys (1994a), *Population Trends,* 77, HMSO, London.

Office of Population Censuses and Surveys (1994b), *Social Trends 1994,* HMSO, London.

Ricci, I. (1980), *Mom's House, Dad's House: Making Shared Custody Work,* Collier Macmillan, London.

Smart, C. and Sevenhuijsen, S. (eds) (1989), *Child Custody and the Politics of Gender,* Routledge, London.

Sullivan, O. (1986), 'Housing movements of the divorced and separated' *Housing Studies,* 1, pp. 35-48.

Wallerstein, J. and Kelly, J. (1980), *Surviving the Break-Up,* Grant McIntyre, London.

Williams, C. (1988), 'Ouster orders, property adjustment and council housing', *Family Law,* 18, pp. 438-443.

6 Teenage motherhood then and now: A comparison of the pattern and outcomes of teenage pregnancy in England and Wales in the 1960s & 1980s

Peter Selman

Introduction

Recent debates on lone parent families have drawn attention to the growing number of such families headed by single women and linked this to the rising number of teenage births outside marriage in the 1980s. Some argue that this is a result of failures of sex education and contraceptive provision (Belleman 1993, David 1992, Francome 1993). Others argue that it is a consequence of welfare and housing policy (Murray 1990, Green 1991, Coleman 1993) or of a lack of any meaningful alternative in jobs or education (Campbell 1993, Gress-Wright 1993, Blaikie 1994). Several recent comments have looked back to the 1960s. In a *Sunday Times* special report, entitled 'Wedded to Welfare', Charles Murray (1993) wrote:

> Turn back the clock restoring the benefit system for single mothers that Britain had in the mid-1960s...and there is every reason to think that you will turn back the proportion of babies born to single women to 1960s levels as well.

Another article in the same feature carried the headlines: 'Once illegitimacy was punished - now it is rewarded.'

Bea Campbell (1993), criticising the Government's Health of the Nation initiative has written:

> In the sixties, a girl became a woman not through motherhood, but through employment: adulthood was achieved by autonomy, work and a wage, a place, peers and then planned parenthood.
>
> ...The adolescent ambitions of Virginia Bottomley's generation were formed in an era of full employment and randy permissiveness that was none the less panicked by unplanned pregnancy.

In fact the number of teenage births was higher in the 1960s than at any time this century; teenage birth rates outside marriage rose as rapidly in the 1960s as in the 1980s; and the number of teenage births conceived outside marriage was higher in the late 1960s, although then the most common outcome was a birth within marriage and one in five of children born outside marriage was placed for adoption (Selman 1976). Even so there was concern over the increase in teenage births and over what Hartley (1966) called 'the amazing rise of illegitimacy in Britain'.

In this chapter I examine patterns of teenage motherhood in England and Wales over the past forty years, paying special attention to the social policy issues - including policies designed to meet the needs of young mothers, especially those without partners; policies which seek to influence the level and outcome of teenage pregnancy, such as sex education, abortion, contraceptive provision and adoption; and policies which are assumed to influence decisions, such as housing allocation and social security payments.

Teenage pregnancy in the 1960s and 1980s

Teenage birth and conception rates rose sharply in both the 1960s and the 1980s, but fell during the 1970s. However any choice of period by strict calendar years is arbitrary and I have chosen rather to concentrate on what we might call the 'long' 1960s and 1980s, following Wrigley's concept of the long eighteenth century (Wrigley 1983). I shall, therefore, discuss the demography of teenage pregnancy by contrasting trends within the two periods from 1959 to 1971 and 1979 to 1991.

Teenage births in England and Wales since the Second World War

The largest annual number of teenage births (86,746) in post-war years occurred in 1966. The teenage birth rate peaked five years later in 1971 at 50.6. Both number and rate fell sharply during the 1970s and by 1977 there were only 54,500 births and the birth rate had fallen to 29.8. In the next 15 years numbers and rates fluctuated but remained well below the level of the late 1960s (see Table 6.1).

The early 1960s were marked by rising fertility both inside and outside marriage and throughout the later years of the decade (from 1966 to 1971) there were over 60,000 'legitimate' births a year, alongside the 20,000 births out of wedlock.

Table 6.1
Live births to women under age twenty; 1959-1991

	Total Births	Rate[1]	Births inside marriage	Rate[2]	Births outside marriage	Rate[3]	Ratio[4]
1959	46,067	31.6	38,090	420	7,977	5.8	174
1961	59,786	37.3	47,890	449	11,896	8.0	199
1963	71,640	40.2	56,037	478	15,603	9.4	218
1966	86,746	47.9	66,164	489	20,582	12.3	237
1968	82,075	49.2	60,266	490	21,809	14.1	266
1971	82,641	50.6	61,086	434	21,555	14.6	261
1977	54,477	29.8	34,426	305	20,051	11.7	368
1979	59,786	30.3	35,138	332	24,005	13.2	406
1981	56,570	28.1	30,140	325	26,430	13.7	467
1983	54,059	26.9	23,636	330	30,423	15.7	648
1986	57,406	30.1	17,793	361	39,613	21.3	690
1988	58,741	32.4	14,099	284	44,642	25.3	760
1991	52,396	33.1	8,948	264	43,448	28.0	829

[1] per 1,000 women aged 15-19
[2] per 1,000 married women aged 16-19
[3] per 1,000 single, widowed or divorced women aged 15-19
[4] per 1,000 live births

Source: OPCS *Birth Statistics - Series FM1*

105

In contrast the 1980s saw falling numbers of marital births and rising numbers of births outside wedlock so that by 1982 the latter outnumbered the former and by 1991 there were fewer than 10,000 marital births a year, one sixth of the level found in the late 1960s. The total number of teenage births was substantially higher in the 1960s.

Births outside marriage

The number of teenage births occurring outside marriage increased sharply in the late 1970s, rising from 21,643 in 1978 to a peak of 44,642 in 1988, doubling in a decade. Rates rose even more dramatically - from 12.2 in 1978 to 28.0 in 1991. However, the number of births outside marriage rose more rapidly in the 1960s, doubling in the six years from 1959 to 1964, and rates increased from 5.8 in 1959 to 12.3 in 1966 and 14.6 in 1971. The proportion of teenage births outside marriage increased in the 1960s from 17 per cent in 1959 to 26 per cent in 1971. By 1979 it was 40 per cent and in 1991 83 per cent of teenage births occurred outside marriage.

The decline of 'shot-gun' marriages

In 1959, 48 per cent of all teenage births in England occurred in the first eight months after marriage - i.e. they were conceived *before* marriage. The number of such births rose in the early 1960s to a peak of 36,745 in 1966 and as late as 1971 42 per cent of all births were premaritally conceived legitimate births. Ten years later the number had fallen to 14,950 (26 per cent of births) and by 1991 they represented only 6 per cent of all births (Table 6.2).

If we aggregate these births and those occurring outside marriage, we find that the number of births conceived outside marriage in the 1960s rose from 30,226 in 1959 to 57,327 in 1966 and 57,484 in 1968. Such births were in excess of 50,000 from 1964 to 1972. In the 1980s the number of extra-maritally conceived live births rose above 50,000 in only one year, 1988.

The rise of cohabitation

There have also been changes in the context of out of wedlock births (Table 6.2). Since 1964 there have been published data on birth registrations indicating whether a birth outside marriage was registered by the mother alone or jointly with the father. In 1964, 81 per cent of births

Table 6.2
Extra-marital teenage births by registration

Year	Total Births	Registration Sole	Registration Joint Different Address	Registration Joint Same Address	Premarital conceptions
1964	17,400	14100 [81]	3300 [19]		33,340
1967	21,600	17300 [80]	4400 [20]		35,793
1969	21,600	16400 [76]	5200 [24]		35,256
1971	21,555	15431 [72]	6124 [28]		34,598
1979	24,005	13700 [57]	10300 [43]		17,417
1981	26,430	13675 [52]	12755 [48]		14,950
1983	30,423	14400 [47]	7000 [23]	9100 [30]	12,004
1987	41,957	16800 [40]	11352 [27]	13818 [33]	7,294
1990	44,583	16200 [37]	12068 [27]	16261 [36]	4,429
1991	43,448	15200 [35]	11844 [27]	16358 [38]	3,267

Source: OPCS *Birth Statistics - Series FM1*

outside marriage to women under the age of twenty were registered by the mother alone. By 1971 this had fallen to 72 per cent and by 1981 to 52 per cent. In 1991 65 per cent of births at this age were jointly registered. Since 1983 there has been further information on the addresses of parents jointly registering a non-marital birth. A majority of the joint registrations now show the same address for both parents so that in 1991 38 per cent of all out of wedlock births were to couples living together.

The number of births registered by the mother alone changed little over this period. The bulk of the increase in births outside marriage is accounted for by those which are jointly registered. The number of joint registrations rose from 6,124 in 1971 to 28,199 in 1991. During the same period, the number of pre-maritally conceived births within marriage fell from 34,598 to 3,662. The chances of conceiving outside marriage were greater in the 1960s than in the 1980s.

Relatively little is known about such cohabitations (Kiernan and Estaugh 1993, McRae 1993) and in particular about their stability, although the breakdown of such relationships may account for part of the rise in the number of single-parent families headed by never-married women (Haskey 1993). It is thought that as many as 50 per cent of teenage marriages contracted in the 1960s ended in divorce (Haskey 1983) and it seems likely that teenage cohabitations of the 1980s will prove even less stable (Hoem and Hoem 1992).

Teenage conceptions 1969-1991

Since 1969, OPCS has published tables of conceptions, where births and abortions are allocated to a year by the date when the pregnancy is assumed to have started. This was made possible by the collection of data on legal abortion following the implementation of the 1967 Abortion Act. It has led to a more precise monitoring of changes in the level and outcome of teenage pregnancy. Table 6.3 shows trends in the number and outcome of teenage conceptions from 1969 to 1981.

In 1969 there were 75 conceptions per 1,000 women aged 15-19. In 1970 the rate was 82.4, which meant that over 40 per cent of 15 year olds would experience a pregnancy by the time they were 20. By 1983 the rate had fallen to 56, less than three quarters of the 1970 level, but then rose to 69 in 1990, the highest level since 1974.

There were many fewer conceptions inside marriage in the 1980s and the number of conceptions outside marriage which ended in a maternity inside marriage also fell sharply. In contrast the number of conceptions leading to a maternity outside marriage doubled between 1969 and 1986 and there

108

Table 6.3
Outcome of teenage conceptions, England and Wales 1969-1991

Year	Inside marriage	Outside marriage		Legal abortion	Total	Rate
		Maternity inside marriage	*Maternity outside marriage*			
1969	43.4	43.5	25.3	11.3	123.4	**75.0**
1970	46.5	43.9	26.1	17.9	134.3	**82.4**
1971	43.9	39.9	25.7	23.3	132.7	**81.3**
1975	34.7	23.8	23.7	29.7	111.9	**64.1**
1979	31.0	22.7	30.5	36.7	121.0	**62.0**
1980	28.5	20.1	32.2	36.4	117.1	**58.7**
1983	20.6	14.6	39.8	37.3	112.4	**56.0**
1986	15.6	11.3	52.3	39.6	118.8	**62.3**
1989	11.8	7.5	56.4	41.8	117.1	**67.6**
1990	10.7	5.9	57.5	41.0	115.1	**69.0**
1991	9.4	5.0	53.4	35.5	103.3	**65.3**

Conceptions (1,000s)

Source: OPCS *Birth Statistics - Series FM1*

was a large increase in legal abortion - mainly to unmarried teenagers. During the 1970s growing numbers of abortions to teenagers seemed to have halted the growth in teenage births outside marriage of the 1960s, but since 1977 abortions have increased alongside out-of-wedlock births. By 1991, more than 50 per cent of conceptions ended in a birth outside marriage and more than a third ended in abortion (Table 6.7).

Conceptions to younger teenagers

Table 6.4 shows the trends in the number and rate of conceptions to women under the age of 16. Total numbers have been falling since the mid 1980s but this has been the result of a fall in the number of girls aged 13-15, so that rates rose throughout the 1980s and have only begun to reverse in the last few years.

Summary

The annual number of teenage births peaked in England and Wales in the mid and late 1960s when births were predominantly within marriage. In contrast the level of births was lower in the 1980s, but progressively dominated by births outside marriage (Table 6.1).

In the 1960s teenage fertility became an increasingly important part of total fertility with the proportion of all births occurring to women under the age of twenty rising from 6.2 per cent in 1959 to 11 per cent in 1972. In this period the rise is the result of higher marital fertility rates and an increase in the proportion of teenagers who marry, combined with a rise in non-marital fertility. It is the impact of the former two factors which is dominant - of the 40,000 additional births in this period 28,000 were within marriage.

In the 1980s teenage fertility was a less important component of total fertility with the proportion of all births occurring to women under twenty falling from 9 per cent in 1979 to 7.5 per cent in 1992. The significance of this period lies rather in the increasing proportion of births outside wedlock, but this is a feature common to all age groups and the proportion of non-marital births to teenagers fell sharply. The rising birth rate in the late 1980s is mainly due to higher fertility rates outside marriage and an increase in the proportion of unmarried teenagers.

Table 6.4
Conceptions to women under age 16

	Total [1,000s]	Maternities [1,000s]	Abortions [1,000s]	Rate*
1969	6.5	4.8	1.7	**6.8**
1971	8.8	5.5	3.3	**8.8**
1976	9.1	4.3	4.8	**8.2**
1981	8.6	3.7	4.9	**7.3**
1983	9.4	4.0	5.3	**8.3**
1985	9.4	4.2	5.2	**8.6**
1987	9.1	4.2	5.0	**9.3**
1989	8.4	4.0	4.4	**9.4**
1990	8.6	4.3	4.4	**10.1**
1991	7.8	3.8	4.0	**9.3**

* per 1,000 women aged 13-15

Source: OPCS *Birth Statistics - Series FM1*

In 1969 70 per cent of conceptions ended in a maternity within marriage (half of which were conceived before marriage); by 1991 over 50 per cent ended in a non-marital birth (two thirds of which were jointly registered) and more than a third ended in abortion. The proportion ending in a non-marital birth registered by the mother alone remained remarkably consistent (Table 6.7).

Analyzing the rise in out of wedlock births to teenagers

One feature common to both the 1960s and the 1980s is a rise in the number of out of wedlock births to teenagers. This rise is in fact almost continuous from 1951 through to 1990, but is interrupted between 1968 and 1978 during which time the numbers fluctuate between 20,000 and 22,000 (see Table 6.1). There are two ten year periods of continuous increase: 1959 to 1968 and 1979 to 1988 (see Table 6.5).

Table 6.5
Changes in teenage non-marital fertility 1959-1988

Period	Rise in Numbers	Rise in Rates
1959 to 1968	7,977 to 21,809	5.8 to 14.1
1979 to 1988	24,005 to 44,642	13.2 to 25.3

A useful framework for analyzing this rise in fertility outside marriage is provided by Hartley's *concatenated theory* (1975) which demonstrates that the level of illegitimacy in a country is determined by a number of inter-related factors:

i)   the proportion of women of childbearing age
ii)   the proportion of these who are unmarried
iii) the proportion of unmarried women who are sexually active
iv)   the proportion of these who become pregnant
v)   the proportion of pregnant unmarried women who marry before giving birth
vi)   the proportion who have an abortion.

Using this framework we can examine a number of factors which could explain the rise in out of wedlock births in each period:

a)   *an increase in the number of teenagers and in particular in the number of single teenagers.*

The changing teenage population is shown in Table 6.6. In the 1960s the number of married teenagers rose both absolutely (until 1966) and as a proportion of all aged 15-19. The increase in out of wedlock births, therefore, owes nothing to changes in marriage patterns, as the proportion of unmarried teenagers falls. The contribution of births within marriage was dominant throughout the 1960s although a majority were conceived outside marriage. Marital birth rates were consistently high (see Table 6.1) peaking at 523.3 in 1965.

By the 1980s things were changing. In 1979, 60 per cent of teenage births still occurred in marriage but this fell steadily to 16 per cent by 1992. The proportion of teenagers who were married also decreased, although after 1983 the total number of unmarried teenagers fell - reflecting the decline in the birth rate from the mid-1960s. The increased proportion of unmarried is clearly crucial to the rapidly shifting ratio of non-marital: marital births, but the rapid rise in rates indicate that changes in population structure are only a small part of the overall change in numbers.

b) *an increase in the proportion of sexually active unmarried teenagers.*

Evidence of increased sexual activity in unmarried teenagers in the 1960s can be seen in the studies of Schofield (1965) and Farrell (1978) and the case for the centrality of this factor in explaining the rising illegitimacy is put by Illsley and Gill (1968), who argue that unmarried teenagers were influenced by their awareness of the sexuality of their married peers who were becoming more numerous through the decade. The births are seen as an unintended consequence of the sexual revolution and the parallel rise in pre-marital conceptions is taken as further evidence of this.

Table 6.6
Female population aged 15-19 [1,000s]

	Pop 15-19	Unmarried	Married	% Married
1951	1,384	1,328	56	4.2
1959	1,457	1,368	89	6.1
1966	1,825	1,684	141	7.8
1971	1,641	1,510	131	8.0
1979	1,912	1,817	104	5.4
1981	2,015	1,923	93	4.6
1983	2,007	1,935	72	3.6
1987	1,864	1,812	49	2.6
1990	1,668	1,628	40	2.4

Shorter (1976) compares the period to the late eighteenth century of which Lawrence Stone (1977) has commented:

The number of prostitutes plying their trade, the number of brides led to the altar when already pregnant and the number of bastard children born all rose together in the 18th and early 19th century and it is reasonable to assume that these three phenomena are all interconnected.

113

Recent research (Wellings 1994) shows that the proportion of sexually active teenagers was greater in the 1980s than in the 1960s. This seems to be especially true of the number of teenagers having sex before the age of 16. There are two features to the increased sexual activity - one is a fall in age of first intercourse; the other is the growing number of unmarried teenagers cohabiting. However there is no reason to believe that this increase in sexual activity accelerated after 1983. Indeed, concern over AIDS in the latter part of the period was expected by some to lead to a rethinking of heterosexual sexual activity, although this seems to have been modest (Wellings 1994). Increased sexual activity cannot explain the rise in teenage birth rates outside marriage after 1983.

c)   an increase in the proportion of sexually active teenagers who become pregnant - e.g. as a result either of less effective contraception or of increased fecundability.

Over longer periods changes in age at menarche can lead to more sexually active teenagers becoming pregnant without any fall in age of first intercourse (Cutright 1972). Over a single decade it would have only a marginal effect.

In the 1960s the arrival of the pill and IUD initially had little impact on younger unmarried women (Kiernan, 1980), but there is no reason to believe individual contraceptive practice worsened, although the falling age of sexually active teenagers may have meant that the rise in the number sexually active was not matched by a rise in contraceptive use.

There has been some concern over prolonged pill use since the 1970s and more recently pressure on teenagers to use condoms rather than the pill as a protection against AIDS. This may have had an overall effect of lessening contraceptive effectiveness. But the real question is why there has not been any sign in the late 1980s of improved contraception as has been seen in most other European countries. Uncertainties over sex education and birth control advice for the under 16s may have had some impact and the importance of policy in these areas will be discussed later.

d)   an increase in the proportion of pregnant teenagers proceeding to motherhood i.e a fall in proportion having an abortion.

Although abortion was not legalised until 1967, there seems to have been a gradual increase in medical abortions throughout the 1960s and no evidence to suggest any reduction in total abortions (whether medical, back-street or self-induced). Likewise in the 1980s the proportion of

114

conceptions ending in abortion changed little after 1983 and was rising before that (see Table 6.7). The impact of abortion in the intervening period was to halt temporarily the rise in births outside marriage. What is clear is that abortion has not become less common and any increase in the proportion of pregnancies aborted has been more than offset by the rise in the number of teenage conceptions. In contrast in countries such as Denmark a falling conception rate amongst teenagers has been accompanied by a rise in the proportion of pregnancies aborted leading to a rapid fall in the number of teenage births.

e)   a fall in the proportion of pregnant women marrying before birth.

During the 1960s the number of births outside marriage and the number of marital births conceived before marriage both rose, although the proportion of extra-maritally conceived live births occurring after marriage fell from 74 per cent to 63 per cent. The common factor behind both increases was the rise in teenage sexual activity which led to the increase in all extramarital conceptions.

Table 6.7
Percentage distribution of teenage conceptions by outcome:
1969-1991

Outcomes	1969	1971	1979	1985	1991
	%	%	%	%	%
Abortion	9	18	30	34	34
Marital Births conceived					
- inside marriage	35	33	26	15	9
- outside marriage	35	29	19	11	5
Non-marital births					
- jointly registered	6	7	11	24	34
- sole registration	15	13	14	17	18
Total (1,000s)	**123.4**	**114.5**	**121.0**	**119.3**	**103.3**

Source: OPCS Conception Monitors; Birth Statistics

In the 1980s there is a very different story. Between 1979 and 1988 the number of births outside marriage rose by more than 20,000 (86 per cent) while the number of marital births fell by 21,000. The proportion of extra-maritally conceived births occurring after marriage fell from 42 per cent to 7 per cent. This rejection of marriage as a solution to extra-marital pregnancy was linked to a rise in jointly registered non-marital births.

Summary and conclusion

The rise in births outside marriage in the 1960s reflected mainly an increase in sexual activity in unmarried teenagers, which manifested itself also in the rise of pre-maritally conceived births within marriage. The proportion of teenagers who were single fell and marriage continued to be preferred to single parenthood or cohabitation. The greater availability of contraception had not extended to younger women and did not keep up with the growth in sexual activity; abortion remained illegal until the end of the period, but there is no reason to think it was becoming harder to get. Many of the pregnancies were unplanned and the solution was seen in terms of better fertility control services and improved sex education.

In contrast the rise in births outside marriage in the 1980s seems to reflect a major shift in attitudes to marriage and parenthood. Fewer teenagers were marrying and marriage was no longer seen as an acceptable solution to a pregnancy out of wedlock. There is evidence that there was some growth in sexual activity, especially at younger ages, and access to contraception was affected by the Appeal Court ruling in the 'Gillick' case that, except in an emergency, it was illegal for doctors to give contraceptive advice or treatment to girls under 16 without parental consent (Jackson 1985). Although the ruling was reversed by the House of Lords (Simpson 1985), uncertainty continued and services were further affected by cuts in family planning clinic provision. Abortion rates continued to rise and thus limited the increase in births to teenagers. An increasing proportion of non-marital births were jointly registered and the assumption of most being unwanted or even unplanned was increasingly questioned. Many saw teenage motherhood as a rational response for certain groups in society. It is to such wider issues that I turn in the next section.

Teenage pregnancy and social policy in the 1960s

Plotnick (1993) has argued that the incidence and outcome of teenage pregnancy may be influenced by social policies. In this final section I look at some of the key policy issues of the 1960s, with a brief contrast with more recent policy developments which I have discussed in detail elsewhere (Selman and Glendinning 1995).

116

In the 1960s there was much greater pressure on the minority of unmarried teenage mothers to relinquish children for adoption. For most of this period an estimated 20 per cent of all illegitimate children had been placed for adoption by the time they were 10 years old, the majority in their first two years (Leete 1978, Selman 1976). For mothers under the age of 20 at the time of birth, the proportion adopted was probably higher (Grey 1971): in Kiernan's study (1980) 33 per cent of teenage mothers who had a birth outside marriage had relinquished their child for adoption.

Table 6.8 shows the trends in such adoption since 1959. By 1980 the ratio of non-parent adoptions to out of wedlock births had fallen from 20 per 100 to 5 and by 1983 the ratio had fallen to 3. After 1964 published data do not distinguish parental adoptions (Selman 1988) but the number of children born outside marriage continued to rise, while the number adopted has fallen further. Even if we relate adoptions only to 'sole registrations', there is a clear fall in the proportion of children being offered for adoption.

In the 1960s adoption was seen as a 'neat and sensible solution' (Benet 1976) to the problems of the child and both birth and adoptive parents. Follow up of adopted children (Seglow 1972) seems to indicate their success when compared with other 'illegitimate' children, but there has also been growing awareness of the problems of closed adoption.

The issue of an adopted person's right of access to their birth records was raised by the Houghton Committee which was appointed in 1968. Such a right was granted by Section 26 of the 1975 Children Act. (Triseliotis 1973, Haimes and Timms 1985). By the 1980s there was growing attention to the rights of birth parents both in the UK (Howe 1992) and New Zealand (Rockell and Ryburn 1988). The needs of such parents are shown by a study of birth mothers carried out by Lesley Tye of the Birth Mothers' Support Group in Cramlington (Tye 1994). A majority of the women had become pregnant in the 1960s and two thirds had been under the age of twenty when they gave birth.

They offered a vivid insight into what it meant to be an unmarried teenage mother in the 1960s and the price paid for doing the right thing by their child. None of the thirty-two unmarried mothers had been using contraception at the time they got pregnant and only three had contemplated abortion. For the majority who gave birth in the early and mid 1960s - before the 1967 Abortion Act - the only alternative would have been a back street abortion. Most of the women had felt pressured to decide on adoption, once it had become clear that the baby's father was unwilling to

Table 6.8
Non-marital births, adoptions and abortions
England and Wales 1959-1984

YEAR	Non-marital births	Children adopted by non-parents	Ratio of non-parent adoptions to non-marital births	Legal abortions (1,000's)*
1959	38,161	7,966	20.9	-
1960	42,707	9,064	21.2	-
1961	48,490	10,065	10.8	-
1962	55,376	11,046	19.9	-
1963	59,104	11,644	19.7	-
1964	63,340	13,470	21.3	-
1965	66,249	13,631	20.6	-
1966	67,065	14,106	21.0	-
1967	69,928	14,222	20.3	-
1968	69,806	14,751	21.1	21.2
1969	67,041	13,129	19.6	26.9
1970	64,744	10,797	16.7	41.7
1971	65,678	9,642	14.7	53.0
1972	62,511	8,170	13.1	61.7
1973	58,100	7,388	12.7	63.8
1974	56,500	6,621	11.7	64.2
1975	54,900	5,774	10.5	63.1
1976	53,800	4,777	8.9	61.6
1977	55,400	4,026	7.3	63.0
1978	60,700	3,926	6.3	69.0
1979	69,500	3,539	5.1	77.3
1980	77,400	3,529	4.6	84.7
1981	81,000	3,270	4.0	86.2
1982	89,900	3,284	3.7	87.8
1983	99,200	3,008	3.0	87.2
1984	110,500	2,910	2.6	96.1

* Single, widowed, divorced and separated women only

Sources: Statistical Review of England and Wales, for the years 1958 to 1973, OPCS Monitor FM3, Marriage and Divorce Statistics.

stand by them. The pressure often came from their own parents:

> When I told my parents, the first thing they said was 'you'll have to get it adopted'.

> She talked of her disgust and shame at having an unmarried mother as her daughter.

Having decided on adoption, the next problem was how to handle late pregnancy and birth. Most had stayed with their parents but were often kept in all the time. Some had been sent to the country. Fourteen of the 32 women had gone to Mother and Baby Homes. For most this had been a traumatic experience which made them feel guilty of a dreadful sin:

> It was terrible! I felt as if I was being punished for my sins... scrubbing floors at six in the morning; chapel at seven and then housework the rest of the day.

Adoption not only saved money but also reinforced the moral message about the wages of sin. The adoption of young babies is rare today and for the most part handled with more sensitivity, but there has been a growth of adoptions of older children (many born to mothers in their teens) who have been admitted to care. Many such adoptions are dispensing with the mother's consent and the needs of such mothers are currently ignored, although there are some pioneering services such as the *Parents Without Children* project which offer help to such 'non-relinquishing' parents (Oliver and Charlton 1994).

There are some who would see adoption as a solution today - a way of providing fathers for children at no expense to the Government. Likewise some recent suggestions about hostels for single parents have revived memories of the mother and baby homes - reminding me of another quotation from the Birth Mothers Study:

> There must never be a return to the hell-holes like...where young innocent girls were treated like sluts.

Abortion

Another major difference between the experience of pregnant teenagers in the 1960s and 1980s is the availability of legal abortion. It is impossible to estimate with any accuracy the number of illegal abortions on teenagers in the 1960s, but the 1967 Abortion Act has certainly put an end to dangerous backstreet abortions and their consequence of sepsis and death

(Selman 1988). There would also have been instances of abortions carried out by doctors - especially in the private sector - and of many largely unsuccessful attempts at self-induced abortion.

The availability of legal abortion has played its part in the reduction in number of children placed for adoption described above (Selman 1976). It has become apparent that few women who decide early in pregnancy that they do not want a child will opt to go to full term and relinquish their child for adoption when safe legal abortion is available.

By the 1980s abortions to women under age twenty were running at 35,000 per annum. By 1985 more than a third of all teenage conceptions were ending in abortion (Table 6.7) and abortions outnumbered maternities for those under the age of 16 (Table 6.5). About a quarter of all abortions were on women who had conceived before their twentieth birthday.

However, the abortion ratio is lower in Britain than in the Scandinavian countries, where the high proportion of teenage pregnancies which end in abortion contributes to the low teenage birth rates (Selman and Glendinning 1995). We need to know more about why a majority of young British women reject abortion - is it on moral/religious grounds; is it still difficult for teenagers to get an abortion; does it reflect ambivalence because unintended births carry few costs (Zabin and Hayward 1993)?

Contraception and sex education

Although it was accepted that in part the rising teenage birth rate of the 1960s was simply part of the general rise in fertility, which led in 1964 to the highest total fertility rate in post-war years, there was a recognition that many teenage pregnancies in the 1960s were unintended and an assumption that most out of wedlock births were unwanted. Concern was also being expressed about the number of higher order births, many of which were thought to be unplanned and unwanted.

Research in the late 1960s established that this was the case. Cartwright (1970) reporting on a survey of married women having a live birth in 1967/8 found that 15 per cent of all the mothers were sorry that their last pregnancy had occurred at all and that a further 17 per cent would have preferred it later. In a similar study in 1973, Cartwright (1976) found that less than half the mothers first pregnant in their teens were pleased to be pregnant and that less than a fifth had been using any method of birth control. Other studies highlighted the absence of any realistic sex education in schools (Farrell 1978).

Selman (1977) found that a third of women having a fifth or higher order birth in 1970 in Newcastle upon Tyne had married before the age of 19;

that 22 per cent had their first child before the age of 19; and that more than half had conceived their first child outside marriage.

As a consequence there was pressure not only to liberalise abortion laws but also to bring family planning into the NHS. Legislation was realised in the late 1960s with the 1967 Abortion Act and the 1967 NHS (Family Planning) Act. The spread of oral contraception and IUDs seemed to offer the means to eliminate unwanted births. There were pioneering attempts to bring contraception to 'problem' parents through domiciliary family planning services (Peberdy 1965) and male and female sterilisation became more common (Bone 1973).

It had been assumed by many that the impact of liberalised abortion and the final incorporation of family planning services into the NHS through the 1973 NHS Reorganisation Act would be to eliminate most unwanted births. The falling birth rates of the 1970s suggested that this was happening. Higher order births became increasingly rare and non-marital fertility rates levelled off. In 1977 the teenage birth rate was lower than in 1958. By the 1980s, however, these trends were reversing. There had been a number of pill 'scares' and the abortion rates continued to rise. Teenage birth rates were no longer falling and an increasing proportion of births were occurring outside marriage. Pregnancy rates rose steadily in girls under the age of 16. This group was still poorly catered for within the NHS contraceptive service with its growing emphasis on GP provision and the task of dealing with young unmarried persons was increasingly left to the voluntary sector in the form of organisations like the Brook Advisory Clinics. The early 1980s saw a prolonged battle over new guidelines for contraceptive advice to under age girls (Selman and Glendinning 1995) and even in the 1990s many younger teenagers lacked confidence in the possibility of obtaining confidential advice especially from their family doctor (Francome 1993). DH statistics for England and Wales show an increase in clinic attendance by those aged under 16 since 1985, when the Gillick case was finally resolved. Numbers rose by 50 per cent between 1990 and 1993 suggesting that there is now a much greater readiness to approach clinics and that this may be a sign of the impact of recent Government initiatives. However, the rate of attendance by all teenagers is still lower than in the early 1980s and there is growing concern over the closure of community family planning clinics (Selman and Calder 1994).

Access to and knowledge of contraception is better now than in the 1960s and this has been a factor in the overall fall in teenage births despite an increase in the number of sexually active teenagers, but progress has been slow and may now be threatened. Certainly, many sexually active teenagers are *not* in contact with contraceptive services (Balding 1994, Hill

121

1988) and this seems to be one reason for the higher levels of unwanted pregnancy compared to other European countries (David 1990, Risor 1989).

However, Bea Campbell (1993) has questioned the Health of the Nation initiative, suggesting that Virginia Bottomley's obsession with reducing teenage pregnancy rates is due to her perceptions about teenage pregnancy being rooted in the 1960s experience, confusing unplanned and unwanted, and implies that measures associated with sex education and family planning are unlikely to succeed. In the final sections of the chapter I shall turn to a consideration of the case that other policies are now more important in determining the level of teenage births.

Welfare incentives and teenage childbearing

The quotation from Charles Murray at the beginning of this chapter is typical of a number of recent statements from Government Ministers and others suggesting that welfare policy is responsible for the recent rise in teenage out of wedlock births. Murray (1993), Green (1991) and Morgan (1995) have argued in particular that additional benefits for single parents have encouraged lone parenthood. In 1993, Housing Minister, Sir George Young, suggested that housing policy favoured and encouraged young unmarried mothers (Selman and Glendinning 1995).

Murray implies that there were fewer births outside marriage in the 1960s because social security policy did not favour single parents, but we have seen that in fact the non-marital fertility rate rose faster in the 1960s, especially for younger women. Indeed it was the rise in one-parent families associated with this and the rising number of divorces that led to the establishment of the Finer Committee and the recommendation for a single parent benefit in the form of a guaranteed maintenance allowance (Millar 1994) and to the subsequent introduction of a small addition to child benefit in 1975.

Thirty years earlier, the rise in 'illegitimacy' in the 1950s and early 1960s had been attributed to the Beveridge reforms. The American writer Shirley Foster Hartley (1966) wrote of Britain in 1962 that:

> ...there were 30,000 mothers of illegitimate children receiving aid amounting to about six and one-half million pounds per year. There was an increase of nine per cent in the number of mothers receiving assistance during 1962. While I would not pretend to suggest that such aid is the *cause* of illegitimacy, I would suggest that its availability may reduce motivation to prevent conception.

It was also widely believed that family allowances led to women choosing to have large families, despite the fact that all evidence (Selman 1977) pointed to such families being largely the result of unplanned pregnancy and lack of access to contraception, sterilisation and abortion.

Few would now argue that the virtual elimination of the large family would have been hastened by the removal of child benefit or indeed that changes in the benefit system over the past twenty years can explain this better than the increased availability of fertility control.

With regard to the particular issue of teenage childbearing, it is important to recall the progressive restriction of income support for younger people and its non-availability to under-16s. (Selman and Glendinning 1995) The country where support for families is strongest and where birth rates have risen fastest in recent years is Sweden, but this increase has been associated with a fall in the number and proportion of teenage births.

Educational and job opportunities

In her study of teenage mothers who became pregnant in the early 1960s, Kiernan (1980) noted that 'the main alternatives to teenage motherhood are continued education or employment'. Contrasting those women from the 1946 birth cohort who had a first birth before they were twenty with those who had delayed childbearing, she found that teenage mothers 'were, on average, the least able academically, unambitious and left school at the minimal age' and stressed the importance of encouraging girls 'to equip themselves with the qualifications needed for satisfactory work'.

In the 1980s the proportion of pregnant teenagers proceeding to motherhood was much lower in Sweden and Denmark than in Britain and the USA (David 1990, Selman and Glendinning 1995) and it has been suggested (Brindis 1993, Gress-Wright 1993) that poorer educational and job prospects in the latter countries may explain why their teenage birth rates have remained relatively high over the past decade. Plotnick (1993) has argued that 'policies that improve teenagers' education and earnings appear to contribute indirectly to reducing teenage pregnancy and childbearing...because better economic prospects lead teenagers to believe that they have something to lose by becoming parents'.

A similar argument has been put forward by Bea Campbell (1993) who suggests that teenage motherhood is a rational choice propelled by economic crisis and that teenage pregnancy is most likely to be reduced by creating employment. Certainly the Tayside study cited by Campbell and the regional variations noted in my earlier paper suggest that high rates of teenage conception today continue to be associated with social and economic deprivation (Babb 1994), just as they were in the 1960s (Kiernan 1980).

If this is the case, the proposals to tackle teenage birth rates by withdrawing welfare benefits and limiting access to council housing for young mothers seem likely to be counter-productive. A more appropriate strategy would be to continue an attack on unwanted conceptions by improved sex-education and easier access to contraceptive services and link this to a determined effort to improve educational and job opportunities to increase motivation to avoid premature parenthood.

Conclusion

A review of teenage motherhood in the 1960s and 1980s should make us wary of any suggestion that the former period represents a golden age when traditional values reigned and teenage pregnancy was in some sense less of a problem.

Teenage birth rates were substantially higher in the 1960s than in the 1980s and the number of extra-maritally conceived births was also higher, albeit more ended in marriage. The experience of teenage women who became pregnant in the 1960s was far from happy. Some faced the risks of backstreet abortion; others had children they could not support and were pressured to surrender these children for adoption, many experiencing a lifetime of pain and regret as a result. Those who married, whether before or after the birth of their child, have faced a high chance of subsequent marriage breakdown and divorce and for many it was the beginning of a longer career of more unwanted pregnancies and poverty due to having many children. For those who did not marry, but kept their child, there was often severe poverty due to a lack of support services. The policy responses of the late 1960s seem in retrospect to have been positive - the implementation of legal abortion, the introduction of contraceptive services into the NHS and the recognition of the need for better support for single mothers.

So how do we explain the reversal of the downward movement in teenage pregnancy and birth rates which occurred in the early and mid-1970s? One reason seems likely to be that the contraceptive revolution heralded by the pill and the IUD has not proved as total as some had expected - while deep ambivalences over providing contraception and sex education to younger teenagers have undermined efforts to provide for the growing number of sexually active adolescents. The other explanation that must be considered is that the economic experience of the 1980s has offered little to young women in more deprived areas of this country so that ambivalence over motherhood continues and motivation to avoid pregnancy and parenthood remains low. Taken together these explanations fit well with the very different experiences of Denmark and Sweden in the 1980s.

What is worrying is that alternative explanations in terms of welfare incentives and the fears that explicit sex education will result in more sexual experimentation are leading to a set of policies which will not achieve the goal of reduced teenage fertility and are likely to worsen the lot of teenagers so that 'a heavy price will be paid by young mothers and their children' (Selman and Glendinning 1995). At worst we could see a return to the miseries that accompanied teenage pregnancy in the 1960s.

References

Babb, P. (1994), 'Teenage conceptions and fertility in England and Wales, 1971-1991', *Population Trends*, no. 74, pp. 12-17.

Balding, J. (1994), *Young People in 1993*, Exeter University.

Baldwin, S. and Falkingham, J. (1994), *Social Security and Social Change*, Harvester Wheatsheaf, London.

Belleman, S. (1993), 'Let's talk about sex', *The Guardian*, 19 November 1993.

Benet, M. K. (1976), *The Character of Adoption*, Jonathan Cape, London.

Blaikie, A. (1994), *Illegitimacy, Sex and Society*, OUP, Oxford.

Blaikie, A. (1994), 'Family fall-out', *Times Higher Education Supplement* 4 November 1994.

Bone, M. (1973), *Family Planning Services in England and Wales*, HMSO, London.

Brindis, C. (1993), 'Antecedents and consequences: the need for diverse strategies in adolescent pregnancy prevention' in Lawson, A. and Rhode, D., *The Politics of Pregnancy: Adolescent Sexuality and Public Policy*, Yale University Press, New Haven.

Campbell, B. (1993), 'A teenage girl's passport to womanhood', *The Independent*, 12 May 1993.

Cartwright, A. (1970), *Parents and Family Planning Services*, Routledge, London.

Cartwright, A. (1976), *How Many Children?*, Routledge, London.

Coleman, D. (1993), 'Britain in Europe: International and Regional Comparisons of Fertility Levels and Trends' in Ní Bhrolcháin, M., *New Perspectives on Fertility in Britain*, pp. 67-93, HMSO, London.

Cutright, P. (1972), 'The teenage sexual revolution and the myth of an abstinent past', *Family Planning Perspectives*, 4-1.

David, H.P. (1990), 'United States and Denmark: Different approaches to health care and family planning', *Studies in Family Planning*, 21-1, pp. 1-19.

David, H. P. (1992), 'Abortion in Europe, 1921-1991', *Studies in Family Planning*, 23-1, pp. 1-22.

Department of Health (1992), *The Health of the Nation: A Strategy for Health in England*, (Cm 1986), HMSO, London.

Department of Health (1992a), *The Health of the Nation...and You*, HMSO, London.

Farrell, C. (1978), *My Mother Said...The Way Young People Learn About Sex*, Routledge, London.

Ford, N. (1992), 'The sexual and contraceptive lifestyles of young people', *British Journal of Family Planning*, 18, pp. 52-55.

Francome, C. (1993), *Children Who Have Children*, FPA, London.

Green, D. (1991), *Liberty, Poverty and the Underclass*, Paper presented at PSI seminar, London.

Gress-Wright, J. (1993), 'The contraception paradox', *The Public Interest* no. 113, pp. 15-25.

Grey, E. (1971), *A Survey of Adoption in Great Britain*, HMSO, London.

Grunseit, A. and Kippax, S. (1994), *Effects of Sex Education on Young People's Sexual Behaviour*, WHO, Geneva.

Haimes, E. and Timms, N. (1985), *Adoption, Identity & Social Policy*, Gower, Aldershot.

Hartley, S.F. (1966), 'The amazing rise of illegitimacy in England', *Social Forces*, 44-4, pp. 533-545.

Hartley, S.F. (1975), *Illegitimacy*, University of California Press, Berkeley.

Haskey, J. (1983), 'Marital status and age at marriage: Their influence on the chance of divorce', *Population Trends*, 32, pp. 4-14.

Haskey, J. (1993), 'Trends in the numbers of one-parent families in Great Britain', *Population Trends*, no. 71, Spring, pp. 26-33.

Hill, M. (1988), 'Do family planning facilities meet the needs of sexually active teenagers?', *British Journal of Family Planning*, 13-4, pp. 48-51.

Hoem, B. and Hoem, J. (1992), 'The Disruption of Marital and Non-marital Unions in Contemporary Sweden' in Trussel, J. (ed), *Demographic Applications of Event History Analysis*, Clarendon Press, Oxford.

Howe, D. et al. (1992), *Half a Million Women*, Penguin, London.

Illsley, R. and Gill, D. (1968), 'New fashions in illegitimacy', *New Society*, 14 November 1968, pp. 709-711.

Ineichen, B. (1986), 'Contraceptive use and attitudes to motherhood amongst teenage mothers', *Journal of Biosocial Science*, 18-4, pp. 387-394.

Jackson, H. (1985), 'Effects of the Gillick ruling', *Breaking Chains*, no. 38, p. 3.

Kiernan, K. (1980), 'Teenage motherhood - associated factors and consequences - the experiences of British birth cohort', *Journal of Biosocial Science*, 12-4, pp. 393-405.

Kiernan, K. and Wicks, M. (1990), *Family Change & Future Policy*, Family Policy Studies Centre, London.

Kiernan, K. and Estaugh, V. (1993), *Cohabitation: Extra-marital Childbearing and Social Policy*, Family Policy Studies Centre, London.

Lawson, A. and Rhode, D. (1993), *The Politics of Pregnancy: Adolescent Sexuality and Public Policy*, Yale University Press, New Haven.

Leete, R. (1978), 'Adoption trends and illegitimate births 1951-1977' *Population Trends*, 14.

MacIntyre, S. (1977), *Single and Pregnant*, Croom Helm, London.

McRae, S. (1993), *Cohabiting Mothers: Changing Marriage and Motherhood*, Policy Studies Institute, London.

Millar, J. (1994), 'Lone parents and Social Security in the UK' in *Social Security and Social Change*, (eds. Baldwin, S. and Falkingham, J.), Harvester Wheatsheaf, Brighton.

Morgan, P. (1995), *Farewell to the Family?: Public Policy and Family Breakdown in Britain and the USA*, IEA, London.

Murray, C. (1990), *The Emerging British Underclass*, IEA, London.

Murray, C. (1993), 'No point fiddling with welfare at the margin', *Sunday Times*, 11 July 1993.

Oliver, C. and Charlton, L. (1994), 'Parents without children', letter to the editor, *Adoption & Fostering*, 18-2, p. 6.

Peberdy, M. (1965), 'Fertility control among problem parents' in *Biological Aspects of Social Problems*, (ed. Meade, J.), Oliver Boyd, Edinburgh.

Phoenix, A. (1991), *Young Mothers?*, Polity Press, Cambridge.

Plotnick, R.D. (1993), 'The effect of social policies on teenage pregnancy and childbearing', *Families in Society*, June 1993.

Risor, H. (1989), 'Reducing abortion: the Danish experience', *Planned Parenthood in Europe*, 18-1, pp. 17-19.

Rockell, J. and Ryburn, M. (1988), *Adoption Today*, Heinemann Reed, Auckland.

Schofield, M. (1965), *The Sexual Behaviour of Young People*, Longman, London.

Seglow, J. et al. (1972), *Growing Up Adopted*, NFER, Windsor.

Selman, P. (1976), 'Patterns of adoption in England and Wales since 1959', *Social Work Today*, 7-7, pp. 194-197.

Selman, P. (1977), *Differential Fertility in Working Class Women*, unpublished PhD Thesis, University of Newcastle upon Tyne.

Selman, P. (1988), *Family Planning*, Reviews of UK Statistical Sources Vol. XXV, Chapman & Hall, London.

Selman, P. and Calder, J. (1994), 'Variations in the characteristics of attenders at community family planning clinics', *British Journal of Family Planning*, 20, pp. 13-16.

Selman, P. and Glendinning, C. (1995), 'Teenage parenthood and social policy', *Youth and Policy*, no. 47, pp. 39-58.

Shorter, E. (1976), *The Making of the Modern Family*, Collins, London.

Simms, M. and Smith, C. (1986), *Teenage Mothers and their Partners*, HMSO, London.

Simpson, F. (1985), 'Gillick Judgement', *Breaking Chains*, no. 41, pp. 4-5.

Stone, L. (1977), *The Family, Sex and Marriage in England*, 1500-1800, Weidenfeld & Nicholson, London.

Triseliotis, J. (1973), *In Search of Origins*, Routledge, London.

Tye, L. (1994), *Birth Parents Talk Back*, Birth Mothers/Adoptees Support Group, Cramlington.

Wellings, K. (1994), *Sexual Behaviour in Britain*, Penguin Books, London.

Wrigley, E.A. (1983), 'The growth of population in Eighteenth Century England: a conundrum resolved', *Past and Present*, no. 98.

Zabin, L.S. and Hayward, S.C. (1993), *Adolescent Sexual Behaviour and Childbearing*, Sage, London.

7 Black families and social security: Evidence from fieldwork in Leeds

Ian Law, Alan Deacon, Carl Hylton and Alyas Karmani

Introduction

Social security is central to any discussion of the politics of the family. There is a considerable literature on the adequacy of the benefits paid to families, and a still more considerable - and contentious - literature on the extent to which the provision of benefit affects the behaviour of some claimants in ways which exacerbates poverty. Such discussions of 'behaviourial dependency' have at times focused upon black families, and some commentators, for example, have reported evidence of a link between the stigma attached to single parenthood and racist ideologies (Room 1993, p. 133). In contrast, relatively little attention has been given to the needs and experiences of black claimants. Peter Craig, for example, has noted that 'ethnicity in particular has been neglected' in studies of the take up of benefits (1991, p. 32). This in spite of evidence of both lower take-up and greater poverty within black minority ethnic communities (Sadiq-Sangster 1991, Cook and Watt 1992, Marsh and McKay 1993).

The research which informs this chapter was conducted against a background of widespread concern at the quality of benefit provision (Towerwatch 1991, Social Security Committee 1991, Ditch 1993), and particularly at that provided to black minority ethnic claimants. The existing literature highlights a number of concerns at the quality of benefit provision to black minority ethnic communities. These include; a lack of multi-lingual facilities (NACAB 1991), the extent to which racist attitudes and erroneous cultural assumptions lead to direct discrimination by Benefits Agency staff (CRE 1985, NACAB 1991), and the extent to which residence tests and the contributory basis of some benefits result in indirect discrimination (Amin and Oppenheim 1992). A further source of concern is the apparent lack of an effective racial equality strategy within the Benefits Agency (Law et al. 1994). The purpose of the present chapter is to present the most important findings of a study of the delivery of social security benefits to black minority ethnic communities in Leeds, and to consider the implications of those findings for future policy. This research seeks to contribute to the development of initiatives in this field by providing a fuller understanding of the perceptions and experiences of both claimants and eligible non-claimants within black minority ethnic communities (Alcock 1992, Committee for Non-Racist Benefits 1993, Bloch 1993).

The research, which was funded by the Joseph Rowntree Foundation, included interviews with over 150 respondents drawn from five minority ethnic groups. The interviews explored the respondents' experiences and perceptions of the claiming process and their perceptions of the Benefits Agency, local authority housing benefits provision, and advice centres. This chapter focuses upon two issues. First, it examines some of the reasons for the non-take up of benefits amongst particular ethnic groups and considers the broader influences of ethnicity upon attitudes to claiming. Second, it discusses the important role of local advice agencies in facilitating access to benefits within minority ethnic communities. The chapter also focuses primarily upon the experiences of families although reference is also made to evidence provided by single respondents where this helps to illustrate or clarify particular issues. A further objective is to document the diversity of the positions and strategies adopted by black people, a diversity which is often neglected in the mainstream social policy literature. As Jones has noted, 'important and complex changes' are taking place within ethnic minority communities (1993, p. 159), and these changes are reflected in the attitudes adopted towards the benefits system.

The fieldwork was conducted in Leeds to enable the research to build upon links already established with black community groups, advice centres, and welfare rights services, as well as with the local authority and the Benefit Agency and its local offices. Quota samples were set for five minority ethnic groups; African-Caribbean, Bangladeshi, Chinese, Indian, and Pakistani, structured by type of benefit unit. The benefits covered were Income Support, Family Credit, Housing Benefit and Community Charge Benefit. A screening questionnaire was devised in order to assess eligibility for these benefits as accurately as possible, and a total of 450 screening interviews were carried out in inner city districts with high concentrations of black minority ethnic groups. This produced 47 completed interviews. It was anticipated that the relatively small size of the Bangladeshi and Chinese communities would make it impossible to identify a sufficient number of respondents through systematic screening, and so 67 respondents were drawn from lists of households compiled during previous screening exercises in 1991. In the event, however, it also proved necessary to contact 41 Indian and Pakistani respondents through informal community networks. As a result, a total of 155 interviews were completed. Thirty three interviews were obtained with eligible non-claimants (Table 7.1). Many of the 122 claimants were, of course, receiving more than one benefit and interviews were conducted with over a hundred claimants of both income support and community charge benefit.

A large majority of the interviews were conducted by ethnically matched interviewers. As the samples of respondents were drawn using a variety of methods the results cannot be taken to be representative. African-Caribbeans, Bangladeshis and Chinese were all identified through screening exercises but numbers were small and response rates for the screening questionnaire were low.

Because of this comparisons between groups are made primarily on the basis of the qualitative material.

Table 7.1
Ethnic origin by whether eligible and not claiming
IS, FC, CCB or HB

Ethnic Origin	Claiming	Not Claiming	Total
Afro-Caribbean	25	4	29
Indian	30	1	31
Bangladeshi	23	8	31
Pakistani	22	6	30
Chinese	24	12	36
Total	122	33	155

Some of the issues that emerged from preliminary analysis of the data were subsequently explored in depth through group discussions in order to check the reliability of results and to develop the range of qualitative material. These groups consisted of the following; African-Caribbean lone parents, young male Pakistanis, young male Bangladeshi non-claimants, older male Bangladeshis, Bangladeshi lone parents and Indian Sikh women. Interviews were also carried out with staff from the Benefit Agency, Leeds

City Council's Integrated Benefit Service and thirteen community-based agencies involved in advice work with black minority ethnic clients.

Table 7.2
Ethnic origin by type of benefit claimed

Ethnic Origin	Family Credit	Income Support	Housing Benefit	Community Charge Ben
A/Carib	1	18	18	24
Indian	3	24	7	21
Bangladeshi	1	23	18	21
Pakistani	1	19	6	18
Chinese	6	16	12	21
Total	12	100	61	105

Perceptions of the right to benefit

Most respondents believed that they had a right to claim benefits, and the main reason which they gave for this belief was their previous payment of national insurance contributions (NICs). Indeed it was striking that the payment of NICs was regarded by respondents as conferring an entitlement to all benefits - contributory and non-contributory alike. Nonetheless, the perception of a right to claim was considerably weaker amongst Chinese respondents, whilst the position of Bangladeshi respondents was ambivalent. These differences reflect the influence of cultural and religious factors upon attitudes to benefits and the strength and importance of such influences is the most striking finding of the research.

Some Bangladeshi Muslims, for example, saw benefit as "Lillah", - charity for the poor - and therefore as something which was only for those who were in need. Others, however, felt that they had contributed to the system through NI payments and so they were entitled to it. These latter respondents had a strong conception of "Haq" or right. This was felt particularly by older Bangladeshis and Pakistanis whereas guilt and disapproval were often associated with claiming for younger people in these communities. Strong belief in Islam provided a key context for these perceptions. One man mentioned that in some situations this money is considered as "Haram" (unlawful) and in other situations it was considered as "Halal" (lawful). It was seen as acceptable to claim benefit as a last resort after the individual had exhausted all other possibilities of finding work or seeking other sources of financial assistance, for example from family members. For such a person claiming benefit was justified and "Halal". If however a person is 'deceiving' by working and claiming at the same time, or staying on benefit or living off his family when he is able to find work then this was seen as "Haram". Another view put forward was that the social security/benefit system was similar to the Islamic system of "Bait Ul Mal " (collective fund/community chest) or the "Zakat" fund (alms fund). In such a system a fixed percentage of money is collected from peoples earnings and savings and then distributed to those who are most in need. One man commented:

> I've worked here for so long and paid my dues and so it is due to me and the others, I have not got work and so it is part of the law of this country to support me. I came to this country to work not to go onto social. If there was any work available we would do it. It is not a matter of religion but a matter of need.

Amongst the Chinese, respondents culturally-based notions of shame were more commonly attached to claiming and 'reliance on government' was often strongly condemned. They were less likely to express a sense of entitlement by virtue of citizenship or feelings of inclusion. It will be seen later in the chapter that such feelings are central to an understanding of the low levels of take up found in the Chinese, Bangladeshi and - to a lesser extent - Pakistani communities.

There is, of course, a clear link between the extent to which respondents perceived themselves to be entitled to claim benefit and the degree to which receipt of benefits was seen as constituting or generating an unwelcome dependency upon the state. There was an ambivalence on this issue within all five communities. On the one hand the process of claiming was seen as leading to a loss of control over day to day living and an erosion of dignity and privacy. On the other hand, receipt of benefit was described by some claimants as fostering independence because it made them less dependent upon families and friends.

These conflicting perceptions were expressed most clearly by a group of Bangladeshi women. They said that they felt fortunate to be on benefit in comparison to people in the same circumstances in Bangladesh who would be dependent upon their relatives to support them. One woman, for example, spoke of her dislike of being dependent on others in the community for income:

It feels bad being dependent on other people, instead people should give to you when they see you need it. Traditionally you don't get loans but have to sometimes from friends and family, there is sharam (shame) in approaching others for money.

Taking loans or borrowing from family and being dependent on them was also seen as bad as this may reinforce relationships of dominance and subordination through establishing that the lender has greater status, and that the borrower has failed to become economically independent. Moreover, borrowing from the bank or from credit companies was worse still than borrowing from friends and family since paying interest on loaned money can be considered to be unlawful by Muslims. Hence, some of the women felt that claiming benefit gave them independence because it freed them from this cultural system, particularly as they believed that there was less stigma attached to claiming by women than by men.

Perceptions of the quality of service

Three quarters of respondents who had had direct contact with local offices said that they were satisfied with the services provided by the Benefits Agency and Leeds City Council's Integrated Benefit Service. This finding is broadly in line with that of the Benefits Agency's national customer satisfaction survey for 1992 (Smith and Wright 1993).

It is important to stress, however, that there were considerable differences between the perceptions of the services held within the different minority ethnic groups. Almost all the Sikh and Bangladeshi respondents, for example, said that they had been 'treated with respect' and 'the same as anyone else'. The evidence of African-Caribbean respondents, however, was mixed. Around half felt that they had not experienced discrimination. One man in his sixties, for example, said that Benefits Agency staff 'tried to talk to me good and do what they were supposed to', and a woman in her twenties said that they had been 'very considerate...[and]...provided information when I needed it'. Others, however, said that they had encountered a lack of sympathy on the part of Benefits Agency staff, a dis-inclination to accept what claimants told them and a reluctance to provide explanations for decisions. One woman said 'Sometimes you feel as if you are talking to a brick wall - you don't get a clear explanation of what is going to happen next'. Another that 'they don't talk to you as if you are entitled - they have a funny way of talking - I don't understand'. These quotations refer to the Benefits Agency and most respondents were less critical of the service at the local authority office in Dudley House.

One woman found the local authority staff 'much more understanding and more willing to help...Dudley House is all right because you only have to go to see them once'.

By far the strongest criticisms of the Benefits Agency, however, were made by lone parents, and particularly by African-Caribbean lone mothers. Relatively few difficulties were experienced by Asian lone mothers, who were more likely to be widows or women whose husbands were abroad.

In both individual and group interviews, African-Caribbean lone parents described their encounters with the Benefits Agency in stark terms. Staff were seen as, 'Quite patronising - I was really shouting at them - (they behaved) like it was their money, and I was a beggar, and they were superior to me'. Respondents said they often felt that 'There was that thing about Black single parents - if they proved you wrong in some way, caught you cheating, they would make an example of us' and that, 'It felt that they did not believe: that I was making it up in some way.'

Long waiting times were reported as were inaccuracies in decisions and difficulties in challenging claim errors - 'When I felt that the amount in my book was wrong I used to go down there and they would take the book away - you felt degraded because you had to practically beg to get some money.'

The fieldwork was conducted before the introduction of the Child Support Agency and there were criticisms that the Benefits Agency's demands for information about fathers were overly intrusive and based on racially stereotypical assumptions. Benefits Agency staff appeared to believe that many lone-parents had a history of single-parenthood within their families but the respondents emphasised the stable nature of their parents' marriages and strongly rejected what they felt was criticism of the morality of their family life.

It is important to see this in context. The national customer surveys also found that lone parents were more likely to complain about the service they had received, and it has already been noted that the overall proportion expressing dissatisfaction was no higher amongst the Leeds respondents than amongst the national sample. There are, however, two important qualifications to be made here. The first is that the measure of satisfaction is a very crude one. The authors of the report on the 1991 national survey, for example, noted that respondents who had their claim refused were more than three times more likely to complain than those whose who had received benefit. This 'suggests that it was difficult here to divorce opinion expressed about the way a claim is dealt with from its final outcome' (Russell and Whitworth 1992, p. 13). The same is true of the Leeds respondents. As one Bangladeshi mother commented, 'after all the

135

moaning I am satisfied because eventually I got what I wanted'.

The second qualification is that half of the respondents had not had any direct contact with the Benefits Agency and so did not express an opinion. Those who said that they were satisfied were thus 38% of the total rather than 75%. Moreover, a further one in six said that they were neither satisfied or dissatisfied, and this was largely because their interaction with the Benefits Agency had been mediated by someone else. The proportion who rated themselves in this way has also been found in the national surveys, but the Leeds research found that the role of family, friends and advice workers was particularly important within black and minority ethnic communities.

The role of community-based advice centres

Local advice agencies played a central role in all five minority ethnic communities. They were more conveniently located than the Benefits Agency or local authority offices and the staff could explain the benefits system to clients in their own language. As one older Bangladeshi man put it

> If we have a problem with social security we don't go direct to the office but we come here, it costs too much to go to town, there are no interpreters so we have to find someone. This is convenient for us as we can deal with all our problems in one go.

The proportion of respondents in Leeds who had used an advice centre was much higher than that suggested by the national surveys (Smith and Wright 1993, p. 33). Two thirds of Chinese claimants, for example, had either visited the Chinese Advice Centre or had received advice at the Chinese Elderly Luncheon Club. Around half of African-Caribbean respondents had used an advice centre, though the proportion was higher amongst women than men. Both the Citizens Advice Bureaux in Chapeltown and the local law centre were described as respectful and supportive. A lone mother whose gas and electricity had been disconnected said of the women who helped her,

> she was quite professional about the situation, because she was a woman, and she was a Black woman as well. She understood that I was not on the make, and was not trying to con anything...She understood the benefit system and how it was difficult to live on the amount...[of money]... - she gave me a lot of positive feedback about me being a strong person and coping, and that it was not my fault - and

that kind of thing.

The type of advice centre used by Sikh respondents tended to depend upon where they lived; either Chapeltown Citizen's Advice Bureaux or the more informal benefits surgeries organised at the Sikh Temple in Beeston. Around one third of respondents had used one or other of these, usually claimants with a limited knowledge of English. Language difficulties were also emphasised by Bangladeshi lone mothers in a group interview. At the time the Benefits Agency did not provide an interpreting service in Bengali and the women found the staff lacking in understanding. Instead they turned to two other sources of advice and help: a Benefits Advisor who was funded by the local authority and based in a local community centre and the surgeries run by Asha, a Bangladeshi Women's Centre. Often, however, these women would also look to male relatives for support.

The role of relatives and friends

One point which emerged clearly from the research was that many Pakistani, Bangladeshi and Chinese women did not deal directly with either the Benefits Agency or the local advice centres as the process was frequently regulated by male relatives. This involved 'escorting' women to the office, dealing with paper work and communicating with staff. It was observed by a Pakistani woman that, 'some people...[in the community]...think Muslim women shouldn't go to the DSS'. This practice spared the women much of the hassle of claiming and overcame problems of poor English, but it tended to reinforce patriarchal and dependent relationships, and to maintain the relative social isolation of many of these women. This was particularly evident for Chinese women; one women said, 'my son helped me to fill in the forms, took me to the office and dealt with everything'. There was also some evidence that the Pakistani community included a larger number of older children who were independent and often in professional occupations. As a result Pakistani respondents seemed to rely more on their families for advice and support and to be less dependent upon advice centres.

Ethnicity and claiming

The most striking and most important finding to emerge from the research in Leeds was the extent to which the cultural and religious factors discussed earlier resulted in significant underclaiming of benefits, especially amongst

137

the Chinese, Bangladeshi and Pakistani communities.

In the case of the Chinese community, it is helpful to distinguish between those factors which influence the demand for benefits and those which arise from the way in which claims are assessed and benefits delivered. The latter include the complexity of the benefit regulations, exacerbated by an inadequate provision of information and a lack of interpreters. On the demand side, the chief obstacles to claiming were a vicarious family pride and sense of stigma attached to benefit receipt, together with a lack of basic benefit knowledge, concerns about seeking information from employers in the case of those eligible for Family Credit and worries over residence status and passport checks.

Some of these factors can be seen operating in the cases of seven families who were eligible for Family Credit but not claiming it. In all cases the father was working on low pay in the catering trade. Four respondents felt that after consideration they would claim, one was unsure and two refused. One of those who wanted to claim had no knowledge of the benefit system at all, did not know where to go for help apart from friends and felt the main barrier to claiming to be her inadequate English. Three of those who wanted to claim were broadly aware of their possible eligibility as they had either been informed by friends or had seen TV adverts. But, one person was particularly worried about the difficulty of obtaining information from his employer, one person was put off by the prospect of waiting and being interviewed and he also felt he would be looked down on in the community. The third person disliked the fact that she would 'have to ask people to do everything for me' as her English was very poor. The person who was unsure about claiming had unwarranted concerns about the status of his residence despite living here for eight years and was also worried about his ignorance of the system, having poor English, and 'relying on the government'. The two who rejected claiming had divergent views. One was aware of the benefits available, aware of their broad eligibility, knew where the Benefit Offices and Advice Centres were, took pride in their good English, saw no difficulties in the process of claiming but firmly refused to claim and refused to explain why. The interviewer noted the underlying factors operating here as being feelings of 'shame' and not wanting to rely on 'charity from government'. This was also the only family credit non-claimant interviewed in the 16-29 age group. The other respondent was unaware of the relevant benefits and had no perception of his eligibility. Claiming was seen to involve many difficulties. These included long waiting times, problems in form filling and communication due to poor English and consequent dependence on other people. Similar problems were evident for another Chinese respondent who was eligible but did not claim Income Support. There was no basic knowledge of the benefits available, little knowledge of English, no knowledge of where to apply or where to obtain advice and assistance apart from friends and a general feeling that it would be too troublesome to claim. In this case there were no negative feelings about state dependency and it was perceived that the wider family would support claiming.

Amongst young Bangladeshis and Pakistanis reluctance to claim stemmed partly from cultural and community pressures and, particularly, from the perceived demands of their religion - Islam. These 'ethnicity' factors had a number of effects. Several respondents referred to the hostility directed towards young people on benefit. One commented that, 'Elders in the community look down on you, as to say "why are you not working, when I was your age...", so it is best to avoid benefit.'

Another said,

> As a young person I don't want to go on the dole, I don't think people would approve of a young person being on benefit when I could find a job. This is why I have decided not to claim benefit yet. I wouldn't claim unless I had absolutely no money to buy necessities.'

A third respondent had just returned from Bangladesh. 'I recently got married there, its not going to look good on my reference if I start claiming benefit.'

A further factor is that Bengali families are close-knit and the family is often there to support its members despite the low levels of household income. One respondent said, 'I don't approve of people like myself who have a very supportive family claiming benefit'.

This was discussed further by an older Bangladeshi man,

> The family system supports while out of work, we are not like the white community, our religion does not let us let go of our children at the age of 16. It may be a burden but we have to sacrifice so we eat less and buy cheaper things for ourselves so we can support our children, we don't let go of the children.

This was confirmed by some young men in a group interview. They said that the family could always be relied upon when in need and so men would first turn to their family and when they become too much of a burden then they would claim benefit. These young Bangladeshis acknowledged that stigma was real and that it was a major factor in preventing them from claiming Income Support. On the other hand, Housing Benefit or Community Charge/Council Tax Benefit were seen differently as they were not felt to be linked so directly to unemployment.

One man stated unequivocally that he would never claim IS because of the shame involved and another, who had claimed IS, said that he had delayed claiming and had only done so as a last resort. All of the participants in the group interview felt that the worst thing about receiving benefit was being seen to do so by other members of the community.

It should be emphasised that there is little evidence that the eligible non-claimants were as well off as those receiving benefits. This may seem a somewhat unnecessary statement, but the point is significant because a recent national survey by Marsh and McKay found that those eligible for but not claiming Family Credit were not placed in severe hardship as a result.

> Their total income should have been lower than that of the claimants, and so it proved. Every logic suggests that they should therefore have experienced more hardship than the claimants, but this was not true... The eligible non-claimants seemed to be far better off than their relative incomes would predict (1993, p. 192).

Marsh and McKay suggest that the explanation for this lies in the fact that the eligible non-claimants were owner occupiers who had enjoyed higher incomes in the past and were still enjoying the benefits of the housing and other possessions they had acquired then. The position with the Leeds respondents is that the proportion who said that they experienced regular financial difficulties was lower amongst eligible non-claimants than amongst those receiving benefits - 45% compared with 56%. It should be remembered, however, that the numbers are small and these differences are on the margins of significance. Moreover, it is possible that in some cases the reported absence of difficulty was because the respondents were receiving help from relatives and friends which they would not have called upon if they had been aware of their eligibility for benefit.

This is clearly a complex issue, and a closer examination was made of the circumstances of the 12 Chinese eligible non-claimants. Of these eight said that they were experiencing regular difficulties, while there were four Chinese households who experienced regular difficulties, who appeared to be eligible for family credit, and yet had no knowledge of that entitlement. If the implication of the findings of Marsh and McKay is that the problem of low take up is less severe than previously thought, then the results in Leeds suggest that that is not the case amongst minority ethnic communities.

Conclusion: the implications for policy

The evidence reviewed in this chapter suggests that there are significant differences between the perceptions and experiences of claimants from different black minority ethnic communities, and between those claimants as a whole and white claimants. Black minority ethnic claimants make a much greater use of community advice agencies, and rely more heavily upon family and friends as sources of advice and help. There is also compelling evidence that cultural and religious influences inhibit claiming and lead to lower levels of take up within black minority ethnic communities. A summary of findings for each minority group is given below.

Such evidence demands a response from the Benefits Agency. It should be recognised, of course, that there appears to have been a very substantial - and very necessary - improvement in the service provided to black minority ethnic claimants since Steven Cooper observed the explicit racism of some officers of the then Supplementary Benefits Commission in 1981/2 (Cooper 1985, pp. 67-70). This is not to say, however, that there is not a pressing need for further change.

Particular attention needs to be given to improving the perceptions and knowledge of benefit and employment rights amongst Chinese households as basic knowledge is limited and there are a range of constraints which undermine perceptions of the utility of such rights particularly when households or individuals are linguistically and socially isolated. Targeted take-up initiatives and campaigns are required which must be particularly sensitive to traditional notions, such as vicarious family pride, a dislike of state dependency and a sense of shame involved in claiming benefit, as well as to language. Our findings support those of Bloch (1993) in pointing to productive joint work carried out by Chinese Advice and Community Centres and benefit providers. There does appear to be evidence that such welfare rights advocacy work can be effective in improving levels of take-up (Law et al 1994).

Similarly, attention needs to be given to encouraging claiming amongst Bangladeshis and Pakistanis. Further discussion needs to take place with these communities to identify appropriate and effective ways in which such an objective can be pursued. The role of advocates using informal community networks to stimulate an awareness of the reality of economic opportunities, benefit rights and perceptions of benefit utility could be a possible way forward. Also measures to improve privacy in the provision of benefits would be of particular value.

The eradication of unwarranted passport checks (evident in the Chinese sample), racially and ethnically stereotypical judgements, and overly intrusive questioning based on such assumptions (evident in the African-Caribbean sample) remain long-standing matters that require attention by the Benefit Agency. Also effective provision of interpreting facilities particularly for Cantonese/Hakka and Bengali speakers and increasing the employment and promotion of black and minority ethnic staff are still areas where urgent change is needed. The issue here is not what needs to be done but how it will be managed, financed and implemented. Measures to implement policy, such as staff training and the development of necessary staff guidelines and procedures, will only be effective when policy development has taken place and when there is explicit management leadership both centrally and in district offices that acknowledges inadequacies and builds on good practice. Ethnic monitoring, identification of areas of concern and subsequent positive action planning, the core elements of a racial equality strategy, need to be put in place as a matter of urgency. The attention to needs of minorities in the new 'quality framework' for service review in the Benefit Agency attempts to facilitate positive initiatives at local level in the context of inadequate central policy planning and inadequate incorporation of ethnic origin data collection in management information systems. Only when such developments have taken place and when they have become a daily consideration in the management and administration of benefit provision, will the pre-conditions for change have been established. The integration of multi-cultural needs criteria in the new 'quality framework' will have the effect of devolving policy to local offices and is likely to encourage diversity in provision. The extent to which this diversity will be ethnically sensitive requires further research as problems in how local needs are identified, avoidance of stereotypical and fixed cultural notions of need, prioritisation of needs, and the formulation of how needs can be best responded to may raise recurring problems in policy implementation.

The value put on community-based advice work by black and minority ethnic respondents indicates its importance in reducing racial differentials in benefit take-up. Increasing the quantity and availability of this ethnically-sensitive benefit advice provision must therefore be one key dimension of any strategy to establish racial equality in benefit provision. The present uneven, and sometimes overlapping provision, provided by local authorities and voluntary sector agencies requires review, but the need for simplified and collaborative benefit advice and provision between the Benefit Agency, local authorities and the voluntary sector is clearly evident.

The Leeds respondents made a number of recommendations for changes in the administration of benefits which largely echoed those reported in the Benefit Agency's National Customer Survey (Smith and Wright 1993). There is, however, one final point which requires emphasis. The findings in Leeds confirm those of other recent research regarding the poverty of many black and minority ethnic claimants (Sadiq-Sangster 1991, Cohen et al. 1992), and the work of Bradshaw (1993) and others on the inadequacy of the present levels of benefit. Low and inadequate income was a characteristic feature across all minority ethnic groups we interviewed.

References

Alcock, P. (1992), 'Poverty, debt and indifference: A study of household debt and advice needs in a Pakistani community in Sheffield', in *Benefits*, Sept/Oct. MacMillan,

Amin, K. with Oppenheim, C. (1992), *Poverty in Black and White, Deprivation And Ethnic Minorities*, CPAG, London.

Bloch, A. (1993), *Access to Benefits The Information Needs of Minority Ethnic Groups*, Policy Studies Institute, London.

Bradshaw, J. (1993), *Household Budgets and Living Standards*, Joseph Rowntree Foundation, York.

Cohen, R., Coxall, J., Craig, G. and Sadiq-Sangster, A. (1992), *Hardship Britain: Being Poor in the 1990's*, CPAG, London.

Committee for Non-Racist Benefits (1993), *Charter for Non-Racist Benefits*, CNRB, London.

Commission for Racial Equality (1985), *Submission in Response to the Green Paper on Reform of Social Security*, CRE, London.

Cook, J. and Watt, S. (1992), 'Racism, Women and Poverty', in C. Glendinning and J. Millar (eds.) *Women and Poverty in Britain: The 1990's*, Harvester, Hemel Hempstead.

Cooper, S. (1985), *Observations in Supplementary Benefit Offices*, Research Paper 85/2, Policy Studies Institute, London.

Corden, A. and Craig, P. (1991), *Perceptions of Family Credit*, HMSO, London.

Craig, P. (1991), 'Costs and Benefits : A review of research on take-up of income-related benefits', *Journal of Social Policy* 20 : 4, pp. 537-565.

Ditch, J. (1993), 'The Reorganisation of the DSS' in N. Deakin and R. Page (eds.), *The Costs of Welfare*, Avebury, Aldershot.

Jones, T. (1993), *Britain's Ethnic Minorities*, Policy Studies Institute, London.

Law, I., Hylton, C., Karmani, A. and Deacon, A. (1994), *Racial Equality and Social Security Service Delivery: Summary Report to the Joseph Rowntree Foundation*, Sociology and Social Policy Working Paper 10, University of Leeds.

Marsh, A. and McKay, S. (1993), *Families, Work and Benefits*, Policy Studies Institute, London.

NACAB (1991) *Barriers to Benefit*, NACAB, London.

Ritchie, J. and England, J. (1985), *The Hackney Benefit Study: A Study to Investigate the Take-up of Means Tested Benefits Within the London Borough of Hackney*, SCPR, London.

Room, G. et al. (1993), *Anti-Poverty Action Research in Europe*, SAUS, Bristol.

Sadiq-Sangster, A. (1991), *Living on Income Support: An Asian Experience*, Family Service Unit, London.

Russell, N. and Whitworth, S. (1992), *The Benefits Agency National Customer Survey 1991*, Department of Social Security, London.

Smith, N. and Wright, C. (1993), *The Benefits Agency National Customer Survey 1992*, Benefits Agency, London.

Social Security Committee (1991), *The Organisation and Administration of the Department of Social Security*, Minutes of Evidence, 12.11.91, House of Commons Session 1991-2, H.C. 19-iii

Towerwatch Advisory Claimants Action Group with Islington Council (1991), *Shame about the Service*, TACAG, London.

8 Fetishizing the family: The construction of the informal carer

Hartley Dean and Di Thompson

Introduction

One of the key components to the political impetus behind the development of policies of community care has been a particular ideological conception of 'the family' (Wilson 1982). Prime Minister Margaret Thatcher once declared that 'it all really starts with the family...it's the place where each generation learns its responsibility to the rest of society' (Thatcher 1981), but on the other hand she was later to announce 'there is no such thing as society, only individuals and their families' (Thatcher 1988). The essence of this apparent contradiction was an antipathy to collectivised state provision and a reification of the self-sufficient family unit.

Objections have been well rehearsed. Firstly, a policy of community care which places an increased burden of care upon families is a policy which necessarily places very particular burdens on women (Finch 1990). Secondly, it is a policy which valorises a specific ideology of the family while obscuring the real, diverse and changing nature of families: 'there is no such thing as *the* family' (Gittins 1993, p. 8). Thirdly, the policy risks making the economic costs of social care invisible (Glendinning 1992). Social policy is therefore implicated in a process which extends patriarchal power while ignoring the real relationships between families and wider economic processes.

In her study of nineteenth-century employment practices, Judy Lown makes the point that patriarchal power simultaneously takes both an economic and a familial form. Indeed, the needs of capital *and* the interests of men were reflected not only in employment but *also* in marital arrangements. Lown counsels, therefore, that 'we can no more talk about "the economy" as if it had fixed and unambiguous boundaries as we can do

145

about "the family"' (Lown 1983, p. 32). This paper will suggest that such advice, applied to the debate about community care policy, translates into an invitation to take 'a single lens' (*ibid.*) to the interconnected needs and interests of 'the economy', 'the family' and the state.

Familialisation

A contribution to such a task has already been made by McLaughlin and Glendinning (1993). Their starting point is a critique of Esping-Andersen's (1990) treatment of the concepts 'commodification' and 'de-commodification'. McLaughlin and Glendinning suggest an analysis in terms of parallel concepts of 'familialisation' and 'defamilialisation'.

The concept 'decommodification' (which Esping-Andersen develops from Polanyi 1944) stems from the idea that the development of social rights under welfare state capitalism served to diminish citizens' dependency on the market. 'Decommodification' is therefore a tendency which stands in opposition to 'commodification', the process more characteristic of *laissez-faire* capitalism, whereby the citizen conversely becomes more dependent for subsistence upon goods and services in a free market and is her/himself constituted as a commodity in the labour market. The benefits conferred by social rights relate therefore to the capacity of the citizen to detach her/himself from the labour market and/or the cash nexus. However, not only is the significance of such benefits different for women than for men (see Langan and Ostner 1991), but the processes captured by the dichotomy between commodification and decommodification are solely economic: they do not encompass the familial processes by which citizens are also constituted (for example, as dependants, carers or bread-winners). As McLaughlin and Glendinning put it,

> although Esping-Andersen develops very clearly the notion of the processes of commodification and decommodification, as the processes through which we may understand the changing and varied relationships between states and markets, he does not develop any similar notion of the process or processes which underpin the changing and varied relationships between states and families, or for that matter, markets and families (1993, p. 11).

To this end, McLaughlin and Glendinning advance the concept of 'defamilialisation' to describe the tendency (or the potential) for welfare states to allow their citizens to detach themselves from dependency within families. This calls to mind certain of the panacean justifications offered -

146

for example by Jordan (1987) - for Basic Income schemes, which by guaranteeing every citizen's needs before s/he enters a family (or employment) can supposedly give effect to her/his autonomy as an individual. However, McLaughlin and Glendinning envisage an analytical framework which encompasses a wide range of state provision including access not only to cash benefits but also to services such as child care and respite care.

The countervailing tendency of 'familialisation' receives less attention from McLaughlin and Glendinning in so far that this is seen as a subject for analysis by revisionist historians, whose task must be '...to trace out the way a patriarchal process of familialisation in western societies resulted in advantages for men as receivers of care, and disadvantages for women and children as both givers and receivers of care' (*ibid.*, p. 13). In this way, McLaughlin and Glendinning point tantalisingly to the prospect of a theoretical model which would somehow define the complex interrelationships between markets, families and welfare states.

A revisionist history?

A question must be raised, however, as to whether indeed the elements of a 'revisionist history' are not already to hand, not least in the historical syntheses of feminists like Diana Gittins (1993), to whom we have already referred, and the work of post-structuralists like Donzelot (1979). From Gittins we have an analysis which, while emphasising the diversities and continuities of family forms, clearly recognises the sense in which in England at least the dismantling of feudal hierarchies of power and the rise of Protestantism were associated with the transfer of power to patriarchal family heads. She further isolates a very particular familial ideology associated with the nineteenth-century middle class and demonstrates how this achieved ascendancy as, for example, trade unions began to campaign for a 'family wage', sufficient to support a male worker and his dependent wife and children.

Donzelot offers rather different insights. He uses the term 'familialisation', albeit in almost the opposite sense to that of McLaughlin and Glendinning. Writing about France, not England, and sharing ground to some extent (though not explicitly) with functionalists, Donzelot implicitly acknowledges that the 'modern' family was weakened firstly through the loss to the market of its productive functions and more recently through the loss to the state of many social functions (particularly in relation to health, personal care and education). In the course of the twentieth century, however, not only have families become increasingly deskilled, they have also become the focus for a variety of psychiatric, medical, social work and disciplinary interventions by which they are constructed and regulated. This is the sense in which Donzelot speaks of familialisation: he uses the term to explain how an ideologically constructed family form is imposed and enforced. The thrust of his argument is that there has been a process of transition, from a family which represented a *form* of government to a family which has become an *instrument* of government.

If we are to hold to the sense in which McLaughlin and Glendinning use the terms, the argument might be that processes of commodification during the industrial revolution and of *de*familialisation during the birth of the welfare state fundamentally altered the basis of relations between families, markets and the state. From here, the conventional wisdom of functionalists (e.g. Parsons 1964) would argue that the family has become a specialised institution dedicated to the primary socialisation of children and the maintenance of adult personalities. Gittins' argument, however, is that a pervasive family ideology has perpetuated patriarchal relations of power within a variety of different family forms. Donzelot goes further: the refinement of the modern welfare state involved, not only the process Esping-Andersen would call *de*commodification, but a process which we could perhaps agree to call *re*familialisation, resulting in the exercise of new forms of power over human behaviour. The post-structuralist perspective provides the sense in which the ideology of the family is translated into discourses, practices and policies by which actual families may be fashioned, disciplined or constrained.

The pressing question is perhaps less historical than contemporary. How are we to apprehend the significance of community care policy in the 1990s? Claus Offe (1984), also drawing on Polanyi's work, has predicted that to overcome the inherent tendency to self-paralysis to which welfare state capitalism is subject, one of the strategies to which welfare state regimes might have recourse is that of 'administrative recommodification'. The term is one which Offe does not elaborate in great detail and appears to be associated in his own mind with the development of neo-corporativism, rather than the kind of new public management which has in fact characterised welfare state capitalism in the late 1980s and early 1990s. The term remains none the less evocative and apposite, associated as it is with Offe's attempts to theorise the emergence of a form of 'disorganised capitalism'. In so far that the shift to 'care in the community' has entailed the promotion of private care provision, quasi-markets and the so called new managerialism into the sphere of the personal social services (Lawson 1993), such policies can be said to involve a process of administrative *re*commodification. In so far as this has also entailed a shift towards informal caring, there has been a parallel process of *re*familialisation; a process by which the care of elderly and disabled people and people with mental health problems may be entrusted to family members. It is important, however, that this should be addressed, not in crude functionalist terms as the reinstatement of 'lost' functions, but very much as an ideological process.

Fetishism and dependency

If we are to examine 'the economy' (or, more particularly, 'the market') and 'the family' through a single lens, and if indeed we are to analyze them as ideological constructs rather than as functional institutions, then there is surely a place for Marx's notion of 'fetishism'. The term was originally applied by Marx (1887) to characterise the ideological distortions peculiar to capitalist social and economic relations. To Marx, the process by which surplus value is extracted from wage labour and by which the products of such labour are exchanged between supposedly autonomous subjects as commodities was truly extraordinary or 'fantastic'. Commodities become socialised, while social life became commodified. It was, he argued, only through fetishized or 'surface' categories and definitions that such phenomena could be made to appear perversely natural: our every day understanding of the 'value' of the goods we buy and of the nature of the 'work' we do is such as to conceal the exploitative nature of commodity production and the wage labour system.

It has been argued elsewhere (Dean and Taylor-Gooby 1992) that, in spite of the growth of the welfare state, our every day understanding of human inter-dependency remains similarly fetishized. Our dependency upon employers for the means of subsistence and/or upon families for material care and support are somehow conjured out of sight, or rather they are made to appear perversely as attributes of individual 'independence' rather than dependence. Dependency itself is thus regarded as unnatural, and dependency on the state for cash benefits tends to appear uniquely visible and especially problematic.

This paper will suggest that the concept of dependency fetishism may assist our understanding of commodification and familialisation. The emergence of the commodity form has tended to obscure the nature of the processes by which we are universally dependent upon the labour of others. The emergence of a particular family ideal has constructed a formally

149

separate 'domestic' sphere within which particular forms of labour and interdependency are hidden from view. The emergence of the welfare state as a regulator of labour power has rendered dependency on various forms of collective provision more or less permissible. Dependency on health and education services for example seems to be more popularly acceptable than dependency on social security. Markets, families and the state are established around a fetishized labour-dependency nexus, in which only certain kinds of labour are valued (and remunerated) and only certain kinds of dependency are acknowledged as legitimate.

The discovery of the 'informal carer'

The shaping of contemporary community care policy represents a significant shift in the labour-dependency nexus since it revolves around a particular form of labour (unpaid caring) and a particular form of dependency (that of elderly and/or disabled family members).

The growing 'burden' of dependency resulting in particular from population ageing, increasing longevity and the consequent increased incidence in chronic illness had been evident for some time, but the political impetus to change came only with the Thatcher governments of the 1980s (Walker 1989). 'Community care' was translated from an idea and a slogan into policies and a discourse. That discourse implied and has promoted an unprecedented notion of what family obligation might constitute. As Janet Finch has put it

> It is meaningless to ask whether people are less willing to look after their elderly relatives than in the past, when this particular family obligation was simply not put to the test for most people in previous generations (Finch 1989, p. 81).

While people may by and large care *about* their elderly relatives, the intention of policy is that increasingly they should also 'tend' or care *for* them (Parker 1981). In practice, of course, caring *about* a family member may lead to caring *for* that person but, as Hilary Graham puts it, this kind of caring '… is experienced as a labour of love in which the labour must continue even where the love falters' (Graham 1983, p. 16). In practice, unpaid caring is a form of labour whose participants may have no more freedom of choice than does a wage labourer with no alternative means of subsistence.

The informalisation or refamilialisation of care has entailed the discovery, even the invention, of the 'informal carer'. The term 'carer' would seem to be of rather recent provenance and to have been associated with a transition in the general usage of the word 'care'. Both 'care' and indeed 'love' are words which may be used as either a noun or a verb. Eric Fromm (1979), in his celebrated polemic about the difference between 'having' and 'being', suggests that the transition to modern industrial society is accompanied by idiomatic changes by which the use of nouns in everyday language increases and the use of verbs declines. In place of the activities and experiences expressed by verbs there emerge the reified abstractions denoted by nouns: instead of 'my head aches', we tend to say 'I have a headache'. In the 'mode of being', 'love' for example is something one does, whereas in the mode of having, it is something which one has or seeks, or by which indeed one is ruled. For Fromm this signals the inherent tendency under consumer capitalism for us to become alienated from our inner selves and feelings. The transition of 'care' from being a word predominantly used as a verb, to one used in a range of new circumstances as a noun, has probably been rather more recent than the trends which Fromm describes. We can none the less detect the sense in which 'care' as an object of policy alienates the actor from the activity and so gives birth to the 'carer' where once there was, for example, a son or (more usually) a daughter.

This was vividly illustrated by one of Clare Ungerson's research respondents, a middle-aged woman looking after both her aged parents, who remonstrated

> I'm a *daughter*, not a carer! ... To me you look after your mum and dad. A 'carer' seems to be anybody. I couldn't do this sort of thing for anybody. To me it's the family. I'm a *daughter*. It's family, isn't it? (Ungerson 1987, p. 92).

'Care' is a discursive construct susceptible to a variety of theoretical interpretations, but, analytically, it is still an empirical category (see Thomas 1993). Ungerson's respondent may have preferred to be defined as a daughter rather than a carer, but what is significant is the process of transition by which she has emerged as an object of scrutiny and by which what she does has become visible. What seems to be at stake is not a single process by which 'care' (the everyday verb) has become 'care' (the policy maker's new noun), but parallel processes of refamilialisation (the manipulation of family dependency as an instrument of policy) and administrative recommodification (the new managerialist approach to public services). It is argued in this paper that, at the level of discourse, these transitions are manifest in a shift from moral and political discourses concerning the nature of obligation and the patriarchal family, to fetishized technical discourses about the nature of normality and the informal carer. Ungerson's respondent is in one sense like a modern day Cordelia, bridling against her father's demand for a public demonstration of her love for him:

Unhappy that I am, I cannot heave
My heart into my mouth; I love your majesty
According to my bond; nor more nor less.
(William Shakespeare, *King Lear*, Act I, Scene 1)

Community care robs the parent-offspring bond of its social and moral character by making it a requirement or technical feature of state policy. Just as Marx argued that social goods are fetishized when they are pressed into service as commodities, so we might speak of family relationships being fetishized when they are pressed into service as 'informal care'.

New public management: the political discourse of administrative recommodification

The growth of a political 'doctrine' of new public management (NPM) arose in the 1980s. This was part of a transnational movement in public administration aimed at slowing down or reversing public spending trends and shifting responsibility away from 'core government institutions' (Hood 1991) towards the private or quasi-private sector. The implementation of this doctrine within the public welfare sector has meant a greater stress on private sector style of management practice, increased competition, a shift towards decentralisation and tighter, more efficient, control over the management of scarce resources.

The emerging discourse of NPM went hand-in-hand with the concept of welfare pluralism: an emphasis upon service provision within a mixed economy of care incorporating 'informal', voluntary and commercial sectors in addition to the statutory sector (see, for example, Johnson 1987). As a political concept, welfare pluralism could appeal to either the political Right or Left as it is anti-bureaucratic, anti-professional and concerned with decentralisation as well as participation. The Thatcher governments, however, endorsed welfare pluralism as a way of assisting in 'rolling back the state', promoting private enterprise and reducing public spending.

The discourse of welfare pluralism was absorbed into the developing doctrine of NPM in the course of various reviews of welfare and community care. The technocratic language of NPM was applied to community care by the 1986 Audit Commission's review *Making a Reality of Community Care* with its emphasis upon cost containment and value for money, and Sir Roy Griffiths' Report *Community Care: Agenda for Action* produced in 1988. Griffiths expounded a specific political and social construction of 'informal caring'. It was the recommendations of these reports which lay the foundations for the Government's 1989 White Paper and the 1990 NHS and Community Care Act. The influence of NPM and a particular construction of caring can clearly be seen in the language of the six key objectives of the White Paper:

- To promote the development of domiciliary, day and respite services to enable people to live in their own homes wherever feasible and sensible.

- To ensure that service providers make practical support for carers a high priority.
- To make proper assessment of need and good case management the cornerstone of high quality care.
- To promote the development of a flourishing independent sector alongside good quality public services.
- To clarify the responsibilities of agencies and so make it easier to hold them to account for their performance.
- To secure better value for taxpayers' money by introducing a new funding structure for social care. (DH 1989, p. 5)

A major change intended by these reforms is the transformation of local authorities into 'enablers' rather than the primary 'providers' of services. Local authorities are now required to promote and develop a flourishing mixed economy of care. They are also charged with the responsibility of ensuring 'consumer choice', for listening to the needs of their customers and tailoring services to meet these needs. This requirement for local authorities to become commissioners and purchasers of services as well as providers has sweeping implications for structural, organizational and managerial change.

Refamilialisation and informal carers: from morality to normality

Informal carers fulfil an essential role within the doctrine of NPM, particularly in the development of a mixed economy of care. The Thatcher government's view that economic growth rather than social policy was the aim of government entailed laying responsibility for 'welfare' strongly upon individuals and families. Johnson argued that 'the family is seen by Mrs Thatcher as an important element in her strategy for transforming British society...a shift from an interventionist state to a minimum state gives a central role to the family' (1987, p. 87). Webb and Wistow contend that the Thatcher government constructed a series of political myths surrounding the family, neighbours, charity and volunteering which were woven into the political dogma of the 1980s. These myths were based on the moral rhetoric of 'social obligation' which supposes that:

> people have become neglectful of their social obligations to kin and neighbours and that a vast reservoir of informal care can be tapped simply by enforcing these obligations; that 'genuinely voluntary' provision, staffed by volunteers and paid for by charitable giving, can be rekindled with little difficulty (Webb and Wistow 1987, p. 93).

'Informal carers' had become a target for a political discourse and the social construction of a moral imperative to care which concealed an underlying economic need by the government for informal carers to undertake this task. The intervention in what had primarily been a private arrangement within families and the attempt to translate the informal caring role into the public arena of the politicisation of welfare pluralism effectively negated choice and laid the burden of care on carers.

However, the impact of the merging of the concept of welfare pluralism into the developing political doctrine of NPM could, potentially, have tempered the Thatcherite 'moral imperative' through discourses based on 'consumer choice'. Griffiths approached his review of the way in which public funds were used to support community care policy from both a consumerist and managerialist perspective. His report (1988) stresses the key role informal carers provide in welfare provision, and acknowledges the need for government to support them in this role. It does not, however, address informal carers as potential consumers through offering alternative choices to caring. The report continues to encompass the Thatcherite moral imperative to care but conceals this, or masks it, through developing further a social and political construction of informal caring based on a concept of 'normality'.

People, the report argues, choose to be carers because this is the most rational, efficient and cost effective way of providing services. It is the normal thing to do. In this way informal caring is perceived as natural, common sense and as 'taken for granted':

> Families, friends and neighbours and other local people provide the majority of care in response to needs which they are uniquely well placed to identify and respond to. This will continue to be the primary means by which people are enabled to live normal lives in community settings. The proposals take as their starting point that this is as it

should be (Griffiths 1988, p. 5)

The contradictions within the doctrine of NPM become manifest when placed in the context of the role of informal carers. The economic and technocratic imperative of the doctrine demands that informal carers continue to bear the brunt of the material burden of caring. This is in order to maintain a reduction in public spending and create a shift away from public to private responsibility for welfare.

The construction of an ideology based on the concept of normality reinforces informal carers' roles within the mixed economy of care. However, informal carers are not just providers of services, they also need to be recognised as potential users of services, and this is where the question of putting the 'customer first' comes in to play. In order to meet the philosophy of the doctrine, informal carers as 'customers' should be able to choose whether or not to be 'carers' from a range of alternatives within the mixed economy of care. The contradictions within the doctrine mean that informal carers are faced with: the government's need for them to remain as carers in order to maintain cuts in public expenditure; difficulty of gaining access to services for themselves due to scarcity of financial and material resources; and potential conflict between their needs as carers and the needs of the person they are caring for.

Griffiths' statements also reflect the patriarchial and 'gender blind' nature of the social construction of the political discourse of NPM. His supposition that people will be enabled to live in the community through the support of families, friends and neighbours depends heavily on the constructed 'normality' of informal caring. The majority of such 'support' will undoubtedly be provided by women, who will consequently be economically and socially disadvantaged. This structuring of gender relations subordinates women and constructs and defines them within an androcentric concept of normality.

In the 1989 White Paper, which developed many of Griffiths' recommendations, informal carers have acquired even greater status within central government thinking, having been elevated to inclusion in the 'six key objectives' for implementing the community care legislation. The White Paper states:

> The Government acknowledges that the great bulk of community care is provided by friends, family and neighbours. The decision to take on a caring role is never an easy one. However, many people make that choice and it is right that they should be able to play their part in looking after those close to them. But it must be recognised that carers need help and support if they are to continue to carry out their role (DH

155

1989, p. 4).

The White Paper appears, at first sight, to take some account of the contradiction within the doctrine of NPM through its acknowledgement that people may 'choose' to become informal carers. However, the emphasis of the White Paper and the 1990 Act is upon the implementation of the reforms within existing scarce resources and, therefore, within the construct of the 'normality' of informal caring rather than promoting alternative choices for informal carers as customers.

The contradiction within the doctrine, therefore, remains unresolved. For informal carers, the fact that the government recognises and potentially acknowledges their need for practical support in their caring role undoubtedly represents an advance. It is not, however, an unqualified advance.

Community Care Plans: a study

An attempt has been made to explore the issues around NPM and 'informal' carers through a textual analysis of the 1992/93 and 1993/94 Community Care Plans published by a sample of thirty-four English and Welsh local authorities (for a full account see Thompson 1993). It is important to emphasise that findings from this exercise do not represent definitive statements of what local authorities are, or are not, doing. They can only act as markers of possible 'intent'; as discursive signals. Subject to this limitation, key aspects within the language of NPM were identified as indicators of local authorities' commitment to that doctrine. Six of these indicators were treated as components of a NPM 'Conformity' Index. A seventh indicator, relating to the claims which local authorities make with regard to the development of practical support for carers, was analyzed separately and used to generate a proposed 'Good Practice' Index.

The New Public Management 'Conformity' Index

Judged by the content of their Community Care Plans, the performance of local authorities against each component of the NPM 'Conformity' Index is described below, with the components appearing in rank order according to the frequency with which the claims made by local authorities 'conformed' in either their 1993/2 plan, their 1993/4 plan, or both.

1st Stimulating a 'mixed economy of care': (32 out of 34 authorities).
This criterion constitutes a central plank of NPM and represents recommodification in its purest form. The 1989 White Paper outlined specific ways in which a mixed economy of care might be promoted, including contracting and tendering arrangements, the stimulation of 'not for profit' agencies and voluntary sector activity, and the 'floating off' of self-managing units (DH 1989, para. 3.4.6). All but two of the local authorities studied endorsed a commitment to such objectives and, from the 1993/4 plans, the level of that endorsement appeared to be increasing.

2nd Undertaking consultation processes: (31 out of 34 authorities).
Consultation is an important concept within the doctrine of NPM, because it represents a form of accountability more in tune with commodified service provision than with democratically determined public services. On the question of consultation, however, there was a problem of definition. It is unclear from the plans when they refer to consultation with carers, carers' groups or carers' forums as to whether they are referring specifically to informal carers. The overwhelming majority of authorities indicated that they had, as they are required, established consultation 'forums'. However, some authorities may have established carers' forums which are attended by voluntary organisations and/or 'caring' professionals such as social workers, community nurses etc. These 'carers' may speak on behalf of informal carers, with or without their knowledge, but equally may be representing their own 'caring' needs/interests. All but three local authorities claimed to be developing consultation processes, but these findings remain ambiguous. It is unknown to what degree these consultation processes reach out to informal carers.

3rd Promoting 'choice' for individuals: (29 out of 34 authorities).
The emphasis on individual choice is symbolically significant because it presupposes the existence of commodified services within a mixed economy. The government states in the 1989 White Paper that 'promoting choice and independence underlies all the Government's proposals' (Paragraph 1.8). Most authorities claimed to be enhancing choice through the processes of needs assessment and individual care plans; through the use of flexible contracting arrangements; through the promotion of complaints procedures and information provision; and/or through advocacy projects and opportunities for individuals to have a 'voice' in the planning of services.

4th Introducing devolved budgets: (25 out of 34 authorities).
Although there is clearly a trend towards the new managerialist device of devolved budgeting, it is noticeable that the main budget holders (particularly where specified in later plans) were upper management within localised centres or specialised service teams. Very few authorities had delegated budgetary control to individual Care Managers.

5th Being an 'enabling authority': (24 out of 34 authorities).
Over two thirds of the local authorities expressly adopted NPM rhetoric by claiming to being an enabling authority.

6th Introducing a 'purchaser/provider' split: (18 out of 34 authorities).
The purchaser/provider split represents a sophisticated administrative device for recommodification and progress with this aspect of the NPM agenda seemed to be less well developed. Barely half the authorities claimed to be ready to implement the major organisational restructuring required.

Finally, compiling the different cumulative 'scores' which individual local authorities achieved against the six components of the NPM 'Conformity' Index produced the frequency table in Figure 8.1.

Figure 8.1 NPM 'Conformity' Index

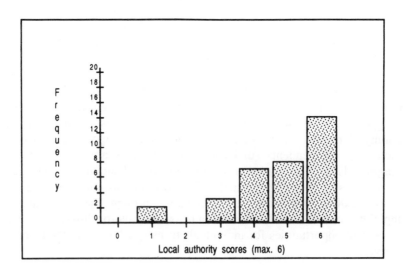

158

The 'Good Practice' Index

The other focus for the study related to practical support to informal carers. The object was to 'de-construct' the degree of commitment demonstrated in 1992/3 and 1993/4 plans towards supporting informal carers. To this end a proposed Index of 'Good Practice' was devised, based on eight separate indicators of commitment. Judged by the content of their Community Care Plans, the performance of local authorities against each indicator or component is described below, with the components appearing in rank order according to the frequency with which the claims of local authorities 'conformed' in either their 1992/3 plan, their 1993/4 plan, or both.

1st   Examples of specific support to carers: (32 out of 34 authorities).
All but two authorities gave examples of the ways in which they were providing specific practical support to informal carers. That support included delegated or increased funds for specific services (e.g. respite care); designated posts (e.g. support workers); the establishment of Carers' Forums, Panels, Units or Support Groups.

2nd   Carers involved in the assessment process for the cared-for person's needs: (30 out of 34 authorities), and

3rd equal Carers eligible for an independent assessment of their own needs if they wished: (28 out of 34 authorities).
These two components of the 'Good Practice' Index address the question of the needs-led assessment process in relation to carers. The 'proper assessment of need and good case management' is, according to the 1989 White Paper, 'the cornerstone of high quality care' and the Department of Health's Policy Guidance indicates that 'The preferences of carers should be taken into account and their willingness to continue caring should not be assumed...Carers who feel they need community services in their own right can ask for a separate assessment' (DH 1990, paras. 3.28 and 3.29). However, the contradiction within the doctrine of NPM here becomes apparent through the question of the eligibility criteria for services. In order to ensure the most effective use of limited resources the guidance also states that services should only be offered to those 'with the greatest needs' (*ibid*, para. 1.10). This rationing of services is dealt with through local arrangements for determining appropriate eligibility criteria and, therefore, restricts the degree of choice open to both users and carers. Although local authorities did not always indicate their eligibility criteria in their plans, it must be assumed that the commitments they made apply

only to carers of those users who have met eligibility criteria.

4th equal Carers included in joint working, joint planning, or other initiatives: (28 out of 34 authorities).
Where such claims were made it was difficult to ascertain whether carers were involved in the formal joint planning processes or simply informal joint working arrangements. It was also difficult to ascertain the precise role of 'forums' when these were mentioned. It was unclear whether they were primarily self-help forums or open forums with the opportunity of commenting to statutory authority personnel. Only a minority of authorities mentioned more practical forms of joint involvement, through training or advocacy, for example.

5th Distinction drawn between users of services and informal carers: (26 out of 34 authorities).
Most but not all authorities recognised that, in the provision of services and arrangements for consultation, service users and informal carers should be treated as separate categories.

6th Central commitment to supporting carers: (24 out of 34 authorities).
This component or indicator was concerned to distinguish whether plans exhibited a central or a peripheral focus on supporting carers. Over two-thirds of authorities were adjudged to have demonstrated a central commitment by fulfilling at least three out of the following five criteria of 'centrality':
- was there a separate section on supporting carers within the plan?
- were carers' needs included within the client group sections of the plans?
- were carers included in joint planning/joint working initiatives?
- were carers' needs included in general Statements of Principles?
- were there specific targets within the plans for implementing proposals for supporting carers?

7th Acknowledgement there may be tensions between carers' needs and users' needs: (16 out of 34 authorities).
Only a minority of local authorities were openly accommodating the likelihood of such tensions. This may reflect the sense in which informal carers are primarily seen as service providers rather than as 'customers' in their own right.

8th Acknowledgement of a need to develop 'expertise' on how to work with carers: (3 out of 34 authorities).

Very few local authorities were prepared to acknowledge an initial lack of expertise on how to work with carers and to address this, for example, through contacting and working with national organisations responsible for representing carers' needs.

Compiling the different cumulative 'scores' which individual local authorities achieved against the eight components of the Proposed 'Good Practice' Index produced the frequency table in Figure 8.2. Under the 'Good Practice' Index there were twenty-one local authorities' (nearly two-thirds of the plans studied) which recorded positive scores of between 6 and 8, and, therefore, could be regarded as examples of 'Good Practice' in meeting the key objective of the 1990 White Paper; namely, 'to ensure that service providers make practical support for carers a high priority'. The pace at which local authorities are implementing change is variable however and individual authorities are identifying differing scales of local priorities and needs. Taking these findings as a whole, it is clear that, at the level of public pronouncements of intent, local authorities still had a long way to go in recognising and acknowledging that the interests of users and carers may conflict.

Figure 8.2 'Good Practice' Index

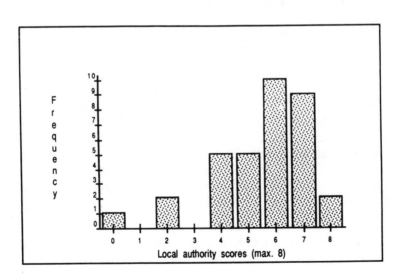

161

Conclusions from the study

The language of the plans studied in this analysis tends to conform to the doctrine of NPM by indicating greater technocratic and managerial reform; a degree of decentralisation and accountability and proposed mechanisms for the transfer of service responsibility. The proposals to transfer responsibility from the state to the 'independent' sector within the developing mixed economy of care appear to have included a substantial acknowledgement of the need to provide practical support to carers so as to enable them to continue in their role as service providers. The difficulty for carers comes, however, with the question of access to services, and therefore the degree to which choice is curtailed. For instance, although over two-thirds of the plans state that carers are involved in the assessment process for the person they are caring for, as well as being eligible for an independent assessment of their own if requested, it is difficult to judge how this fits in with the rationing of services to those in greatest need. The contradictions within the discourses on 'choice' and availability of services are consistent with the conflicts within NPM: namely the question of finance taking precedence over choice. The plans give little credence to the language of 'alternative choices' for informal carers.

This lack of 'real choice' for carers has been highlighted in a recent research project conducted by the Carers National Association (CNA 1992) where nearly 3,000 carers responded to the survey. In a section entitled 'Choice in Becoming a Carer' the report states:

> Virtually no respondent indicated that they had felt there was any real choice about taking on their caring role. Their explanations fell into three roughly equal groups: duty, family relationship and lack of alternative. (CNA 1992, p. 36)

Although the CNA's survey was conducted before the full implementation of the 1990 Act, the language contained within the community care plans we have studied does not indicate any significant shift in emphasis in providing an alternative choice to becoming a carer. A study commissioned by the SSI and conducted by the Nuffield Institute, Leeds University, on a preliminary analysis of a sample of English 1992/3 Community Care Plans has found

> It is quite clear that on this issue [support for carers] authorities across the sample have not only acknowledged the importance of providing support for carers and in most cases have clear plans for doing so. (Nuffield 1993, p. 24)

This finding in no way conflicts with that from our study, but the issue which remains outstanding is the question of how far in practice choice is circumscribed and curtailed in spite of the rhetoric of NPM. We have argued that the doctrine positively engages with, and supports, informal carers through a technocratic view of welfare based on the supposed 'normality' of their role as 'service providers' offering value for money, efficiency and effectiveness within the sphere of private enterprise. However, the construction of a 'normality' principle effectively collapses the question of choice for informal carers to one position only, namely that of choosing 'to care'. To attempt to choose not to care would not only go against the moral notions of love, duty and responsibility but would also place an individual outside the hegemonic definitions, as expressed in the Griffiths Report, of 'the natural, cost effective and as it should be', normality of welfare relations established by the doctrine of NPM.

What our study does suggest is that, in part at least, the community care reforms and the attention now focused on informal carers are intelligible in terms of parallel processes of administrative recommodification and a fetishizing process of refamilialisation. The shift in the welfare mix which has been driven by NPM has involved a refashioning of what we earlier referred to as the labour-dependency nexus. Certain services have been recommodified by a process that is regulated through the state. Other services have not been recommodified so much as refamilialised. Care within families has assumed the fantastic form, not of a marketable commodity which people may choose to sell or but, to give or receive, but of an 'informal service'. Its moral character has been transfigured by a new administratively constructed 'normality'.

References

Audit Commission (1986), *Making a Reality of Community Care : A report*, HMSO, London.
Carers National Association (1992), *Speak Up, Speak Out*, CNA, London.
Dean, H. and Taylor-Gooby, P. (1992), *Dependency Culture: the Explosion of a Myth*, Harvester Wheatsheaf, Hemel Hempstead.
Department of Health (1989), *Caring for People*, Cm.849, HMSO, London.
Department of Health (1990), *Caring for People: Policy Guidance*, HMSO, London.
Donzelot, J. (1979), *Policing the Family*, Hutchinson, London.
Esping-Andersen, G. (1990), *The Three Worlds of Welfare Capitalism*,

Polity, Cambridge.

Finch, J. (1989), *Family Obligations and Social Change*, Polity, Cambridge.

Finch, J. (1990), 'The Politics of Community Care in Britain' in Ungerson, Clare (ed.), *Gender and Caring*, Harvester Wheatsheaf, Hemel Hempstead.

Fromm, E. (1979), *To Have or to Be*, Abacus, London.

Gittins, D. (1993), *The Family in Question*, second edition, Macmillan, Basingstoke.

Glendinning, C. (1992), '"Community Care": the Financial Consequences for Women' in Glendinning, C. and Millar, J., *Women and Poverty in Britain: the 1990s*, Harvester Wheatsheaf, Hemel Hempstead.

Graham, H. (1983), 'Caring: a labour of love' in Finch, J. and Groves, D. (eds.), *A Labour of Love: Women, Work and Caring*, Routledge & Kegan Paul, London.

Griffiths, Sir Roy (1988), *Community Care: Agenda for Action*, A report to the Secretary of State for Social Services, HMSO, London.

Hood, C. (1991), 'A public management for all seasons?', *Public Administration*, Vol. 69, No. 1.

Johnson, N. (1987), *The Welfare State in Transition*, Wheatsheaf, Brighton.

Jordan, B. (1987), *Rethinking Welfare*, Blackwell, Oxford.

Langan, M. and Ostner, I. (1991), 'Gender and Welfare: Towards a Comparative Framework' in Room, G. (ed.), *Towards a European Welfare State*, SAUS, Bristol.

Lawson, R. (1993), 'The New Technology of Management in the Personal Social Services' in Taylor-Gooby, P. and Lawson, R. (eds.), *Markets and Managers: New Issues in the Delivery of Welfare*, Open University Press, Buckingham.

Lown, J. (1983), 'Not so much a Factory, More a Form of Patriarchy: Gender and Class during Industrialisation' in Gamarnikow, E. et al (eds.), *Gender, Class and Work*, Heinemann, London.

Marx, K. (1887), *Capital*, vol.1, 1970 edition, Lawrence & Wishart, London.

McLaughlin, E. and Glendinning, C. (1993), 'Hypertension and Hypotheses: Conflicting Perspectives on "Paying for Care"', paper presented to *Social Policy Association* Annual Conference, Liverpool, 15 July - an amended version of which appears as 'Paying for Care in Europe: Is there a feminist approach?' in Hantrais, L. and Mangen, S. (eds.) (1994), *Concepts and Contexts in International Comparisons: Family Policy and the Welfare of Women*, Cross-National Research Papers, Series 3, No. 3, Centre for European Studies, University of

Loughborough.

Nuffield Institute (1993), *Caring for People: Implementing Community Care. A Preliminary Analysis of a Sample of English Community Care Plans*, Nuffield Institute, Health Services Studies, University of Leeds, DH/SSI, London.

Offe, C. (1984), *Contradictions of the Welfare State*, MIT Press, Cambridge, Mass.

Offe, C. (1985), *Disorganised Capitalism*, Polity, Cambridge.

Parker, R. (1981), 'Tending and Social Policy' in Goldberg, E. and Hatch, S. (eds.), *A New Look at the Personal Social Services*, Policy Studies Institute, London.

Parsons, T. (1964), *The Social System*, Routledge & Kegan Paul, London.

Polanyi, K. (1944), *The Great Transformation*, Rinehart, New York.

Thatcher, M. (1981), *Welfare and the Family*, speech to WRVS, 19 January.

Thatcher, M. (1988), Interview, *Sunday Times*, 9 November.

Thomas, C. (1993), 'Deconstructing concepts of care', *Sociology*, Vol. 27 No. 4.

Thompson, D. (1993), 'New Public Management and Informal Carers', unpublished, University of Luton.

Ungerson, C. (1987), *Policy is Personal: Sex, Gender and Informal Care*, Tavistock, London.

Walker, A. (1989), 'Community Care' in McCarthy, M. (ed.), *The New Politics of Welfare*, Macmillan, Basingstoke.

Webb, A. and Wistow, G. (1987), *Social Work, Social Care and Social Planning: The Personal Social Services Since Seebohm*, Longman, Harlow.

Wilson, E. (1982), 'Women, the "Community" and the "Family"' in Walker, A. (ed.), *Community Care*, Basil Blackwell/Martin Robertson, Oxford.

9 Money, care and consumption: Families in the new mixed economy of social care

John Baldock and Clare Ungerson

Background: the 'new community care'

There is a continuing debate about how far the more than a decade and a half of Conservative government from 1979 has changed the welfare state in Britain. Some argue that the essential achievement has been no more than to contain the inherent tendency to expenditure growth (albeit in a sometimes sharply ideological way) and that the core welfare guarantees remain in place: social security, education and health care. Others, while recognizing that public expenditure on welfare remains as high a proportion of the national product as when the Tories came to government, focus on qualitative changes in the way welfare is produced, delivered and consumed. Those who argue from this point of view have tended to concentrate on organisational matters, the structures and rules which govern the implementation of social policy (Taylor-Gooby and Lawson 1993), but the eventual thrust of their argument is that the experience of receiving and using welfare services and benefits has changed in a fundamental way. This chapter explores the degree to which this may be true in one area of social policy: the delivery of care services to elderly and physically dependent adults in the context of what has been called 'the new community care'.

The new community care in Britain marks a radical shift from the past. It is widely accepted that the implementation in England and Wales of those sections of the National Health Service and Community Care Act 1990 which deal with the support of adults in the community will require that 'a revolution take place over the next decade in the way social services operate' (Audit Commission 1992: 1). The nature of this revolution is not merely administrative and organisational: in addition 'changing from the traditional role requires a cultural revolution...major changes in attitude are needed' (ibid: 19). Central government recognition of the scale of the changes required of the public services in evidenced by the quite unprecedented level of support provided to local authority social services departments by the Department of Health, the Social Services Inspectorate and the Audit Commission in the form of publications, letters of guidance and collaborative training and monitoring exercises.

However, it may not just be the services that will have to adapt but also those who use and consume them. Indeed, as the Audit Commission itself points out, 'the new approach to community care focuses on the service user, not the service' (1992, para 1). The spirit of the reforms is explicitly consumerist : users will be empowered, they will be able to express their needs, they will exercise choice, suppliers will compete to obtain their custom in a 'mixed economy of care' (Cm 849 1989, section 3.4). Yet relatively little attention has been paid to whether the public are likely to find the new community care system acceptable and useable and to investigating how far they may have to change their expectations and behaviour in order to benefit from the new arrangements. Despite the rhetoric of consumerism we know little of what might be called the consumer response to the new community care product.

The study and its findings

We followed a small sample of 32 people who had suffered a stroke and then recovered sufficiently to be discharged from hospital and return to their homes. Over the next six months we observed two broad outcomes that this chapter seeks to explain.

i)   Despite considerable advice and 'care management', the vast majority of our sample experienced great difficulty in adjusting to and accepting the help that constituted their 'care in the community'. We attempt to explain this in terms of what we call the 'conditions of consumption' of community care.

ii) At the end of the six months we observed a variety of patterns of consumption of community care services amongst our sample that could not be explained simply in terms of their objective need, their incomes or even their class. We seek to explain this in terms of a model of four types of welfare consumerism which influence how people use community care services.

168

The study was based upon a consecutive sample of stroke victims who, after a period of rehabilitative treatment in hospital, were discharged into the 'community' rather than into residential care. Stroke victims were chosen for the specific reasons that their dependency tends to be of sudden onset, and therefore they and their families are abruptly introduced to the problems of organizing and providing care, and because the degree of dependency can change quite quickly within the first six months, leading in some cases to a need to change care arrangements. Almost all this sample had been discharged from a specialist stroke unit, catering for patients over 60 years old, located in East Kent. A more detailed account of the sample and methodology can be found in Baltic and Ungerson (1994b).

The findings were a surprise to us. We had chosen this sample because we delivered that they would have been very clearly and deliberately exposed to the workings of the 'new community care' and particularly to the need to find their help from within a more 'mixed economy of care'. We were therefore rather bemused when the bulk of them made no mention of any assessment or care management process and when we observed them, over the six months, for the most part appearing to have considerable difficulty in finding their way through the choices they had to make. We had expected these to be care consumers under a spotlight; instead they appeared to be blundering about in the dark.

Amongst the choices or decisions that some people appeared to find difficult, at least initially, were: paying independent professionals such as physiotherapists; buying private home help; asking family, friends and neighbours for assistance; paying neighbours and friends; paying members of their own families; joining voluntary groups and taking advantage of voluntary services such as speech therapy. In a more general sense people in our sample sometimes found it hard to grasp or to accept that unless they initiated the use of some of these options nothing else would happen. For some their inaction was explained by a form of resignation or fatalism but for others apathy was not the problem but rather uncertainty or fear that these sorts of consumption decisions would in some sense be unwise, inappropriate or risky.

Amongst the choices made more readily and frequently were: paying for and arranging forms of transport; paying for alterations and extra equipment for their homes (extensions, alterations, stair lifts); paying for help in the garden; negotiating those parts of free NHS services that they wanted and avoiding those they did not. In these cases our samples were less surprised that they needed to act and make choices, in other words they expected to behave as consumers.

Most of the difficulties had to do with making payments to others and this respect a certain reluctance might be thought to be rather inevitable. However, payment itself was rarely the problem. People in the sample were ready to change their spending patterns. The shock of a stroke is deep; the impact on daily household routines is substantial when people return home to find they can no longer do many of the ordinary things (dress, bathe, drive, talk) that they hitherto had done without a thought. In the face of this trauma people were ready to make big adjustments to their spending patterns and to draw on long held savings. In a number of cases they made substantial, and possibly unwise, expenditure decisions almost as reflex action. There difficulties did not lie in an unwillingness to spend money.

None the less our sample was not, with the odd exception, a prosperous one. Retirement, for this generation at least, is a great leveller. Out of 32 households, while 28 owned their home, only 6 appeared to have net incomes over £150 a week (June 1991 to December 1992) and 12 couples lived on no more than the basic retirement pension and disability allowances. Yet, by the end of the six months, a shift of expenditure of the order of £30 a week in order to meet some of their new care needs was not uncommon amongst even those on the lowest incomes. The obstacles to payment for care were rarely explained to us in terms of poverty, rather they had to do with issues of habit, appropriateness and principle. It is these issues we explore in the rest of this chapter.

The sociology of consumption

The developing sociology of consumption owes its origins to questions that initially arose in other arenas of empirical and theoretical investigation: from studies of stratification, of political action and voting behaviour, of social and psychological motivation, of the evolution of cultural forms (Dunleavy 1980, Saunders 1984, 1986, Cross 1993, Miller 1987). To a large extent we, in seeking to understand our data, have stumbled across consumption theory for parallel reasons: from a welfare perspective we were searching for an explanation as to why so many of our sample found the consumption of care so difficult to arrange and to benefit from. There is a bewildering variety of theory to choose from. Moreover it is clear that the sociology of consumption no longer serves only to answer questions from outside itself. It has become sufficient unto itself; that is to say further theoretical and descriptive elaboration are pursued for their own intrinsic value and not necessarily to answer questions from beyond its

170

boundaries.

A large part of this elaboration involves unpacking the capacious idea of consumption itself and classifying its variety of forms, contexts and meanings. Many of these developments have obvious relevance to understanding the consumption of care and suggest illuminating ways explaining the processes by which care is received by people. Any selection we make of from the growing literature is somewhat arbitrary. However, what is obvious is that care is a particularly complex good. It is liable to exhibit qualities and demonstrates processes from right across the sociology of consumption. Unlike other more simple goods it does not fit neatly into one part of the field or another.

It is notable, for example, that the consumption of care exhibits many of the features of the consumption of food and that food is often chosen to exhibit the complexity of processes of consumption. Like food, care (for those who depend on to get through the day) is basic survival itself. It can be a necessity rather than an option. It is similarly charged with meaning and emotion. It is consumed in contexts which can be raw, brutal and demeaning (*viz* the poor house and its many institutional variants); while at other times, like food, care may serve as a luxurious or even religious celebration of love and commitment.

Warde (1990), for example, has suggested, that for completeness, any account of consumption should consider at least four discrete elements in the process and he illustrates these largely by referring to food. The distinctions serve as well in a consideration of the consumption of care. They might be called 'the conditions of consumption'.

The conditions of consumption

i) The process of production and provision. Food, and similarly care, may be supplied for profit (and therefore be likely to exhibit degrees of systematization, routinization and bureaucratization), be produced within the household or be supplied directly or indirectly by the state.

ii) the conditions of access. Warde is still writing of food but the argument applies even more aptly to the provision of care services: 'The criteria of access to goods and services provided in...different sectors are analytically distinct: purchasing (food/care), availing myself of the labour of another household member and being in receipt of state-provided service entail diverse relations of access. Typically these three kinds of provisioning are governed, respectively, by the relations of market exchange, familial obligation and citizenship right. It is because services are produced under distinctive conditions and access to them is regulated accordingly, with subsequent consequences for their enjoyment, that the shifting of service between sectors - from the state to the market sector, from the state to the household, or out of the household - is so important politically' (pp. 4-5).

iii) the manner of delivery. The service offered by different providers (private, for-profit suppliers, family members, or public sector employers) will vary in style, manner and perceived meaning and these differences become differences in the quality of the good itself.

iv) the social environment of enjoyments. 'The social environment in which final consumption takes place (for example in the presence of strangers, or family or professionals) is an integral part of the experience but cannot be directly attributed to any other of the processes involved' (p. 4).

Part of the point is that some goods, indeed most goods, occupy a relatively stable and simple position in each Warde's 'elements in the process of consumption'. Take for example a highly standardized good like petrol: process of provision = sold by commercial suppliers; conditions of access = monetary payment; manner of delivery = little variation in petrol station forecourts (even self-service is almost universal); environment of enjoyment = on public roads in a motor car (there is perhaps some room for variation depending on the quality of your car and who you choose to travel with).

This is very much the pattern in a developed market economy such as Britain. We know the conditions of consumption and they remain relatively fixed and simple. Even quite complex goods are consumed under routinized and well-understood conditions. For example medical care, after nearly half a century of the national health service, is consumed under highly predictable conditions for most people: there is the GP and the local hospital and not much else in most people's experience (Busfield 1990, Flynn 1992, pp. 174-5).

Then, as we have already said, there are other goods like food where the conditions of consumption are much more varied and complex (art, sex and alcohol are other commonly considered examples). It is these goods that are generally of more interest to the sociologists of consumption for they are interested in the social significance and cultural loading that comes with the variety. However, even in these more complex cases the conditions of consumption tend to be relatively stable and fixed; they are just more varied and therefore take longer to learn and offer more choice for personal and social differentiation.

The more difficult cases occur when the conditions of consumption are both complex *and in flux* and this would seem to be true in the case of social care. For a variety of reasons the consumption of care is undergoing a period of uncertainty and change. The forces behind the change are many: government policy is only one and it is itself a response to many of the others - demographic change, the restructuring of family relationships, greater longevity and the growth of chronic dependence in old age (including that due to mental frailty such as Alzheimer's disease), labour market changes (particularly those affecting women), better housing and a preference for homecare. All these factors are forcing changes in the conditions of consumption of care for old people. Again the patterns of change can be considered in terms of Warde's four divisions:

The uncertain conditions of consumption of care in the community

i) the process of production and provision. Except for three particularly well informed households in our sample, our stroke sufferers and their family carers all expressed themselves thoroughly confused about who was responsible for producing what care and in which manner. Where they had expected help from their GP it was not forthcoming; where they expected direct assistance from social services they received instead enabling advice followed by approaches from commercial service providers the existence of whom they had never even imagined. Even the day hospital, one of the more fixed beacons in this sea of change, operated in ways that surprised them. Only slowly did they begin to grasp the importance that private and voluntary assistance would have to play in their care.

In essence, they faced new confusions added to existing complexities. While the goal of the Conservative government's community care reforms is frequently described as seeking to create a mixed-economy of social care, even the key policy documents admit that the support of dependent people is already and always has been very varied (Cm 849 1989, Audit Commission 1992, Griffiths 1988). A more complete description is to recognize that the new policies seek to reorder the already complex process of production and provision, replacing direct supply by the state with delegated and contracted-out services and substituting tax-financed entitlements with for-fee and for-profit provision. However, the shift to the new pattern is not distinct and well-focused. Rather, as we have already

173

pointed out, the method of reform is not to establish a new but sharply defined set of responsibilities (as for example is happening in Germany and the Netherlands where the debate about care reform is precisely about the strict allocation of roles between state, private and voluntary sectors and the family) but simply to create a set of financial and regulatory conditions which will allow a different mixed economy of care to emerge.

Thus, for the moment, there is great uncertainty amongst care producers as to their roles in the new system and that uncertainty is to a large degree planned and deliberate. The reports of the new community care that are currently emerging from research evaluations (Lewis et al. 1995, Pahl 1994) and in the professional press (Community Care 1994) document this confusion amongst service providers. What we discovered was an equal and parallel level of confusion amongst the current consumers of social care.

ii) the conditions of access. One of the paradoxes of the new community care is that it is tending to substitute one form of citizenship, that built round a liberal conception of choice, in place of the established, more collectivist, entitlement to social services (Baldock and Evers 1991, Offe 1987). The justification is that some of the implicit state guarantees of the past (to publicly-provided home help, to longstay beds, to local authority residential homes) are simply no longer deliverable in the face of growing demand and costs. The new community care is monetizing the conditions of access in many areas: by obliging local authorities to contract out 85% of their new social care budgets; by substituting payment for care allowances for the direct provision of services; by making the assessment of total social network support the key local authority function; and by means-testing most of the public out of entitlement to state-funded provision. The result is that access to social care is less built around a core of entitlements to state provision. Instead state provision has become a residual, fallback option once services accessed through payment, family obligation, neighbourly reciprocity and charity have been exhausted. The fundamental rules of access have been quietly and fundamentally changed.

This was a deep source of confusion for the people in our sample. They would often say to us like 'Well we thought we'd at least be entitled to an hour a week' or 'We never expected them to stop the physio right away' or 'I kept expecting social services would come round and sort it all out, but there was never a peep out of them'. The fundamental rules of access and the hierarchy of entitlement that they had internalized through a lifetime as citizens of the British welfare state had, from their point of view, suddenly been turned upside down. You could not start with what the state offered and then supplement it with family and private resources, rather you discovered that state assistance was secondary and contingent upon what you found for yourself. This basic confusion over the fundamental rules of access and entitlement may account for the degree of incomprehension and even non-recognition between the care-managers and members of our sample. The care-managers, having come through to a barrage of retraining and organisational change over the last few years, had internalized the new rules and assumptions. Our elderly stroke sufferers and their spouses knew nothing of these changes. The two sides were simply not talking the same language.

Professionals were not reported to have raised the issue of private expenditure in an explicit and systematic way. Public physiotherapists do not appear to discuss adding on more intensive private provision to the very limited time they tend to ration out to the patients. Social workers mights mention a private home-care agency or even pass on the name of the patient but not make it clear that they had done so. We came across no evidence that they had spent time discussing in detail the difficulties our sample had in dealing with the private sector: where private help could be obtained, how to negotiate over price and provision, how to establish the appropriate price with neighbours and friends who did odd jobs or who had been drawn into providing regular help. Similarly, doctors might say in passing 'Oh you could get that privately but it will cost a bit' but seemed reluctant to get into any specific and helpful detail. Our respondents tended to try to use our interviews with them as a way of exploring the difficulties they had encountered in becoming private care consumers. They would clearly have liked the interviewer to approve or comment on the solutions, in terms of source and price, that they had often struggled to reach: was this a good way to compensate a neighbour, had they been right to make such a request, would such a decision be disapproved of by the social workers or the day hospital?

iii) the manner of delivery. The people in our sample found the manner of delivery of many of the services they began to use in their homes, or which it was suggested they should use, somewhat disturbing and uncomfortable. They were not sure what to expect, often disliked the way things were done and were uncertain to what extent their worries or reservations were legitimate.

One reason was that they had become accustomed to the manners of the national health service. Most of our sample of stroke sufferers had been inpatients in the stroke unit of the local for many weeks. They had grown used to the slightly bossy but all-encompassing and reassuring care that entailed. To an extent they had become institutionalized. They were not used to exercising choice about the care they received. Also, because they were in hospital, they tended to attribute a degree of medical legitimacy to the mainly social and emotional care they received in the stroke unit.

Going home was looked forward to but deeply disturbing when it happened. When we interviewed our sample a week after they had arrived back home many expressed a feeling of desertion. The care they then began to be offered was not delivered in the manner of the NHS hospital they were used to. The closest in style was the day hospital some were attending. They felt comfortable there, though, after a few weeks most of them began to express concern about the fact that a day at the day hospital involved very little time actually getting treatment (such as physiotherapy) or seeing a doctor.

What most surprised people was the commercial manner of some of the community services they were introduced to. Some felt they had been given the 'hard sell' by local home help businesses put in touch with them by social services. Others found what the private suppliers offered rather limited: 'She offered shopping for food and that sort of thing. And I said well it was kind of her, but it didn't seem to me to be necessary put like that'. Others felt unwilling to trust the private sector: 'I'm sure you feel that with a government sponsored person there must be some integrity. They don't employ people without vetting them to some extent'. It took time for many of them to adjust to commercial relationships as ways of meeting needs that they had come to see as an area of public sector responsibility. In the end, however, most of our sample did make the necessary adjustments to a more commercial manner of delivery.

People had similar difficulties initially with voluntary sector provision, a source which, after six months, more were finding an essential part of their care. At the voluntary Stroke Association's speech therapy groups for example, the casualness about whether you came or not and who was in charge worried some; so did the unexpected mixture of paying for some things (lunch and transport) but not for others. These were not minor or marginal issues for people in our sample. Their strokes had made them feel vulnerable; the care they needed was fundamental to the quality of their lives, it was very personal and touched closely upon their sense of autonomy and identity.

Some care products have made the transition to being legitimate objects of independent consumerism. We came across frequent consideration of whether to buy a chair lift. This is product has apparently legitimated itself as a private purchase through many years of advertising in home consumer magazines. It also has many of the other characteristics that assist a care product gain acceptance as a private purchase: it is fitted to the house and not the person and so does not require the hands-on contact that people believe should be the province of professionals; it can be used in private rather than in public (unlike an electric wheelchair for example), it is large, technical and contains manifest value (unlike some other aids for the disabled that look rather crude, home-made and poor value and unlike services such as physio- or speech-therapy where the value and skill involved is hard for people to grasp let alone agree to pay for).

iv) the social environment of enjoyment. Most of the care consumed by our sample was consumed in their own homes, much of it in territory that had hitherto been private; in their bedrooms and their bathrooms. Here there were a whole series of complex adjustments to be made. Whether it was with spouse, or child, neighbour or professional home carer, in every case subtle and difficult adjustments to established social relationships were necessary.

('I feel like a baby' said one distressed woman, and later her husband/carer echoed the sentiment: 'It's not the same. She's my wife but I have to do everything for her.' Another woman commented on the change involved in having to ask her fifteen year old nephew to help her in the toilet).

Care comes into that class of goods that have the quality of having to be 'enjoyed' at the point of production - you cannot take it home with you and consume it privately. This, together with fact that without the care you may be quite stranded and helpless, means that the consumption of care can be a 'public' enactment of a dependent relationship. This is partly why professional rather than simple commercial suppliers are thought to be more appropriate in the provision of personal social services. It is also why many people prefer care to come from non-family sources (Wenger 1984). The disability rights literature describes routes round this problem of dependent social relations in care (Morris 1993). In this literature commercial relationships are actually seen as a solution rather than a problem because they permit control and autonomy by making disabled people the employers of their assistants. But that is an approach to consumption relations that takes time to learn and was not one that our newly dependent sample had had time to reach.

At first our stroke sufferers wished to avoid the cost of these adjustments and based a lot on their hopes of recovery and assumed much was temporary. Some did regain their full independence, but most had to make the difficult journey to the acceptance of new kinds of consumption in a place, their home, which in the past had been a haven of entirely voluntary and pleasant choices.

Different people, different journeys to care

In our interviews, the stroke survivors and their carers describe in great detail and in their own terms the journeys they made in the first six months after they left hospital. Some of these journeys ranged quite widely across the map of care, others did not move far at all. They had very varied starting points; some began on their own with little support while others were at the centre of a household rich in caring resources. Similarly the journeys had varied end points; even when their needs appeared to an outsider to be relatively similar, people were dealing with them in quite different ways at the end of the six months.

Implicit in the new community care policy is that people's experience of exercising choice throughout their adult lives will be a resource in reaching solutions. They will be able to use their family and kinship network, their links with friends and neighbours, their experience of acting as consumers and shoppers in the market and their understanding of the public services in order to assert their needs and their preferences. Where they are uncertain the implication is that it will be in connection with practical information about what is available and from where. They will then be able to use their accumulated skills as consumers in the market and as users of public services in order to make the care system work for them. In fact our research appears to show that our respondents' accumulated skills and understandings of the way things work operated as obstacles to, rather than facilitators of, their new roles as consumers in the mixed economy of care.

What emerged from our interviews was confirmation that what people are prepared to buy or use is not a simple function of wants and an ability to pay. Advertisers have long been aware that the decision to make a purchase is determined by a very complex cocktail of habit, knowledge, values and, perhaps most important of all, largely 'irrational' emotional responses. We found that there were similar cultural and emotional obstacles to effective participation in a care market. Even where people knew of services or products, needed them and could afford them they still found the prospect of buying them uncomfortable or inappropriate in some way. These, what might be called loosely, cultural and psychological blocks to the full flowering of a care market are complex and difficult to capture. People do not so much explain them, they are largely unaware of them, as demonstrate them in their behaviour; in the choices they make and, often more importantly, in those they do not. A qualitative survey such as this is probably the only way to begin to tease out these behavioural phenomena but it remains an inexact process. What is offered below is an interpretation of what people told us they had done and not done.

'Habits of the Heart': the values that inform the search for social care

So far in this chapter we have treated the members of our sample as a single group, suggesting that they all share, if in differing degrees of intensity, the same kinds of emotional distress and patterns of consumer behaviour. In this section we will try to incorporate into our account the considerable variety in outlook and expectations that also characterized our sample.

By the end of the period each family had, in each case, to some extent established care régimes that fitted with their expectations about what was right and possible, that were consonant with their pre-existing scripts about how life is lived. They had also, in a variety of ways and to varying degrees, learnt and adapted to new ways of living their lives. As we hope we have shown, these were difficult lessons, or scripts, to learn and required, for some more than others, difficult adjustments. They had had to learn to do things that went 'against the grain' rather than with it.

How are we to characterize the varieties of 'script' according to which people reached decisions (or non-decisions) about how they would live with their new disabilities? We are not seeking to explicate their ideological commitments, such as support for freedom or justice, opposition to poverty or racial discrimination, but rather what sociologists have called 'norms' and intermediate values' which drive choice in their everyday lives. Here we would suggest the use of a term first used by Alexis de Tocqueville in his early nineteenth century study of America. He drew attention to what he termed the mores ('moeurs') of daily life. He characterized these as:

> Habits of the heart; notions, opinions and ideas that shape mental habits; the sum of moral and intellectual dispositions of people in society; not only ideas and opinions but habitual practices with respect to such things as religion, political participation and economic life. (Bellah et al. 1988, p. 37)

In a recent and very influential study of the culture and character of American life, a group of sociologists has built upon this idea to construct a typology of 'habits of the heart' (Bellah et al. 1988). Here we attempt to use the same approach to capture the variety of behaviour in the care

179

market amongst our sample.

Figure 9.1, 'Habits of the heart' describes the distinctions we wish to draw. It positions people along two axes. The horizontal axis describes the degree to which the stroke survivors and their carers expected their care to be provided from their own resources or from some kind of collective provision; it distinguishes an individualistic from a collectivist view of welfare. The vertical axis measures people's views of how active they would need to be in order to obtain services; it is a measure of participation. Thus, the diagram presents a model that distinguishes four types of disposition towards the provision of care at the beginning of our study: consumerism, welfarism, privatism and clientalism. What we are presenting are 'ideal types' of care consumers. Rarely were any of our sample solely of one category or another. The function of ideal types is to represent the theoretical range of individual examples. No particular individuals or households corresponded exactly to one or another of the categories; in fact most cases demonstrated elements of each. We shall characterize the qualities of each category by constructing cases that typify them but which are no more than composites of cases we found in our sample.

Consumerism

At its extreme this is a view that expects nothing from the state and intends to arrange care by actively buying it in the market or providing it out of household and family resources. There were relatively few examples of this view in our sample. Such people were not ignorant of public provision but were sceptical about whether it would suit them. They might doubt its quality but more often they found it inconvenient and time-consuming to use. For example they objected to the inflexibility of the day hospital or, at the other extreme, the uncertainty about who would come and when in the case of public domiciliary services. Clearly this is a view which is easier to hold if one has enough money to pay for what one wants but it was not a position limited only to the better off in our sample. People in this category are used to the control and autonomy that being a customer brings and do not like the uncertainty about who is in charge that using voluntary or public services may bring. Thus we found some people with low incomes who would always prefer a private, for-payment arrangement where possible. For example one elderly couple, both of whom were disabled, appeared to have over the years established very reliable relations with a local taxi-driver, a local jobbing builder, a nearby grocer and a butcher (both of whom would deliver) and a number of neighbours who would do odd tasks for payment. For quite small amounts of money this couple appeared to be able to obtain very prompt and flexible attention which they could control. Their instincts were always to use their own initiative. They did not wish to be indebted to anyone and they regarded the increasingly occasional visits of social workers or community nurses as almost purely social events. It must be added that these two people were immensely charming, even jolly; their 'business relationships' had a large non-commercial component.

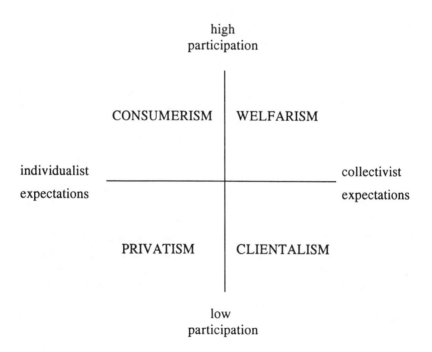

Figure 9.1
'Habits of the Heart'
Modes of participation in the care market

high
participation

CONSUMERISM | WELFARISM

individualist   collectivist
expectations   expectations

PRIVATISM | CLIENTALISM

low
participation

Privatism

People who fell largely into this category did the least well in terms of support. Many sociologists have commented on the growth of what has been termed 'privatism' in British life (for a summary see Saunders 1990, pp. 275-282). It is associated with owner occupation and thus, in retirement, quite often with moving to a new home in an unknown neighbourhood. Attention is 'devoted overwhelmingly to home and family based life rather than to sociability of a more widely-based kind' (Goldthorpe et al. 1969, p. 103). Privatism has also been closely associated with the growth of mass consumerism. 'Ordinary people now demand ever-increasing amounts of consumer goods which they place and use in their own homes. The result is that external and community facilities' become marginal to their way of life (Saunders 1990, p. 277)'. This is a rather passive form of consumerism where most of the work is done by the producers and retailers and requires little initiative from consumers other than the act of purchase itself.

Such a privatized existence may work well when people are fit and well and the things they want are the products of mass consumerism. When they become ill and dependent and require products and services that are not available 'off the shelf' they have much more difficulty. In our sample these people had tended to refuse help when it was initially offered at the point of discharge. In some cases they very determinedly would not accept an assessment or any care management. They strongly valued their autonomy and would say things like 'we've never depended on other people. We've always looked after ourselves'. At home, as the months went by, we found them increasingly puzzled, embittered and, in some cases, frightened. Few of the skills and attitudes they had accumulated during their fit years seemed to serve them well now. What they needed was not advertised nor available in the ready way of the consumer good they were used to buying. Neither were they accustomed to the ways of the voluntary and community-based support system. Some found their few unavoidable encounters with neighbours or voluntary help very difficult. For example one carer-wife whose husband had always done the driving found the process of negotiating her way round the local parish lift scheme quite excruciating. She felt her privacy invaded, that she was having to beg and to justify her private choices. In seeking to take advantage of a private and market-based approach to home care, policy makers do not seem to have appreciated how impersonal and passive much of more conventional 'participation' in the market is.

Welfarism

This is a set of attitudes and an approach that is associated with such ideas as citizenship and welfare rights. These are people who believe in the welfare state and their right to use it. This implies the active pursuit of one's entitlements. People in this group tend to be educated, articulate and may well have worked in the public sector. The clearest example in our sample was a retired physiotherapist married to an ex-headmaster. She was impressively effective in obtaining the best of what was available in the public and voluntary sector. By the end of the six months she was attending the day hospital three times weekly but only for so long as was required to receive the physiotherapy she wanted. She had used an NHS domiciliary dentist and an NHS chiropodist who also visited her at home. She attended the stroke club but had refused an offer from a private domiciliary agency because she 'didn't like their money-making approach'. This stroke survivor's most outstanding, but very rare, characteristic was the way she had very explicitly participated in the assessment made by her case-manager. They had reached a clear agreement on what she needed, what she might need in the future and how she would go about contacting the social worker when necessary. However, much as this whole approach was in tune with a citizenship-based conception of welfare, it was equally obvious that if more than a very few people operated in this way the public sector would rapidly be overwhelmed.

Clientalism

This was a common approach amongst our elderly and often low-income sample. It is the 'traditional' way of using the welfare state; passive, accepting, patient and grateful. These people, unlike the privatists, did not refuse or question what was offered. They are accustomed to using what the welfare state offers, adjusting to its rigidities and accepting its omissions. It is a stance that works well where one's needs are high and manifestly so, such as where the stroke survivor was bed- or chair-bound. One does best if one does not get better; indeed more services will tend to appear the longer one is known to the services and less well one does. However, this approach also brings with it the classic and well-known disadvantages of public provision. It is inflexible and time-consuming. Those services one does receive (day hospital, home care) are rigid in what they can provide and when.

At the same time the public provision leaves gaps. There were things it could not do; for example, put one to bed late. One wheelchair-bound stroke survivor preferred not to go to bed before about 11pm because otherwise her very frail husband would have to help her to the toilet during the night. Although a care assistant came each evening largely to help the woman to bed that is not in fact what happened. In other cases the classic inflexibility of public services was not a matter of timing but rather a bureaucratic inability to deal with a quite simple problem: for instance removing a carpet that made it impossible for an elderly woman to use her walking frame or, in another case, providing a much-promised bed-board that might have allowed the client to sleep and so greatly improved the quality of life of an elderly couple who still shared a double bed.

It was most commonly amongst those in our sample who most nearly fitted this category that we found the puzzling denial of having been assessed or even of having a care-manager where we now know one was very much involved. In its most extreme form, the passivity of this stance seems to hide from people even the organizing and planning that it being done for them. They find the ways of the welfare system and its staff unpredictable and do not attempt to understand or change them.

Conclusion

The 1992 Conservative Party election manifesto emphasized 'a society in which government doesn't try to take responsibility away from people' and which gives 'the power to choose - to say for yourself what you want' (Conservative Central Office 1992). This is a theme which has been pursued in many policy documents and in important legislation such as the National Health Service and Community Care Act 1990 which prescribes more explicit roles for the family and voluntary and private services in the provision of welfare. The argument is that these policies fit more closely with the preferences and habits of the British people.

We did *not* find this to be a false assumption but rather that the issues involved are far more complicated than has been allowed for. In the case of care in the community, we have discovered that the emergence of a satisfactory mixed-economy of care will require that people behave not according to the established 'grain' of everyday life, but that will mean that many of them have to make considerable adaptions. Most people are indeed capable of making such adaptions but the changes involved are not simple ones to do with obtaining information or with receiving assistance with the organization of care. Both of those were offered in abundance to our sample but often fell on deaf ears and provided a rather poor return on effort.

What has been misunderstood is that effective participation by needy people in the mixed economy of care requires that they change values and assumptions that are quite fundamental to how they have lived their daily lives hitherto. We have called these 'habits of the heart' in order to emphasize how deeply embedded they are in people's existence. We have also tried to show that these habits of the heart are not similarly and universally shared and that the adaptions people need to make to obtain adequate care vary from individual to individual.

Acknowledgement

The Joseph Rowntree Foundation has supported this project as part of its programme of research and innovative development projects which it hopes will be of value to policy makers and practitioners. The facts presented and views expressed in this chapter, however, are those of the authors and not necessarily those of the Foundation.

References

Audit Commission (1992), *The Community Care Revolution*, HMSO, London.

Baldock, J. and Evers, A. (1991), 'Citizenship and Frail Old People: Changing Patterns of Provision in Europe' in N. Manning (ed.), *Social Policy Review 1990-1*, Longman, London.

Baldock, J. and Ungerson, C. (1993), 'Consumer Perceptions of an Emerging Mixed Economy of Care' in A. Evers and I. Svetlik (eds.), *Balancing Pluralism: New Welfare Mixes in Care of the Elderly*, Avebury, Aldershot.

Baldock, J. and Ungerson, C. (1994), 'A consumer view of the new community care: the homecare experiences of a sample of stroke survivors and their carers', *Care in Place*, 1 (2), pp. 85-97.

Baldock, J. and Ungerson, C. (1994b), *Becoming Consumers of Community Care: Households Within the Mixed Economy of Welfare*, Joseph Rowntree Foundation/Community Care, London.

Bellah, R. et al. (1988), *Habits of the Heart: Middle America Observed*, Hutchison Education, London.

Busfield, J. (1990), 'Sectoral divisions in consumption: the case of medical care', *Sociology*, 24(1), pp. 77-95.

Challis, D. and Davies, B.P. (1986), *Care Management in Community Care*, Gower, Aldershot.

Cm 849 (1989), *Caring for People: Community Care in the Next Decade and Beyond*, HMSO, London.

Community Care (1994), 'One Year On', pp. 15-22, 31st March edition.

Cross, G. (1993), *Time and Money: The Making of Consumer Culture*, Routledge, London and New York.

Dieck, M. (1994), 'Reforming Against the Grain: Longterm Care in Germany' in R. Page and J. Baldock (eds.), *Social Policy Review 6*, Social Policy Association, London.

Dunleavy, P. (1980), *Urban Political Analysis: The Politics of Collective Consumption*, Macmillan, London.

Esping-Andersen, G. (1990), *The Three Worlds of Welfare Capitalism*, Polity Press, Oxford.

Flynn, R. (1992), *Structures of Control in Health Management*, Routledge, London and New York.

Goldthorpe, J.H. et al. (1969), *The Affluent Worker in the Class Structure*, Cambridge University Press, Cambridge.

Griffiths, Sir Roy (1988), *Community Care: Agenda for Action, a Report to the Secretary of State for Social Services*, HMSO, London.

Lewis, J., Bernstock, P. and Bovell, V. (1995), 'The community care changes: unresolved tensions in policy and issues in implementation', *Journal of Social Policy*, 24(1), pp. 73-94.

Miller, D. (1987), *Material Culture and Mass Consumption*, Basil Blackwell, Oxford.

Morris, J. (1993), *Community Care or Independent Living*, Joseph Rowntree Foundation, York.

Newby, H. (1977), 'In the Field: Reflections on the Study of Suffolk Farm Workers' in C. Bell and H. Newby (eds.), *Doing Sociological Research*, Allen and Unwin, London.

Offe, C. (1987), 'Democracy against the welfare state: structural foundations of neo-conservative political opportunities', *Political Theory*, 5(4), pp. 501-37.

Pahl, J. (1994), 'Like the Job - But Hate the Organisation: Social Workers and Managers in Social Services' in R. Page and J. Baldock (eds.), *Social Policy Review 6*, SPA, London.

Saunders, P. (1984), 'Beyond housing classes: the sociological significance of private property rights in means of consumption', *International Journal of Urban and Regional Research*, 8(2), pp. 202-25.

Saunders, P. (1986), *Social Theory and the Urban Question*, 2nd ed., Hutchison, London.

Saunders, P. (1990), *A Nation of Home Owners*, Unwin Hyman, London.

Taylor-Gooby, P. and Lawson, R. (1993), *Markets and Managers: New Issues in the Delivery of Welfare*, Open University Press, Buckingham.

Warde, A. (1990), 'Introduction to the sociology of consumption', *Sociology*, 24(1), pp. 1-4.

Warde, A. (1990), 'Production, consumption and social change: reservations regarding Peter Saunder's sociology of consumption', *International Journal of Urban and Regional Research*, 14(2), pp. 228-248.

Wender, G.C. (1984), *The Supportive Network: Coping With Old Age*, Allen and Unwin, London.

10   Exploring dominant ideologies and disability: Masculinity, marriage and money

Gillian Reynolds

Introduction

This chapter explores the experiences of some white, Western men whose social locations as 'disabled' do not fit the dominant social stereotype of a 'real man', as 'provider' and 'protector'. Specifically, I address aspects of their life experiences within the home, their relationship with the dominant ideology of 'work', and perceptions of the tensions which emerge from being masculine and being disabled. Clearly, disablement also influences the self-identities of women, but here I explore the issue of masculinity as a dominant ideology.

The discussion concerns the ways in which disabled men might renegotiate dominant ideologies, thereby managing to survive - rather than remain victims of - social oppression. Oppression is perceived as emerging through material practices which are informed by dominant ideologies. Using these perspectives, the complexity of the interface between dominant ideologies concerning the distribution of the means of survival, and the reality of the struggle to maintain a quality of life which goes beyond the concept of 'existence', becomes clearer.

Within the growing body of literature concerning the definition of disablement within 'social oppression theory', it is possible to identify two main theoretical strands, reflecting radical perspectives, and feminist perspectives. The former strand (e.g. Finkelstein 1980, Oliver 1990) deals with conceptual issues surrounding the definition of disablement as a structural and social construction or creation, which oppresses those who are classified as disabled. The latter strand (e.g. Lonsdale 1990, Morris 1992) emphasizes the experiences of disabled women as part of an oppressed or subordinated group. It also addresses the issues embedded in the privatization of caring within the community (which frequently means women members of the family) by calling for more structural and social means of organizing care. This inevitably brings the two strands into some conflict (Parker 1993), but both strands, in my view, continue to hold in common a perception of disabled people as 'victims'.

The data for this discussion were collected, interpreted and analyzed as part of a doctoral thesis during 1991 and 1992 (Reynolds 1994). The research began as an exploration of employment problems experienced by disabled people. However, for various reasons, many of the eventual respondents had not experienced the kinds of problems which my preparatory reading had led me to believe were prevalent. As a consequence, I lost temporarily the power invested in my position as a researcher to define the 'problem', and I found myself listening to a body of very different accounts of people's lives, *as they were defined by* the experiencing, observing and theorizing 'knowers' of those lives (Stanley 1990).

The overarching theme of the multiple interviews was that of a person's perceived social location within the acquisition, exchange and distribution of both material and emotional means of survival. This social location is embedded within the sub themes of work (paid employment, domestic chores, and voluntary work), the home (marriage and family relationships, and domestic roles) and 'charity' (state benefits, fundraising, images of beneficiaries, and the giving or receiving of help).

Definitions and language

The definition of disablement used here has emerged from the radical stream of disabled sociologists. Oliver (1993), for example, argues that impairment is socially created within the context of time and space. Causes include poverty, poor living and working conditions, wars, accidents from technology, and the current state of advance in medical knowledge of cure or prevention. Disablement is the socially constructed experience of having an impairment. It is experienced within the contexts of physical, educational and cultural access, and attitudes of ablism and pity.

The question of finding language which is sensitive without contributing to objectification and dehumanization is always difficult, since the very idea of politically correct language also assumes a homogeneity among the group which the language is still seeking to define. Within recent years a number of suggestions have been made for changing the linguistic definitions of people with impairments, mostly by ablebodied people. Two definitions have been widely accepted now into everyday speech by those who are identified, or identify themselves (the two are frequently not synonymous) as disabled.

Some liberal and humanist groups have argued for the general use of the term 'people with disabilities'. This is seen as a way of ensuring that someone is perceived, firstly as a whole person, and only secondly, as someone who has an impairment. However, Michael Oliver argues that this perspective...

> flies in the face of reality as it is experienced by disabled people themselves who argue that...disability is an essential part of the self...(and) are demanding acceptance as they are, as disabled people (Oliver 1990, p. xiii).

I propose, therefore, to use the term 'disabled people' throughout this chapter, not only to recognise Oliver's point, but also, during fieldwork I have found that most of the disabled people to whom I have spoken, use this term themselves.

Dominant ideologies of home, gender and work

This section looks at the milieu of dominant ideologies connected with the themes and issues discussed here. The history of the concept of ideology is well-known (e.g. Larrain 1979, Barratt 1988), and therefore will be passed over. Billig et al summarize the attendant problems, maintaining that

> Different theorists have used the concept in very different ways, whilst disputing each other's right to do so (Billig et al 1988, p. 25).

Arguing that ideological thinking is inconsistent, and that ideologies are not received uncritically, they reject

> any assumption that the relations between lived and intellectual ideology are in any sense simple...Instead it is necessary to consider the contradictory themes both between and within...them (op cit, pp. 31-2).

In this chapter I consider these contradictions between the ideologies surrounding disablement, gender, the home, and work. However, I am unhappy to refer to the formalized ideologies embedded in philosophies which have contributed so much to the ethics and principles of capitalist thinking, as 'intellectual', for this ignores the outcomes of inequality which the thinking has generated. Instead, I refer to these historically powerful notions concerning the acquisition, exchange and distribution of both material and emotional means of survival, as dominant ideologies, because, in everyday language, they frequently have the 'loudest voice'.

Ideology of home and gender

Ideologies have deeply mythologized and romanticized the modern, Western concept of home as a place of sanctuary, safety, support, and sentiment. Many social scientists have, in my view, colluded in this ideology by emphasizing the economic concept of the 'household'. This collusion enabled ideologies of privatized gender roles to remain unchallenged. More recently, 'realism' research into family life (Finch and Morgan 1991) has made more visible the connections, and disjunctures, between actual social processes in the home, and social and political ideologies.

Ideologies surrounding gender roles within the home are now well known and well understood. Only a brief review is necessary here. A central ideological assumption is that the 'co-resident' nuclear family is the normative ideal. Thus, the sexual division of labour in which the woman is the housewife and mother and mainly located in the 'private' world of the family, and the man is wage earner and breadwinner and mainly located in the 'public' world of paid work, is also normatively desirable. This suggests that many of those who live alone, or 'unconventionally', may still perceive a nuclear family as the ideal standard by which all other forms should be judged.

There is another form of gendered ideology which needs to be addressed at this point, and that is the construction of gender *within* an ideology of familialism. As Michele Barratt argues...

> Ideologies of domesticity and maternity for women, of breadwinning and responsibility for men, are articulated very strongly in families themselves in contemporary society...Families clearly play a crucial role in constructing masculinity and femininity (Barratt 1988, p. 207).

Thus, through the socialization by families, education, media and the state, people tend to take it for granted that men are strong and tough, and the public world belongs to them. Included in the dominant ideology of masculinity is an assumption that men seek to dominate by competitiveness (Brittan 1989). Women, on the other hand, are perceived as submissive, gentle and relational, and should remain in the private world of the home to care for men, children and elderly relatives.

192

Max Weber's well known critique of historical materialism argues that Christian teachings, especially to an 'ascending class' of people in the seventeenth century, were fundamentally influential in creating an ethos in which a system of production oriented capitalism could develop. Through the 'subversion' of 'natural' work (that which is necessary for the basic survival of the individual), the earning of money became an end in itself, and by the twentieth century the spiritual element was no longer a part of economic acquisition (Weber 1976).

The secular version of this 'Protestant ethic', argues Anthony (1977), was refined by liberalism, which simultaneously explained and defended the relative positions in the new social order. This ideology of democratism and egalitarianism purports to offer the possibility of success to all who try, and the essential quality of success is hard work. Meanwhile, those who work hard and 'fail' can apparently draw a sense of pride and dignity from their efforts in the struggle. Victim blaming ideologies (Ryan 1971) have, with varying degrees of success, rendered invisible the structural contributions to 'failure'. The principle of self help, individuated through the process of schooling with its philosophy of 'achievement', provides both a motivating and a hopeful ideology.

The theme of a work ideology may therefore be conceptualized as a moral appeal to self effort, an encouragement of independence from 'benevolence', an emphasis upon success as 'proof' of ability, an objectification of the self under the guise of 'self discipline', and personal responsibility for success or failure. This ideology of work as a moral value is deeply entrenched, not only in the schooling system, but also in the mass media, organized leisure activities, and - for the most part - within the family unit.

These ideologies of home, gender and work provide the theoretical underpinnings for this chapter. The next section introduces the subjects and describes the data. Jenny Morris (1993) points out that the social construction of gender has an important part to play in the lives of disabled men and women, and so I end the chapter with a discussion of the ways in which these men appear to renegotiate their images of disability and sense of oppression within their construction of masculinity. However, whereas Morris emphasizes the characteristics of the gendered body image, it is gender ideologies and roles which are addressed here.

Introducing the subjects

Edward's story

Edward lives with his wife, Sarah, and a variable number of their own, and fostered, children, in a small terraced house. Having left school in the late sixties, he gained a degree and moved into industry. He is in his early forties, and has multiple sclerosis (MS).

After a few days of attempting to return to work following the first major attack of MS, Edward conceded that employment was no longer an option. Money problems became paramount for a while, and it was necessary to move house, in order to reduce the mortgage. In this way, Edward illustrates the well understood trajectory of downward social mobility experienced by many disabled people. His previous employers had an insurance policy to cover disablement of employees, and he was eventually able to take advantage of this, which has guaranteed him and his family a very small income and relieved the most damaging aspects of poverty.

Edward still finds it difficult being at home all day and every day, and still perceives the home as Sarah's 'domain'. Even though they both say they enjoy being in each other's company, and their world revolves around their home, Edward is self conscious, and concerned that neighbours may be suspicious about his willingness to work. Despite his recognition that fathers are often visible during the day, because of shiftwork and unemployment patterns, he still endeavours to protect their children from possible peer group victimization, by using strategies such as putting his former occupation on school forms.

Jeff's story

Jeff is in his late forties and married with a young adult family. He lives with his wife, Jane, and the youngest of his daughters, in a semi-detached council house in a central city location. He left school with no qualifications, and did various industrial unskilled and semi-skilled jobs. Then he developed rheumatoid arthritis throughout his body. Other health complications followed, such as heart attacks.

He gave up his job, and initially undertook a role reversal with Jane, while his health held out sufficiently to cope with the demands of young children. Later he began to find a feeling of usefulness in voluntary work. This continued until his health deteriorated to such a degree that he was more or less confined to his home.

He finds it difficult and degrading to be pushed in a wheelchair, especially by a woman, and feels emasculated by his arthritis, which he feels precludes him from performing his 'proper' role in the home. He sees this role as undertaking jobs such as changing plugs and replacing locks. Much of his everyday life now revolves around doctors, hospitals, and drugs.

Jim's story

Jim is in his early fifties and married to Rena, with several young adult children, two of whom still live at home. They live in a semi-detached council house on a large estate on the edge of the city. After finishing school in the late fifties without qualifications, Jim worked for several employers, before an accident at work left him with spinal problems, when he fell through some rotting boards. He has since developed severe arthritis.

A lifelong strong supporter of the Labour Party, he now finds life boring, and appears to concentrate on 'armchair' politics to pass the time away. My first impressions were that he and Rena seem to have settled into traditional gender roles, to deal with their mutual centredness on the home. Jim undertakes the 'outside' chores - the garden, the window cleaning, refuse disposal, and the car; Rena is 'in charge' of chores connected with the 'inside' - the cooking, cleaning, and clothes maintenance. She is also responsible for the shopping. Jim insists that she likes it that way; Rena, however, does not agree.

Edward, Jim and Jeff clearly share more than the one aspect of life experience as disabled people: they are of a similar age group, and in similar family circumstances of parenthood. Each one became disabled in their adulthood. They also share a similar relationship to roles within the home, and to the concept of work, money and consequently state benefits. These experiences and characteristics can be analyzed as potential resources which are vital for both material and emotional survival (Doyal and Gough 1991), the access to which is largely controlled by dominant ideologies; and also as potential resources for the process of maintaining a self identity. Thus, the 'means of survival' encompass, not simply functional necessities such as food and shelter (or the money with which to purchase them), but also the necessary means of emotional and social survival, such as self esteem, life roles, and helping behaviour; all that 'being human' entails.

Historically, a considerable number of texts have examined the concept of impairment in terms of dependence and independence (e.g. Barnes 1990, Oliver 1993). 'Dependent' and 'independent' represent masculinist and patriarchal symbols (respectively) of subordination, and a reality of self government. Conversely, the concepts of 'control' and 'autonomy' may be viewed as a feminist critique of the ontological states implied by 'dependence' and 'independence'. Control and autonomy thus symbolize the existence of domination by others, and the principle of rights and freedoms - that is, theoretical 'choice', or lack of it, in ways of being.

In some of the issues discussed, the State has the direct means of control. In others, dominant ideologies are seen as the mechanism which seeks control. State control is more indirect here, as the specific dominant ideologies relate to ideologies of marriage and the family, and the ideology of work, based on a 'work ethic' which are founded on a specific concept of masculinity. The policy of service provision, with its emphasis on 'dependency', remains largely informed by these dominant ideologies.

People live out their lives in a specific relationship to these dominant social perceptions of them, and in the midst of the ideologies surrounding identity forming experiences of work. The concept of articulated 'differences' can be perceived as a mechanism by which we all construct our self-identity through constant re-negotiation of social identities (Giddens 1991). It is important to repeat at this point that I acknowledge the relevance of these issues to women, and, indeed, address this in the main research project. Here, however, I specifically want to engage with the concept of masculinity, and its connection with the issues below, as they may apply to disabled men.

Issue 1: relationship to the home and life-roles

The concept of 'home' is heavily romanticized and mythologized in Western industrial society. The mythology implies a concept of home as a site of *power* ('the Englishman's home is his castle'); *freedom* ('I'm coming home, I've done my time'); *familiarity* ('feeling at home', 'home from home'); *ecstasy* ('home is where the heart is', 'home, sweet home'); *satisfaction of needs* ('hearth and home', 'home and dry'); *completion of a task* ('the home run'); and *returning to beginnings* ('the homeland', 'homing pigeons').

For the people involved in this study, being 'on benefits', first of all, meant a redefinition of the concept of home. Home is, for many, no longer primarily a repository for the commodified rewards of employment, or a romanticized place to return to at the end of the day. Instead, it is conceptualized as a site of mundane relations, no longer romanticized; sometimes boring, sometimes causing people to feel extreme guilt, either for not being employed, or because they perceive themselves to be 'without roles'. Learning to live with these dilemmas entails either directly subverting, or renegotiating, dominant ideologies which do not take account of differences in lived experiences.

Many sociologists have historically ignored the concept of home, preferring instead the masculinist concept of the 'household' (e.g. McDowell 1983, Hanmer and Saunders 1983). There has been some movement here, with the concept of 'home' being built around the equally emotive issue of 'homelessness' (e.g. O'Mahony 1988). However, even recently, the concept has largely been reinvested with its mythological beginnings...

> The home is the embodiment of the modern domestic ideal, a suitable place to be occupied by 'a family'...a place of security, privacy and comfort...actively constructed through a process which turns the raw materials of a house plus possessions into a home (Allan and Crow 1989, cited by Finch and Hayes 1994, pp. 417-18).

Josephine Donovan's definition of 'home' for women is a 'domestic sphere, inside enclosures'; a restricted and restricting area (Kramarae and Treichler 1985, p. 194). However, this conceptualization of home was echoed by several male as well as female respondents and thus problematizes the implication of *gendered* space...

> You're between four walls...it's like being in prison...you don't meet anybody, you don't see different faces, it's the same thing, day in, day out, same routine (Jim).

The home has also been defined not only as a physical and material space, but as the site of emotional processes, which are developed over time and within a particular set of historical circumstances (Finch and Morgan 1991). In my study, the site of the home was frequently conceptualized by being juxtaposed to another site, such as the workplace, but it was also often seen as a site of expertise and skill. Sometimes this was gendered, sometimes explained in the context of impairment, and sometimes the two issues were interwoven in an inextricable way...

> Jim: I don't have to do the cleaning or the cooking, Rena does it...she loves her housework, she loves her cooking...I feel awkward about being here, and not working.
> Gillian: do you ever do anything like putting a load of washing in?
> Jim: she always does it, I don't know how to work the washer.
> Rena: I could scream sometimes cos I don't get any help.

This interaction is interesting for several reasons. Methodologically, it is indicative of the frequent ways in which Jim and Rena appeared to use my presence to maybe renegotiate their roles in the home. It is also clear that Jim perceives housework and cooking, not just as a 'woman's job', but as a form of expertise which he might be able to convince Rena to value. Other men in the study expressed their feelings of awkwardness about being in the home for most, if not all, of the time...

I'm in the situation where I'm at home all the time, (but) I - er - I still feel awkward about being put in that situation (Edward).

Although most of the men in my study - and some women - had been quick to deny a territoriality in the home, it became clear that the 'work' largely still belongs to the women...

I try to help Sarah with (the housework). Er, that domain still remains hers, being the housewife er - I try to help as much as I can...because I've been put in the situation... I try not to appear as if I'm sort of taking over, but-er-there's things that I would do automatically; there are other things that need doing that don't always get done straight away (Edward).

However, as the following small interchange between Jim and myself suggests, oppression can also form part of that unspoken contract between many marital partners...

Gillian: do you think of this (housework) as work?
Jim: no.
Gillian: why don't you class it as work?
Jim: you mean me? Because Rena does it.

Thus, not only is the most lowly and oppressed wage slave a 'king' in his own home (Bernardes 1985), but so also is the disabled man, who is not directly connected at all to the relations of production. Bernardes claims that, in the absence of the husband, the most oppressed wife is herself a powerful 'queen' in the home. If this is so, then the onset of disablement of her husband can represent a usurpation of her 'throne'. However, it does not always occur without a struggle...

It was terrible, wasn't it, really; bawling out all the time, arguing out all the time...you just get used to it, I suppose, but first it was terrible...argue over the telly, and what needs doing and what needs clearing up and, you know, that's it - there's me, I'm sitting here, and then got to move over there and then - you know - you just don't know what to do (Jim).

Jim and Rena thus struggled with each other for the control of everyday life in the home. Jeff struggled too, but in a different way. He experienced painfully the lack of autonomy by having to wait for Jane to turn the key in the lock...

> It's the little things that get you - this morning we'd just been to the shop and we came back. The lady across the road called the wife, she gave me the key. I put it in the door, couldn't turn it. I was stuck. Stuck on the step till she could get to me. Little things like that hurt you, when you know as you can't change a plug, you get ready to throw the plug against the wall, you know (Jeff).

Whilst lack of choice and autonomy in this context is frequently part of women's life experiences, it is a more unaccustomed event for men, who are therefore often less practised at dealing with the frustration which it engenders. Edward felt that he and Sarah had managed to renegotiate successfully some of the problems which arise when both partners are sharing the home for the majority of their time..

> It made us realize that some of the things that were important weren't important...some of the things that we thought weren't important took on some importance. Things were turned upside down a lot, a lot of things, including our values. One of the things that took on greater importance was our commitment to ourselves and our family. Keep the family together (Edward).

Jeff, on the other hand, implicitly sees his life at home as more of a mundane existence, lacking the social interchange of the workplace..

> I'm not saying me and me wife get bored with one another's company, we don't, but...it's a different companionship...I used to love the three days a week at the (hospital) physio...talking, exchanging addresses - it was like going to work (Jeff).

For Jeff, the social aspects of his employment had been important, and the physiotherapy clinic, to a degree, had filled that chasm of isolation within the home, by providing different faces and different topics of conversation. Indeed, for some disabled people, clinics and daycentres are the only route to 'public' social relationships. Edward, on the other hand, now sees his whole life as centred on the home...

> We don't mind being together, so in that respect, we know we're all right, whereas some people say, 'oh can't wait to get back to work', we

don't mind being in that situation... Er-the world does tend to revolve around the home now (Edward).

In her work among women caregivers, Judith Oliver points out that most have little choice about taking on their caring role, and that spouses have the least choice of all. There is an assumption that the post of potential carer is bestowed with the wedding ring...

> It was not so much role-change...but...they had to take on both male and female roles. Many said it would be pleasant to be able to ask their husbands to make a cup of tea occasionally...in the sharing sense which they had previously associated with marriage (Oliver 1983, p. 79).

Whilst it seems clear that there is marginally more state help for male carers than female carers (Land and Parker 1978, cited by Oliver 1983), and Oliver's work among women is of great significance, it is easy to overlook the point that disabled men are equally powerless to change the situation - and some do feel it keenly...

> it's the little things...not being able to look after yourself...I know she's me wife - when we got married it was fer better or worse ...If I could do fer me wife like she does fer me...I can't do for her, and I feel - it hurts me, you know, cos I don't feel I'm giving 100 per cent to me marriage (Jeff).

There remains powerful rhetoric which insists that marriage is constructed as a private and individualized domain (Clark 1991). However, disablement of one of the marital partners signals permission for intrusion by the 'public' sphere of institutions. Meanwhile, the privatized concept of 'care' denies the possibility of reciprocity within the relationship. Within existing literature on caring, the emotions and feelings of the care recipient, in their everyday relationships, remain *relatively* unacknowledged (Thomas 1993).

An exception here is the work of Gillian Parker (1993a), who points out that because those who acquire impairments far outnumber those who are born with or grow up with impairments, the most usual experience of disability occurs within the context of previously existing relationships. She argues that, just as literature on marriage has largely ignored the issues of disability and caring, so the literature on disability has excluded the marriage relationship, except as a 'caring' bargain. However, the picture is a little more complex, for this relationship is not just between two partners in isolation, but becomes a three way relationship with the State.

Issue 2: relationship to work, money and benefits

The articulation between the social construction of masculinity, class, and status generated by work in the 'public' sphere, is well known. There is social pressure on men to achieve a sense of self identity through their employment status. Men, more than women, tend to rely upon the public world of employment status for their perceptions, in order to engage in a process of identifying an authentic self. Jim, Edward and Jeff are no exception...

> (Work) - it's your livelihood, in't it? I mean, you have an accident, have it took off you. You had your two good legs that you had to manage on, they're essentials...I've always had good money cos I used to work seven days and seven nights...I've always turned me wages up...and then that happens...you start...running up your debt (Jim).

Jim illustrates the connection between the work ethic (or ideology) and status and control in the home. It is this status and control which he perceives as having lost...

> (Politicians) don't know how disabled people live...they don't know what disablement means. They are fit and er they go and dictate to you how much you get. Wherever you get disabled people, there's people as don't know how much suffering, and the pain they have, and they're scratching their heads, you know, there's fixed income from year to year, never gets - and your wife's got that much and no more...That's the hurtful thing about it (Jim).

Jim thus perceives State control of his income as hurtful to his masculine identity as the 'provider' of the family. Edward voices sentiments similar to those of Jim...

> We had hardly any money coming in, the house was going to be repossessed, what were we going to do for money?... 'Well, I'd better try to get back to work to get back into some money'...Getting back to work was more for our future (Edward).

Mortgaged beyond his current ability to pay, Edward was clearly worried about his future ability to hold the family together, and keep control of it in the face of 'hostile forces'...

> Getting out of that mess we were in...with not much money coming in, Building Society sort of knocking on the door...the insurance company for the car and the insurance company for the life-cover, and all those sort of things. You take so much for granted, and it all came to the

201

fore (Edward).

Both men appear to seek a means of keeping control in the home. Jim seeks to control the incoming finances which Rena receives; Edward seeks to protect his family from outside forces which he perceives as a threat to their stability.

Jeff, on the other hand, relates differently to the ideology of work, and to issues of control. He seems generally less concerned than Jim or Edward about money, even though his circumstances are similar to theirs...

(Money) isn't so important now. It was, it was when I was first whatsit, cos all me children were young, you know, me eldest was 14. I mean, she's now 27...it's easier (if) you've no longer got to provide for them, look after them...it isn't easy, but I - I'm happy as long as I can pay me rent, and I've got a meal in front of me (Jeff).

A possible analysis of these differences is that whilst Jeff and Edward share a perception of paternalism in holding the family together, the different ages of their children mean that Jeff can relax his feeling of responsibility. Conversely, whilst Jeff and Jim share a similar experience of family age-range, Jim's attitude to money is more a function of his marital relationship.

The relationship to work, because of its articulation with the medium of money, is also, for these men, a relationship to welfare. Unlike other unemployed people, they must not only repeatedly justify their social status with regard to not being self financing, but must also justify their right to claim benefits by demonstrating the maximum extent of their disablement. This means that situations intimately connected with the body, which are taken for granted as being 'private' by most people, become the object of public scrutiny. Again, this is sometimes perceived as an affront to the masculine image of keeping control of a situation...

It's a terrible feeling, I mean, when they send for you for a medical down (assessment centre)...they don't treat you like disabled, they don't treat you like people...
(Gillian - how do they treat you?)
...Like dirt! They sent for me three times in three months, didn't they? Three times in three months, and it's - I've had some medicals, you know, and I've seen some doctors - but I've never been treated like them people down there...one day I'm going to go down there, they're going say, 'you got go work', and I haven't been able walk...you've never seen nothing like it, you want go down there and talk to the people what are going in there...they get treated worse than - I've never

been treated like it. You can't explain to anybody what it's like being in that place (Jim).

Jim's anger faced in three main directions: the physical and emotional effects of anxiety when an impending 'visit' to the centre is due; the subjectivity and variability of doctors' perceptions which alter the assessments; and the necessity to 'prove' the disablement. Thus, people in Jim's situation may experience their lives, not as dependent on a welfare state, but existing under the control of ideological agents of that State. They are thus denied the right to be treated as autonomous citizens (Oliver and Barnes 1993).

Sometimes it seems that the only way to regain control is to 'shoot oneself in the foot', as it were, for, as Jim pointed out, his pride was the one thing that was left to him...

I filled all me form in, took it down to the doctor, and asked the nurse...I said, 'can you sign this?' - 'Oh it's got to go all through the channels of the doctor for reading it and signing it' - so I said, 'oh that's it', I brought the form back, chucked it in the bin...Don't want to be bothered with it. You know, it's too much. People on disablement...they've had enough of medicals...they have more medicals than soft mick (Jim).

Jim's action predictably left Rena with less money than she could have had, but his perceived need to do what he could to maintain his 'public' face of autonomy evidently became of greater importance.

The second major issue which arose in the context of State benefits, revolved around the perpetual debate over welfare as rights or charity. Most of the group in my study felt that state benefits do not constitute a form of charity, but that they have more in common with life insurance policies...

I don't see state benefits as charity because I paid for them, I paid me taxes, I paid me National Insurance from the day I left school when I was working. It wasn't my fault that I was suddenly taken ill...I did work hard, I did 12-hour shifts (Jeff).

Although Jeff's statement is typical, it is important to note that there is a strong difference in the data between the way in which people theorize about welfare, and their experiences of the 'generalized other' in claiming the benefits...

Other people think I'm having charity...because they think they pay for keeping us (Jim).

203

For all three of the men, unemployment and being 'on benefits' meant, not a simple switch to the welfare distribution system, but a complete change of relationship to the material resources for survival. In addition, it indicated a change of articulation with dominant ideologies, which are all structured to facilitate the supremacy of social relations of production within capitalism. In short, the experience meant a renegotiation of ideologies within the concept of 'masculine' reality.

Whilst this experience may be true for all unemployed men, there are essential differences between those who are, for the time being, able-bodied, and those who are classified as disabled. Probably most men, when faced with the loss of their role as provider, find it difficult to know where they fit into marital or family life. The experiences of disabled men, however, are such that their gendered image of masculinity - of strength, assertiveness and independence (Morris 1993) - is also denied by the social construction of the disability.

Theorizing renegotiations

In this final section, I rely largely upon Michele Barratt's work which, although concerned with women, has, I think, much to contribute to the discussion in the areas of oppression, collusion, and survival. Just as Barratt concludes that ideology and economic relations are important sites for the construction and reproduction of women's oppression, so they are for the construction and reproduction of disabled people. However, it is important to distinguish the extra dimension of gender here, for it often represents a radical difference in the experience of disablement. Disabled women may largely experience oppression in which the ideology of their gender is reinforced (through perceived dependency, frailty, embedded in the body). As Jenny Morris puts it, they experience...

> partial congruity between the roles of being a woman and being disabled, in that both are associated with weakness, passivity and dependence (Morris 1993, p. 88).

The experiences of disabled men, on the other hand, may be oppression which denies the image of their gender, through the ideologies of masculinity, which imply, not only that they should be strong and assertive (op. cit.), but also that their appropriate role is that of provider and protector of the family. In the same way that Barratt sees women's oppression as both a category of meaning, and a consequence of the historically identifiable positions in the class structure and division of labour, so, too, is the oppression of disabled men.

It can be argued that, because of the growing body of feminist writing on the subject, disabled women - at least in theory, if not always in practice - have access to resources which give self affirming, alternative views to those of dominant ideologies. Disabled men, I would argue, do not; and here, I return momentarily to the two main strands of contemporary writing on disablement in the social sciences. That which is written by the radical stream of disabled male sociologists attends largely to issues historically connected with the realm of the 'public' sphere - employment, money, transport, access to public places, definitions of disablement, and relations with the State. They do not, on the whole, address the issues of gender - the problematic nature of the ideology of masculinity, and the consequences of this for disabled men - but, rather, assume male gender as given. Contemporary writing by disabled feminists, on the other hand, by examining the gender specific oppression experienced by disabled women, consequently problematizes the concept of masculinity, but largely ignores the theoretical implications of their analysis for disabled men (Jenny Morris's work is a notable exception here).

Barratt also discusses the issue of women's collusion in their own oppression, which she sees as arising from two processes. The first process is that of the manipulation and 'parading' of their 'consent' to subordination and objectification. The second, which perhaps is more painful to examine, is their willing consent to, and internalisation of, their oppression. Arguing that accepting the concept of collusion need not lead theoretically to false consciousness or denial, Barratt points out that politically incorrect elements of consciousness cannot simply be 'willed away'. Connected with the concept of collusion are those of 'compensation', which she sees as practices which elevate the moral worth in order to compensate for material denial of opportunities; and 'recuperation', by which she means...

> the ideological effort that goes into negating and defusing challenges to the historically dominant meaning of gender in particular periods (Barratt 1988, p. 111).

These three interlocking concepts of collusion, compensation and recuperation are valuable in this discussion of masculinity and disablement. Much has already been written about the collusion of disabled people in their own oppression, so I shall not address that here. However, very little has been achieved in describing or analyzing the collusion by disabled men in their gender oppression. On the contrary, the emphases in the writings of male sociologists concerned with impairment - whilst of immense importance - have, I believe, contributed further to the alienation of disabled men from the ideology of masculinity. Essentially, I mean by this that, in concentrating on issues of the 'public' world, which have traditionally been seen as the domain of masculinity, writers have tended to ignore the gendered life experiences of those who spend most of their time in the 'private' sphere of the home.

Compensation, for disabled people, takes place primarily in the sphere of the imagery of disablement. Disabled people are idealised as morally worthy of charity and philanthropy - to be critical of their actions, or of the principles of charity is to be perceived as petty minded. And, indeed, there are major dilemmas inherent in a critique of charity, for so much survival, for disabled people, is at present literally dependent upon precisely these practices.

Recuperation occurs largely in the home, and frequently at the expense of women. In addition to the economic issues already well addressed in this volume, the current political move away from formalized 'care in the community' to informalized 'care in the community' (i.e care by - largely female - relatives) may also be viewed as ideological recuperation for the concept of masculinity. As we have seen with Edward and Sarah, and Jim and Rena, the neighbourhood and the home - when inhabited by both partners all the time - can become the site of gendered struggle for control. Loss of control in the public sphere of employment and money demasculinizes; the gaining of control in the home recuperates some of the ideology of masculinity. Barratt cites Ann Foreman as arguing that..

> Men struggle to succeed in the public world of business and industry, but failing that they rule in the family (Barratt 1988, p. 192).

She points out that the home is a site where relations between occupants are ones in which women are systematically dependent upon, and unequal to, men. Jim, Jeff, and Edward, in their different ways, all use their masculinity to seek control in their homes, even though, in attempting that, they also collude in their own emasculation by the dominant ideologies of masculinity in the public world.

Conclusion

In this chapter I have explored some of the contradictions and ambiguities involved when people's lives do not fit the dominant stereotype of their social location. The tensions arising in the discussion emphasize the struggle for some disabled men in recuperating their gender identity, made problematic by not being the 'provider' and 'protector' of their families. It may be, of course, that other commonalities between these three men - their age, family circumstances, and geographical location - are also relevant to the discussion. However, as in all qualitative research, I have sought to identify some themes and issues to the exclusion of others.

I do not attempt to put forward any answers to this complex dilemma. Just as women are having to rewrite their own history, and disabled people generally are working out ways in which to do that, so must disabled men conceptualize and problematize their own social locations with respect to their gender. As a woman researcher who is also a feminist, and as someone who is personally committed to addressing the human need for affirmation and self esteem, I am concerned for those who do not find their lives emotionally fulfilling. Put simply, if Edward, Jeff and Jim had been women, there are several texts which could have been available to them, written by women who are active in 'public feminism'. As it is, they will continue to struggle and renegotiate their gender in a privatized and individualized way, which may well contribute to further oppression of their partners. The discomforting consequence of accounting for gender in any discussion of disability is that we must also account for the oppressive relations embedded within the social construction of masculinity (Reynolds 1993).

References

Allan, G. and Crow, G. (eds) (1989), *Home and Family: Creating the Domestic Sphere,* MacMillan, Basingstoke, (cited by Finch and Hayes 1994).

Anthony, P.D. (1977), *The Ideology of Work*, Tavistock, London.

Barnes, C. (1990), *Cabbage Syndrome: the Social Construction of Dependence*, Falmer, Basingstoke.

Barratt, Michele (1988), *Women's Oppression Today (2nd ed),* Verso, London.

Bernardes, J. (1985), 'Family ideology: identification and exploration', *Sociological Review,* Vol. 33, pp. 275-297.

Billig, M., Condor, S., Edwards, D., Gane, M., Middleton, D. and Radley, A. (1988), *Ideological Dilemmas*, Sage, London.

Brittan, A. (1989), *Masculinity and Power,* Blackwell, Oxford.

Clark, D. (1991), 'Constituting the Marital World: A Qualitative Perspective', in Clark, D. (ed), *Marriage, Domestic Life and Social Change*, Routledge, London.

Doyal, L. and Gough, I. (1991), *A Theory of Human Need*, MacMillan, Basingstoke.

Finch, Janet and Morgan, D. (1991), 'Marriage in the 80s: A New Sense of Realism?' in Clark, D. (ed), *Marriage, Domestic Life and Social Change*, Routledge, London.

Finch, Janet and Hayes, Lynn (1994), 'Inheritance, death and the concept of home', *Sociology,* Vol. 28, No. 2, pp. 417-433.

Finkelstein, V. (1980), *Attitudes and Disabled People*, World Rehabilitation Fund, New York.

Foreman, Ann (1977), *Femininity as Alienation: Women and the Family in Marxism and Psychoanalysis*, Pluto, London, cited in Barratt (1988).

Giddens, A. (1991), *Modernity and Self-Identity*, Polity/Blackwell, Cambridge/Oxford.

Hanmer, Jalna and Saunders, Sheila (1983), 'Blowing the Cover of the Protective Male: a Community Study of Violence to Women', in Gamarnikow, Eva, Morgan, D., Purvis, Jane and Taylorson, Daphne (eds), *The Public and the Private*, Heinemann, London.

Kramarae, Cheris and Treichler, Paula A. (1985), *A Feminist Dictionary*, Pandora, London.

Land, H. and Parker, R. (1978), 'Implicit and reluctant family policy - United Kingdom', in Kamerman, S. and Kahn, A. (eds.), *Family Policy: Government and Families in Fourteen Countries,* Columbia University Press, New York.

Larrain, J. (1979), *The Concept of Ideology*, Hutchinson, London.

Lonsdale, Susan (1990), *Women and Disability*, MacMillan, Basingstoke.

McDowell, Linda (1983), 'City and Home: Urban Housing and the Sexual Division of Space', in Evans, Mary and Ungerson, Clare (1983), *Sexual Divisions: Patterns and Processes*, Tavistock, London.

Morris, Jenny (1992), 'Personal and political: A feminist perspective on researching physical disability', *Disability, Handicap and Society,* Vol. 7, No. 2, pp. 157-166.

Morris, Jenny (1993), 'Gender and Disability', in Swain, J., Finkelstein, V., French, Sally and Oliver, M. (eds), *Disabling Barriers - Enabling Environments,* Sage, London.

Oliver, Judith (1983), 'The Caring Wife', in Finch, Janet and Groves, Dulcie (eds), *A Labour of Love: Women, Work and Caring*, Routledge and Kegan Paul, London.

Oliver, M. (1990), *The Politics of Disablement,* MacMillan, Basingstoke.

Oliver, M. (1993), 'Disability and Dependency: a Creation of Industrial Societies?', in Swain, J., Finkelstein, V., French, Sally and Oliver, M. (eds), *Disabling Barriers - Enabling Environments*, Sage, London.

Oliver, M. and Barnes, C. (1993), 'Discrimination, Disability and Welfare: from Needs to Rights', in Swain, J., Finkelstein, V., French, Sally and Oliver, M. (eds), *Disabling Barriers - Enabling Environments*, Sage, London.

O'Mahony, B. (1988), *A Capital Offence: the Plight of the Young Single Homeless in London*, Routledge, London.

Parker, Gillian (1993), 'A Four-way Stretch? The Politics of Disability and Caring', in Swain, J., Finkelstein, V., French, Sally and Oliver, M. (eds.), *Disabling Barriers - Enabling Environments*, Sage, London.

Parker, Gillian (1993a), *With This Body: Caring and Disability in Marriage*, Open University Press, Buckingham.

Reynolds, Gillian (1993), "'And Gill Came Tumbling After..': Gender, Emotion and a Research Dilemma", in Kennedy, Mary, Lubelska, Cathy and Walsh, Val (eds), *Making Connections: Women's Studies, Women's Movements, Women's Lives,* Taylor and Francis, London.

Reynolds, Gillian (1994), *Work, Charity and Physical/Sensory Impairment: Biographical Accounts of the Re-negotiation, or Subversion, of Dominant Ideologies,* unpublished doctoral thesis, Staffordshire University.

Ryan, W. (1971), *Blaming the Victim*, Pantheon, New York.

Stanley, Liz (1990), 'Feminist Auto/Biography and Feminist Epistemology', in Aaron, Jane and Walby, Sylvia (eds), *Out of the Margins: Women's Studies in the Nineties,* Falmer, Basingstoke.

Thomas, Carol (1993), 'De-constructing concepts of care', *Sociology*, Vol. 27, No. 4, pp. 649-669.

Weber, M. (1976), *The Protestant Ethic and the Spirit of Capitalism,* Allen and Unwin, London.

Acknowledgements

Grateful acknowledgement is offered to those friends and colleagues who read and commented upon an earlier version of this discussion.

11   Generations, inheritance and policy relevant research

Janet Finch

Policy relevant research on families

The topic of families, and how they organise their collective lives, is now unequivocably at the centre of the political agenda in the UK. Though of considerable importance over the last decade, family policies seem set to achieve even greater prominence for the rest of the century whichever political party is in power. On the Conservative side, the political importance of the topic is highlighted by the designation in 1993 of a government minister with special responsibility for the family. In discussions about the future prospects of the Labour Party under its new leader, there has been much talk amongst political commentators about the importance of capturing the 'family agenda' and transforming it into a socialist rather than a Tory vote-winner. Pressures coming from the European Union are likely to accelerate rather than diminish the tendency for family issues to remain high profile, though the approach to family policies still varies widely between different member states (Lewis 1993, Hantrais 1994).

As new policy agendas emerge - some of which will, of course, be old agendas in a new guise - what should be the role of research in the public debate which will ensue? In particular, how can social policy researchers make an effective contribution to current and future debates about families? I shall use this chapter to suggest some answers to these questions in general, and I shall develop some of my key points by drawing for illustration on some of my own recent work, which concerns the inheritance of property and how families handle this.

If social policy researchers are to achieve maximum impact on future public debates about the family, at a tactical level the most obvious priority is to anticipate issues which are likely to come onto the policy agenda before they arrive, in order to be ready with research findings which can be fed into the public debate at the relevant time. Developing a shrewd capacity to 'spot the right topic' is vital, and happily it is a skill which many social policy researchers already possess.

However of equal importance is the need to be very clear about *how* research can contribute to public policy debates about families and *what kind* of research is the most appropriate. This is a particular issue on which I want to concentrate in this chapter, because I see it as a relative weakness in social policy research. As I have argued elsewhere (Finch 1991), social policy and administration has produced less critical reflection than many other social science disciplines on philosophical and methodological issues which underpin empirical research. On the central issue of thinking through appropriate relationships between research and policy-making, clearly there is an awareness of this in the social policy literature, though much of the basic research upon which this draws has actually been generated from within political science or sociology, rather than as a product of work within social policy and administration *per se*. I think for example about discussions concerning the 'engineering' and 'enlightenment' models of policy research, developed by a number of writers but probably associated principally in this country with Martin Bulmer's work (Janowitz 1972, Bulmer 1982, Finch 1986).

Given this relative weakness within social policy research, I see a danger that - in a set of policy debates about the family which are likely to be fast-moving - researchers will rush to produce work which feeds into current policy thinking, but which in fact is inappropriate for its purpose. In particular, there is a danger that many will fall too readily into a type of research which is applied in the narrowest sense - beginning with the specific questions about families as defined within the political process, and attempting to produce quick results which will influence the making of policy directly.

There may be some issues on which this approach is entirely appropriate. However it is a mistake to view social policy research as confined to approaches which are 'applied' in this narrow sense. I would make the distinction here between 'policy-led' research on the one hand, which is work of the type aiming to begin with questions as defined in the public domain and to feed directly into policy-making; and on the other hand 'policy-relevant' research, which certainly can inform policy making, but which is not geared to a particular set of questions as currently defined by government or other policy-making bodies. Both approaches are legitimately encompassed within the field of social policy research.

212

However research which is policy-*relevant* may well look more like 'basic' than 'applied' research, to borrow the language of the 1993 White Paper on science and technology (*Realising Our Potential*, 1993). The importance of encompassing basic as well as applied research in policy-relevant work on the family can be appreciated simply by considering the range of questions currently being debated. In almost every case, if one looks just a little below the surface, some very fundamental questions are being posed about how family relationships actually work.

How can parents be made to control their adolescent sons more effectively? How can we ensure that working-class parents get their children to school on time and insist that they do their homework? How can separated and divorced fathers be made to recognise their continuing financial responsibilities to their children? How can adult children's responsibilities for their elderly parents be reinforced? These are the kinds of questions which engage various government departments at the present time, and of course they embody certain normative assumptions which many people would not share. They do, however, form the basic agenda for much contemporary social policy research on families, however diluted and qualified. Each of them requires that we understand the workings of family relationships in some detail if we wish even to comprehend, say, *why* parents may find it difficult to control their adolescent sons, still more if interventions are being planned to change this situation.

The basic problem is that, in applied research, it is easy to move too quickly to assumptions about how families actually work, without properly considering the evidence for those assumptions. The reasons for this are understandable, not least the pressure of time to produce research outcomes before the policy debate has moved on somewhere else. However if policy-makers are operating on the basis of unexamined - and possibly quite erroneous - assumptions about how families actually work, it is fatal for researchers to begin by taking for granted the same flawed assumptions. Not only is this dubious on intellectual grounds, but also it is bound to reduce the value of research outcomes to public debate.

By way of a concrete illustration, I would argue that a common failing is to assume far too readily that family relationships work on a rather straightforward version of economic rationality. In essence, it is assumed that people's actions will be governed by a desire to maximise resources to themselves as individuals and to those members of their family with whom they have a common stake. This of course is a gendered assumption, given the differing command over resources enjoyed by men and woman in many families.

Some research in social policy has been successful in exposing the

213

weakness of this assumption, but too little in my view. There is, for example, the excellent work done in the 1970s and 80s by Jan Pahl and others who studied women living in refuges who had been the victims of violent relationships with men (Pahl 1978, 1985). This research demonstrated that, in many cases, the income available to these women and their children was considerably less once they had left home than had been the household income when they were living with a man. Yet these women actually felt better off once they were living independently, largely because the money which they did have access to was fully in their own control. The powerful forces associated with gender relations in families served to counteract any tendency on the part of these women to maximise income. Interestingly, the very recent work done by Clarke, Craig and Glendinning on the operation of the Child Support Agency points to similar factors in determining whether women actually do want their former male partners to be pursued for money to support their children. Again the power associated with money, symbolically as well as materially, and the way in which this works in gendered relationships is the key to understanding why many women do *not* welcome pressure being brought to bear on the fathers of their children even though it would be in their economic interests (Clarke et al 1993).

If we are going to develop research on families which is both high quality and policy relevant, it is therefore inadequate to build in unexplored assumptions about how families work, including what kind of incentives people will respond to in their family relationships. We need to know much more about how they *do* work, and disentangling that is a complex matter. The kinds of research required to do that will look much more like basic social science than applied research, but in a real sense this is vital in order to produce high quality research which is policy relevant. I shall develop this point with an example drawn from my own current research.

Inheritance and generational relationships

For several years I and my colleagues have been conducting research on inheritance of property and other material possessions, focusing on how inheritance is actually handled within contemporary families [1]. One starting-point for this research was a belief that questions concerning inheritance are likely to be a more relevant and potent factor in more families now than in the past, since the spread of home ownership means that many more people have something valuable to bequeath. Though we know something of how these matters work in the small minority of wealthy families for whom inheritance has always been an issue (Scott 1982), very little was known about how inheritance issues are handled in ordinary families.

We set out to find out how people handle questions of inheritance, both in terms of outcome and process, and how questions of inheritance interact with other aspects of family life, especially with the responsibilities and obligations between generations. Though this certainly lies more at the basic than the applied end of the research spectrum it relates to a range of issues which are highly relevant to social policy. How do the structures of support within families develop under different conditions over time? How far is family solidarity either enhanced or undermined when there is significant money at stake? How far do families exploit the opportunity to deploy financial resources in order to assist younger generations to improve their economic and social position? The answer to these questions about the role of money in generational relationships is highly relevant to assessing likely changes in the balance over time between state support and family support, and in indicating to any government interested in stimulating changes in that balance what are the opportunities and the limitations.

In considering such questions there is a great temptation to assume that families will work on the basis of a rationality which essentially is economic. That is tempting but it is wrong, as I shall show. I shall refer briefly to two issues which, in different ways, show that inheritance works in families in ways which do not mirror simple economic rationality. As I have written about both of these more fully elsewhere, I shall not present the data in detail, but simply refer to these other published sources.

My first illustration concerns the question of what we can call 'jumping a generation'. Because of the demographic structure of contemporary families, the statistically average child can expect to be age 56 before both her or his parents have died (Anderson 1985). This means that inheritance passes to the first descendent generation at a point when the child will be contemplating retirement if he or she has not indeed retired already. It is certainly well after a point where it could make a significant difference to life chances though it may help to finance a more comfortable old age for the next generation of elderly people. In these circumstances some commentators have assumed that increasingly inheritance will pass directly to the grandchild's generation, either through the grandparent's will, or because the parental generation receives it and passes it straight on. Certainly there is a strong economic case for families using inheritance in this strategic way. In the statistically average family the grandchild's generation would be at the point where money could make a difference -

215

to enter or to enhance their position in the housing market, to provide the resources to gain additional qualifications or to start a business, to pay private school fees for the great grandchild's generation.

The evidence of our study is that none of this is happening, except unusually. Certainly our analysis of a random sample of 800 probated wills shows that it is very rare for grandchildren to be named as major beneficiaries. That does not settle the matter of course. It is quite possible that the testator's children inherit through the formal process, and then pass on much of the wealth received direct to their own children. However we do not believe that this is happening either. Our evidence from interviews with 98 individuals, of all ages, about how inheritance is handled in their own families, gives no inkling that people who inherit from their elderly parents are inclined to pass on most of these assets directly and immediately to their own children[2]. It is possible that we have yet to see these processes developing as the effects of increased home ownership work their way through to an impact on inheritance. But other evidence from our interview study leads me to suppose that there are actually points of resistance to the strategic use of inheritance in this way (see Finch 1995 for fuller discussion).

Essentially this resistance stems from the idea that grandchildren should wait their turn. The strong message in our data is that generational relationships work on the assumption that the oldest living generation has the right to control - and indeed to dispose of - any money which has been passed on from previous generations. Our interviews suggest that this is widely taken for granted as a basis for family relationships, and that is entirely consistent with the pattern of bequeathing which we find in our random sample of wills. However we need to understand this in a slightly broader context, namely that there is also a strong assumption that parents will continue to assist their children in adult life wherever they can do so (Finch and Mason 1993).

When we put these two principles together, we can see why inheritance does not 'jump a generation' either directly or indirectly. In the 'ordinary' families whom we have studied, the oldest living generation expects not only to have assets under its own control but also to use those assets as part of the *normal* processes whereby parents go on helping their children. Inheriting resources from one's parents in late middle age enhances one's capacity to give financial help to one's own children, but at a time and on a scale of one's own choosing. Conversely it would deny the opportunity to go on being a good parent to one's adult children if the resources went over the head of the first descendent generation, as it were, straight to their own children.

Thus the strategic use of inheritance in a way which maximises its material value is not favoured in most ordinary families, I would argue, because it would disrupt seriously the basis on which generational relationships normally operate and would deny to one generation the capacity to be a good parent. A rather similar theme recurs if we look at quite a different issue in our data -the possibility of care bargains. By 'care bargains' I mean the phenomenon which has been widely predicted, namely that the increased pressures on family members to provide care for frail elderly people will combine with the increased number of people who have something to bequeath, to produce bargains whereby one child agrees to be the main carer in return for an enhanced share of the parent's estate after he or she dies. Again, the economic rationality is impeccable, and in this case it is reinforced by a rather obvious sense of fairness to the child who has been the main carer. But again our data give cause for scepticism that this is going to develop except unusually (see Finch and Wallis 1994 for fuller discussion).

As with the phenomenon of jumping a generation, our data from will show that care bargains are not being enshrined explicitly in bequeathing practices, though it is possible that some wills embody them without being explicit. In our interview data, again one can detect points of resistance to deploying inheritance in this strategic way. Even in situations where a care bargain seemed an obvious possibility - and we had several in our data set - it seemed unlikely to occur. The clue to understanding this is giving by one of our interviewees, a woman of 78 who was still living independently but was receiving significant regular help from one son and daughter-in-law. Meanwhile she had another son of whom she saw little and whose lack of attention was resented by the whole family. This is precisely the kind of situation in which one might expect a bargain to be struck, with a greater share of inheritance going to the son and daughter-in-law who have invested strongly in the caring role. However in this case the elderly mother clearly had no such thoughts. She resisted the idea that she should do anything other than bequeath her sons equal shares of her estate, commenting that just because she saw rather little of one son, this did not mean that she 'thought any less' of him.

This idea of 'thinking less' of one child gives the clue, I believe, about why care bargains are likely to be resisted, at least by the parental partner to the potential bargain. To favour one child over another in your will is to make a statement that your relationship with your children is not on equal terms. Though on one level this may be an entirely rational statement to make if it is tied up with a care bargain, in fact it is experienced in a more complex way. It raises the possibility that one child *means* more to you than another which in turn may reflect on your own life-long conduct as a parent, inviting the charge of favouritism. This is a particularly potent statement if it comes at the end of your life, if literally it is the last statement which you make about your children (Finch and Wallis 1994).

In different ways, the examples of care bargains and jumping a generation point to the continuing potency of the parental role for elderly people. They suggest that the ability to continue to be a 'good parent' through to the end of one's life is a significant factor shaping elderly people's priorities. It may well over-ride considerations based on economic rationality. It is of course likely to be more powerful for women than for men, certainly in the present generation of elderly people in which many women will have invested a great deal of their identities in being good mothers. The gendered consequences of continuing to be a parent throughout one's life - motherhood and fatherhood in old age - is certainly an issue about which we need to know more. In relation to the specific issue of inheritance, our own study indicates that women think and act differently from men in respect of passing on their property, especially women who have outlived their husbands or who have never been married. One important difference is that men focus on material resources, and think about inheritance as a practical question of dividing up their property. Women however, are more likely to focus on the more symbolic aspects of inheritance, seeing the passing on of property as a way of acknowledging relationships (Finch and Hayes 1995).

We did not set out to study the continued importance of the parental role in old age, for those elderly people who do have surviving children. Its significance was something which we stumbled across in the course of trying to understand how families handle inheritance. However if we are right - and certainly a wider range of studies on this topic is needed - there are implications across a range of social policy issues concerned with both the support of elderly people and their financial circumstances. It implies that we need to start thinking carefully about the consequences of policy initiatives which remove from elderly people the capacity to continue to act as good parents.

But my main point is that this example illustrates the importance of understanding how family life actually works, which may not always match commonly held assumptions and may sometimes seem counter-intuitive. Without having set out to understand how this particular aspect of family life works, we might well have fallen into the trap of assuming that care bargains and jumping a generation are likely outcomes of present trends. In fact the evidence points in the opposite direction.

218

Conclusion

In this chapter I have tried to use the issue of generational relationships in families to show the importance to social policy of research which lies more at the 'basic' end of the research continuum. Basic, but policy-relevant, research is an essential underpinning to research which sets out to be more directly applied. Without it, one inevitably gets sucked into making dubious assumptions about the basis of human actions. Certainly in relation to work on families, an empirically grounded understanding of how families actually work is crucial to any research which is going to make a high quality contribution to either the analysis or the formulation of social policies.

More generally, I would argue that social policy research can and must cover the full spectrum from basic to applied research, for the reasons which I have given in this chapter. It is easy automatically to equate social policy with applied research but the idea that it should cover a fuller range is embedded in the development of the discipline of social policy and administration, if one looks carefully. The point is made indeed by Richard Titmuss in his classic essay on 'Social administration in a changing society'. As it happens, he also uses the example of research on the family in his discussion and his emphasis is - in the terms which I have been using - on the importance of basic research to the social administration enterprise. Writing about social change and its impact on families he says,

> We know little of the forces which are shaping family life. We do not understand the fundamental reasons for the falling birthrate, for the greater popularity of marriage, for the rising esteem of children in our society, or the significance of the large increase in the number of married women who now leave their homes to work in factory and office. These are some of the important problems at present challenging the social sciences. They are of practical concern to social administration which, as a humble partner in this broad field of study, cannot hope to understand the working of social institutions without understanding the needs which arise from changing ways of living. (Titmuss 1958, pp. 32-3).

Though nearly forty years on public pre-occupations about families look rather different, the point about research remains the same. Understanding - as Titmuss put it 'the needs which arise from changing ways of living' - is an essential component of policy-relevant research, which enhances our capacity to apply our understanding to current policy proposals.

219

Notes

1. I am grateful to the ESRC for their financial support for this project, entitled 'Inheritance, Property and Family Relationships' (Grant No. ROO 232035). I would also like to thank Jennifer Mason, Lyn Hayes and Lorraine Wallis, my co-researchers on the inheritance project. Though the responsibility for the argument in this chapter is my own, the analysis of families and inheritance on which it draws has been very much a common enterprise.

2. The study of wills was based on a sample of 800, selected randomly from wills which have passed through probate, 200 for each of four sample years (1959, 69, 79 and 89). The interview study was linked conceptually but concerned a separate study population. Within a total of 98 interviews, we built up sets of interviews with several members of the same family where that was possible. People were interviewed about how questions related to inheritance are handled in their own families, using semi-structured techniques.

References

Anderson, M. (1985), The emergence of the modern life cycle, *Social History*, vol. 10, no. 1, 69-87.

Bulmer, M. (1982), *The Uses of Social Research: Social Investigation in Public Policy-Making*, Allen and Unwin, London.

Clarke, K., Craig, G. and Glendinning, C. (1993), *Children Come First? The Child Support Act and Lone Parents*, Barnardos, Children's Society, NCH, NSPCC, SCF, London.

Finch, J. (1991), 'Feminist Research and Social Policy' in Groves, D. and Maclean, M. (eds), *Women's Issues in Social Policy*, Routledge, London.

Finch, J. (1986), *Research and Policy: The Uses of Qualitative Methods in Social and Education Research*, Falmer Press, Lewes.

Finch, J. (1995), 'Inheritance and financial transfer in families' in Walker, A. (ed.), *The New Generational Contract*, UCL Press, London.

Finch, J. and Hayes, L. (1995), 'Gender, Inheritance and Women as Testators' in Lyon, S. and Morris, L. (eds), *Gender Relations in Public and Private*, Macmillan, London.

Finch, J. and Mason, J. (1993), *Negotiating Family Responsibilities*, Routledge, London.

Finch, J. and Wallis, L. (1994), 'Inheritance, care bargains and elderly people's relationships with their children' in Challis, D., Davies, B. and Traske, K. (eds), *Community Care: New Agendas and Challenges*, Ashgate Publishing/British Society of Gerontology, Aldershot.

Hantrais, L. (1994), 'Comparing family policies in Britain, France and Germany', *Journal of Social Policy*, vol. 23, no. 2, 135-160.

Janowitz, M. (1972), *Sociological Methods and Social Policy*, General Learning Systems, Morristown, NJ.

Lewis, J. (ed.) (1993), *Women and Social Policies in Europe*, Edward Elgar, Aldershot.

Pahl, J. (1978), *A Refuge for Battered Women*, HMSO, London.

Pahl, J. (1985), 'Violent Husbands and Abused Wives - A Longitudinal Study', in Pahl, J. (ed.), *Private Violence and Public Policy*, RKP, London.

Realising Our Potential: A Strategy for Science, Engineering and Technology (1993), Cm. 2250, HMSO, London.

Scott, J. (1982), *The Upper Classes. Property and Privilege in Britain*, Macmillan, London.

Titmuss, R. (1958), 'Social Administration in a Changing Society' in Titmuss, R., *Essays on the Welfare State*, Unwin, London.

221